Living in the Borderland

D0220454

Living in the Borderland addresses the evolution of Western consciousness and describes the emergence of the "Borderland," a spectrum of reality that is beyond the rational yet is palpable to an increasing number of individuals. Building on Jungian theory, Jerome Bernstein argues that a greater openness to *transrational* reality experienced by Borderland personalities allows new possibilities for understanding and healing confounding clinical and developmental enigmas.

In three sections, this book examines the psychological and clinical implications of the evolution of consciousness and looks at how the new Borderland consciousness bridges the mind–body divide. Subjects covered include:

- Genesis: Evolution of the Western Ego
- Transrational Data in a Western Clinical Context: Synchronicity
- Trauma and Borderland Transcendence
- Environmental Illness Complex
- Integration of Navajo and Western healing approaches for Borderland Personalities

Living in the Borderland challenges the standard clinical model, which views normality as an absence of pathology and which equates normality with the rational. Jerome S. Bernstein describes how psychotherapy itself often contributes to the alienation of Borderland personalities by misperceiving the difference between the pathological and the sacred. The case studies included illustrate the potential this has for causing serious psychic and emotional damage to the patient.

This challenge to the orthodoxies and complacencies of western medicine's concept of pathology will interest Jungian Analysts, Psychotherapists, Psychiatrists and other physicians, as well as educators of children.

Jerome S. Bernstein is a Jungian Analyst in private practice in Santa Fe, New Mexico.

Living in the Borderland

The evolution of consciousness and
the challenge of healing trauma

Jerome S. Bernstein

Routledge
Taylor & Francis Group

LONDON AND NEW YORK

First published 2005 by Routledge
27 Church Road, Hove, East Sussex BN3 2FA

Simultaneously published in the USA and Canada
by Routledge
270 Madison Avenue, New York NY 10016

Reprinted 2006, 2007 and 2008

Routledge is an imprint of the Taylor & Francis Group, an Informa business

Typeset in Times by RefineCatch Ltd, Bungay, Suffolk
Printed and bound in Great Britain by
MPG Books Ltd, Bodmin, Cornwall

British Library Cataloguing in Publication Data
A catalogue record for this book is available from the British Library

Library of Congess Cataloging-in-Publication Data
Bernstein, Jerome S., 1936–
 Living in the borderland: the evolution of consciousness and the
 challenge of healing trauma/by
Jerome S. Bernstein.
  p. cm.
 Includes bibliographical references and index.
 ISBM 1-58391-756-X (hardcover)—ISBN 1-58391-757-8 (pbk.) 1.
Psychoanalysis and religion. 2. Liminality. 3. Cerebral dominance. 4.
Nature. I. Title.
 BF175.4.R44B457 2005
 150.19′8—dc22

2004025714

ISBN 13: 978–1–58391–756–5 (hbk)
ISBN 13: 978–1–58391–757–2 (pbk)

We see and hear what we are open to noticing.

Jerome S. Bernstein

Contents

PART II

PART III

Dedication

This book is dedicated to my elders, some of whom are chronologically younger than I.

Nathan Bernstein – my father, an immigrant from Russia at the age of 20, who, had he had the opportunity for a formal education, would have become a medical doctor. He became a healer of wayward youth in his retirement years. It is from him that I come to many of the clinical gifts that I do have.

Edward C. (Christopher) Whitmont – Jungian analyst and homeopathic physician, whom I fondly think of as "Yoda," who journeyed with me through the depths of hell, and who led me to and through my second birth to my self.

Herbert (Grandpa) Hamana – Hopi elder and kiva chief, friend and teacher, who took me into his world and into my first religious experience.

Carl Nelson Gorman – Navajo sage, code talker in World War II, artist, teacher of Navajo religion, my personal teacher, tracker of Navajo medicine men, teller of jokes, lover of opera, and one of the most gentle men I have ever known.

Homer Cooyama – Hopi artist, medicine man, teacher, musician and friend, who taught me that intuition and sensation are not true opposites, what magic looks like when it lives in one's hands, and who loved to sing to me.

Roslyn D. Kane – friend, fellow traveler in the federal government's "War on Poverty," my partner in Rj Associates, the one who triggered this path by cajoling me into going on a one week's consultancy to the Chairman of the Navajo Tribe, lover of numbers and statistics, smarter than 95% of the people either of us has ever known, a bit crazy in the same way that I was – but shrewdly more cautious – and someone of very generous heart.

Johnson Dennison – Navajo medicine man, friend, teacher, fellow bridge builder between two worlds, storyteller, and man of many jokes, who values and converses with the healer in me.

Ronald Brown – Navajo medicine man and teacher, who saw the holy in me.

The observant Jew at the Wailing Wall – with whom I never exchanged a single word, and who with his inner light and his inner song, connected me to the roots of my tradition and the agelessness of time.

Max Seeboth – conductor of the East Berlin Symphony, refugee from Nazi Germany, escapee from behind the Berlin Wall, who taught me that without knowing the depths of my first language – music – I would never know my soul.

Helen Keller – who, when I was 14, taught me to notice the sensuous world about me, especially the color green.

Acknowledgments

It seems to me that most books carry acknowledgments of the support of wives for their men in their writing endeavors: The many cooked meals, the absent hours, the dishes washed, the kids taken care of, and, of particular note, their own creative endeavors sacrificed to that of their spouse. All quite true, no doubt, and also true of Susan in the case of this book as well (except my kids are grown).

This book has been one of the most challenging, difficult, and passionate endeavors I have ever undertaken. It has gone through many permutations and in the past year seems as if it has written itself or written me, more than I have written it. At the same time, it had a number of close calls, coming close to being stillborn. There were times I lost my way, lost my faith in the work and in myself to express myself, as well as those very strange times when my left brain and my right brain collided in what seemed to be an unbelievable Gordian knot of mush. Each time I would go to Susan for help, sometimes not even being able to articulate the problem. Each time she unraveled me, explained to me what I was trying to say, supported me, lectured me, shoved me, held my hand, and nursed me through. There were many times when she carried the light of this work more than I.

It seems to me that to be able to know, intuit, and provide so much can only come out of the deepest love. It is that for which I most want to thank her – for the sake of this book which would not have been completed without it, and for my sake.

I love you.

Very special thanks goes to Hannah, who introduced me to, and helped me define, the Borderland. Her willingness to share her process in the context of this book has been most generous. It has been most gratifying to share her journey into wholeness.

Thanks to all other Borderlanders, some my patients, and many of whom I have never met, for introducing me into and sharing their extraordinary world. I am enlightened, enriched, and grateful for it.

A special thanks to my colleague, Donald Kalsched, who read the entire draft of the book and gave most generously of his time, support for the work and his knowledge and clinical experience in assisting me through some quagmires towards its completion.

Thanks and appreciation to Barbara McNeill of The Institute of Noetic Sciences, a friend of 30 years, and who was responsible for the publication of "On the Borderland" in the *IONS Noetic Sciences Review*.

Many thanks to David Barton of The Salt Institute for publishing the first chapter of what has become this book in *The Salt Journal* and for his continuing support for the completion of this work.

There were several people who were "readers" of a near complete draft and who gave me content and editorial feedback, giving generously of their time and input: David Barton, Paul deStefano, Alicia Torres, Liz Williams, and several Borderlanders whom I have never met other than through correspondence. Marilyn Matthews' ardent support of the work is particularly appreciated.

There were a number of people whom I interviewed regarding various aspects of the book who were most helpful and generous in their contributions. Very special thanks goes to Erica M. Elliott, M.D., an environmental physician, who was extraordinarily helpful regarding my struggles to grasp the nature and import of environmental illness (or, she would definitely say, multiple chemical sensitivities). Her enthusiasm and support for the work assisted me through that most difficult of chapters. And, as it turns out, she was a teacher and sheepherder on the Navajo reservation at the same time that I was consultant to the Tribe.

Other interviewees who were particularly helpful were: William A. Shrader, Jr., M.D., Ann McCampbell, M.D., Susan Schmall, Ph.D., and a number of others.

Special thanks to Lee Cartwright for sharing his clinical insights regarding the interface of psyche and soma.

There were other colleagues and friends who provided support for the work at various points along the way: Lola, my faithful companion, who accompanied me on my many hikes in the Santa Fe arroyos where so much of this work came together; David Abram, Michael Benanov, Carol and Francis Marsh, Rob McCullumsmith, Sylvia Brinton Perera, Meredith Sabini, and Barry Williams, among others.

In the six to seven years during which this book took its current shape I had a number of administrative assistants who helped research material for the book: Particular thanks to Carlo Santiago; everyone should have a research assistant as able and thorough as Carlo. Thanks also to Nicolai Bachman, Misty Blakesley, Jena Clouse, and Caroline Knapp. Kittredge Stephenson labored long and hard during the final weeks of its completion to catch the myriad errors that fell through the cracks and to chase elusive sources..

For the past four years Mary Gay Graña, a published author in her own right, has been my editor on the work. There are editors and then there are editors. Her support for and dedication to the work sometimes seemed to exceed my own, and her capacity to cajole, badger, and threaten consequences to move me and the work along was something I came to rely on. More than a first-rate copy editor, she understood and believed in the work and pushed and pulled me through several substantive swamps along the way. One could not have had a better ally.

Thanks to Ronald Brown and Johnson Dennison for permission to use photographs of various aspects of their work as a Navajo medicine man.

My sons, Eric and Matthew, have always been inspiration for life's vigor, challenges, and wonderment. As we have grown older together and the gap between being parent and child has narrowed, enabling more of a feeling of being men with mutual respect for one another, they have grown into my support and at times the kind of intellectual challenge that has pushed me to goals and limits beyond those which I might set for myself. Their light shines ever-brighter on the blessings of being a father. I am so appreciative of all of that.

Many thanks to you all.

Introduction

Whereas in the early scientific era, knowledge had rested on observation and deduction, modern scientific knowledge is based on experimentation and measurement.[1]

Since science is all-inclusive knowledge, it cannot admit the validity of extrascientific healing – hence, the contempt of "official" medicine for all kinds of primitive and popular medicine, the latter containing remnants of primitive and early scientific medicine.[2]

A psychotherapist whom I supervise opened our supervisory session with the following: "So what's with the animals out there? Everyone in my practice is coming in and talking about animals. What's going on?" I replied that I think that what's going on is that the western psyche is being reconnected to nature, and that nature themes in general, and animal themes in particular, reflect what I have called "Borderland consciousness," a phenomenon that is emergent in the culture and becoming increasingly prevalent in clinical settings. I referred her to my article, "On the Borderland," on the IONS[3] website. That article follows here as the Prologue (Chapter 1) and Living in the Borderland (Chapter 2) of this book. I also pointed out that Borderland awareness is beginning to affect her, since she heard those references to animals as valid clinical data worth reflecting on, rather than passing them off as metaphor for something else on a more abstract level. And hers was not the only reference by a clinician to increasingly prevalent animal themes in their practice. I have heard similar statements from many colleagues.

I won't take space here to describe "Borderland consciousness," since this whole book addresses that topic. One point that does require discussion here, however, is what I refer to as "transrational reality." By transrational reality I mean objective nonpersonal, nonrational phenomena occurring in the natural universe, information and experience that does not readily fit into standard cause and effect logical structure. These are the kinds of experience that typically are labeled and dismissed as superstition, irrational, and, in the extreme, abnormal or crazy. A major theme of this book is that there is an increasing number of people who have transrational *experiences* that are *real* – not real seeming, not "as if" experiences, but real.[4] One problem that these individuals experience in our very left-brain, ratio-centrically, cogni-centrically[5] biased culture, is that there is no construct, no frame for receiving and integrating such experience. That bias – culturally and psychologically – does not allow for the *possibility* of transrational reality. Thus people who claim to have such experience often are ostracized, dismissed out of hand, or worse, branded as pathological or crazy.

There are thousands of people in our culture – people I refer to as "Borderland personalities" – whose transrational experience is nothing short of sacred.[6] There are many who would not be able to function in our society without their deep personal connection to that domain. And most of them feel forced to conceal that dimension of their experience, even from their loved ones, out of fear of being ostracized and branded as abnormal.

There are still others who suffer psychological wounding and who pursue psychotherapy in an attempt to heal and to find ways of coping and living in a wounded and wounding world. A number of these people have a Borderland connection that sustains them. Even so, they fear revealing this dimension even in their therapy, lest it be labeled, profaned, and spoiled. Still others are confused by their own Borderland experience and wonder themselves whether what they experience and cherish is not an extension of pathology and somehow must be given up in the name of something they do not understand. And worse, some are wounded by the therapy itself if the therapist, because of his rational bias and lack of receptivity to transrational experience (and perhaps his own discomfort with the very notion of the transrational), labels as pathology what for the patient is experienced as authentic and deeply meaningful. Many testimonials in this regard follow in this book.

Moreover, the western ego construct *is* the organ of rationality. The exclusion of transrational reality from consideration leaves it unchecked by any power outside itself and prone to profound and dangerous inflation. Indeed, I suggest in Part I of this book that such inflation threatens the very survival of our species. The western ego construct buttresses its stance of omnipotence and omniscience with a claim to superior and absolute knowledge through its scientific construct. The phrase "its scientific construct" is used advisedly. For science *is* a construct of the mind, and not, as some would assert, an independent system determining objective knowledge and truth. For all of its correctness and the benefits that flow from it – modern medicine for one – science remains, nonetheless *a* construct of the mind, in the context of other constructs, which, if received, could add to the general well-being of all of life. Alan Lightman, in a review of *Einstein's Miraculous Year: Five Papers that Changed the Face of Physics*, observes, "Modern textbooks on science give no sense that scientific ideas come out of the minds of human beings. Instead, science is portrayed as a set of current laws and results inscribed like the Ten Commandments by some immediate but disembodied authority."[7]

In this amazing scientific and technological age, it is easy to forget that *all* science takes its roots in clinical observation. Chemistry was once alchemy, and before that, experimental ethnobotany; physics takes it roots in the hunter–gatherers who studied their prey, their motion in flight, and adjusted the trajectory and angle of their spears through intuitive observation by trial and error. And these "scientists" developed scientific systems in the age and context in which they lived, which were sufficiently reliable to warrant being taught to others in the community.

George Lakoff, Professor of Linguistics at the University of California at Berkeley, in his book co-authored with psychologist Rafael Nuñez, *Where Mathematics Comes From*, says:

> There are excellent reasons why so many people, including professional mathematicians, think that mathematics *does* have an independent, objective external existence . . . The reason [we think scientific truths to be completely objective] is that they are metaphorically based on our experience of external objects and experiences: Containers, continuous paths of motion.[8]

Lakoff proposes that the ability to mathematize results from our experiences in the world *and our ability to make metaphor*, i.e. that the source of this ability is the mind. It is in linking these metaphors that humans were able to develop the ability to formulate abstract mathematics. As regards the seemingly objective transcendence of mathematics and the mathematical underpinnings of modern science, he suggests that in the evolution of civilization and of science there was a need to break free of old mythic beliefs. Thus new metaphors were developed, ultimately leading to mathematics as we know it today. However, it would appear that the baby was thrown out with the bath water, and that other metaphors of reality and science have been shut out of modern scientific consideration.[9]

What all of this is about, is a plea for openness regarding other metaphors of science and reality. This is a central theme of this book. Along with openness, one needs to be prepared to listen differently and to think differently. Language, too, must be open if we are to make space for other formulations than those with which we are familiar and most comfortable. How we formulate questions very much determines the type of response we are likely to get and hence places constraints on experience.

In this regard, the reader will note that in several places in this book I have refrained from clarifying language and experiences that are ambiguous, even confusing. This constraint is deliberate and employed in the name of being true to the other's experience, and to compel the reader to search for the metaphor being alluded to in the atypical experience/thought being reported.

To insist on a rational response to transrational experience, i.e. "It is or it isn't . . .," aborts the possibility of recognizing a different metaphor of reality. When, for example, my patient Hannah reports "feeling" the sadness of the cows, I consciously avoid the question of what she "really" did experience. That word "really" puts the discourse into a left-brain cause and effect linear metaphor and denies the validity of the truth she was struggling to claim. Truth is what it is – whether it makes sense to us or not. *Our* discomfort with what is alluded to in the moment does not justify denying the other's reality. Whatever Hannah's experience, it was not *that* metaphor. We may not be able to put into words what her metaphor was, but we can share that she experienced something beyond what such questions imply.[10] So in some passages of the book, the reader is thrown back on himself to struggle with what is alluded to and what is conjured up in the reader, both on a mental and on a body level.

I began this introduction with reference to what my supervisee said was taking place in her practice regarding Borderland, i.e. transrational, experience. But these experiences are far from limited to the clinical context alone. Their prevalence becomes more apparent the more one reminds oneself that there are other dimensions of experience to be encountered. *We notice what we are open to noticing.*

The reader will note that, from time to time, I mention a film. Whereas the arts, poetry, drama, the troubadour, and various forms of literature have been the primary carriers of archetypal awareness over the centuries, beginning in the 20th century, film has become a primary mode of incarnating and communicating collective consciousness and evolution. Film is a major vehicle and harbinger of society's psychic evolution. Film oftentimes provides our first peek at mythological and archetypal themes and changes happening in our midst; thus, it often presents a graphic confrontation with emerging positive and negative social consciousness as well as new psychic realities. There has been a spate of films in the past several years that portray Borderland personalities and transrational reality. Some of these are: *E.T. The Extra-Terrestrial*,[11] the *Star Wars* trilogy, *The Sixth Sense*, *The Green Mile*, *Instinct*, *The Matrix* trilogy, the Lord of the Rings trilogy, and *The Wild Parrots of Telegraph Hill*, among others. The prevalence of the Borderland theme in modern film is evidence of an emergent psychic reality that is pressing for incarnation from within the collective unconscious.

Last, this book has been written with a broad readership in mind. It is structured in three parts, any one of which may be read independently of the others. However, it is strongly recommended that the Prologue and Chapter 2 be read first. Part I presents a theoretical formulation for the emergence of Borderland reality and Borderland personality in western culture. Part II is primarily clinical in focus and explores how Borderland dynamics are manifest in the psychotherapeutic setting, as well as their related psychotherapeutic implications. Part III continues the clinical explorations of

Part II, but incorporates the Navajo medical model as a paradigm for bridging the mind–body duality in western medicine. It explores a clinical model that might result from a joining of Navajo and allopathic approaches to medicine and healing. It demonstrates, through multiple case presentations, how modern medicine could benefit from transrational data in the diagnosis and treatment of serious illness.

The reader is strongly encouraged to check for content endnotes (as opposed to citations without content). The explications in these content endnotes amplify the book's content in important ways.

Most of all, I would hope that the reader will be touched as I have been in sharing some of the extraordinary experiences of the Borderland personalities who have generously opened their hearts and souls and their suffering out of a need for others to witness their unique connection to the sacred.

Jerome S. Bernstein

December 2003

Notes

1 Ellenberger, 1970: 47.
2 Ibid.
3 The Institute of Noetic Sciences.
4 Of course, there are people who hallucinate, or are delusional, who also would say that they have experiences that we would consider abnormal or not real. The struggle to differentiate between the two was dramatically highlighted in the film, *A Beautiful Mind*. This book discusses the difference between these two dimensions of experience, one real and the other pathological, and how to make those differentiations, particularly in a clinical or therapeutic context.
5 A term coined by the modern authority on shamanism, Michael Harner.
6 Rudolf Otto says of the holy and the sacred: "There must be felt a something 'numinous' [something outside of itself], to which the mind turns spontaneously . . . these feelings can only arise in the mind as accompanying emotions when the category of 'the numinous' is called into play . . . The numinous is . . . felt as objective and outside the self" (Otto, 1923: 10–11).

   He also distinguishes between what he calls "rational religion," and the "ineffable" (pp. 1–7). And, with the rational comes the *choice* of believing or not in the sacred. In an experience of the ineffable, there is no choice.

   In my usage of the word "sacred" throughout this book, I am referring to the numinous – that which compels a feeling experience of awe and that is outside the self. In the modern context for western culture, that dimension is the western ego's reconnection with nature. It is in this context that the western ego is reconnecting with the "ineffable."
7 Lightman, 1999: 88.
8 Lakoff and Nuñez, 2003: 349.
9 Lakoff, 2003: 337–363.
10 E.g. she didn't "really" feel those cows – it had to be . . .
11 This film, up until the *Star Wars* trilogy and subsequently *Titanic*, held the record for box office attendance, testimony to the compelling nature of the Borderland theme in the American psyche.

Part I

Chapter 1

Prologue

The year 1971 was one of personal endings and personal beginnings. I ended a career in the federal Office of Economic Opportunity, and started a new consulting firm with a friend and business partner. We did social science consulting of the kind that was prevalent in the 1960s and 1970s and that had mushroomed with the War on Poverty.

That year was also a landmark year for American Indian tribes. Richard Nixon initiated what became the Indian Self-Determination Act. For the first time in the history of US tribal relations, American Indians would be given the right to decide for themselves what was in their best interest, to take over the administration of selected programs from the federal government, and, like other Americans, to make their own mistakes and to live with and learn from them.

In the fall of 1971, within weeks of approval of this Act, the newly elected chairman of the Navajo Nation called my business partner and said that he wanted to begin the process of restoring his tribe's culture, language, and dignity through the development of a tribal Division of Education. His plan was that, henceforth, Navajo children would be trained by Navajos in their own language by bilingual teachers who would teach Navajo culture and religion with pride. No such tribal-wide program had ever existed, and the chairman was well aware that starting this project on the Navajo Reservation (comprising one-third of all tribal Indians in the United States, with a land-base about the size of West Virginia) would set a precedent and establish a model for all Indian tribes and for the federal government as well. We determined that I would go for a week's consultation.

I did know something about the administration of school programs, but I had never been on an Indian reservation and had never met a tribal Indian. The assignment was daunting, but something deep within me said that there was a purpose in this calling.

When I arrived in Window Rock, Arizona, the capital of the Navajo Nation, the town was cold and lonely, desolate even. The desolation was accentuated by the ever-present wind, which seemed to remind me of a silent, persistent history that demanded to be heard. I met with the Division of

Education staff and the staff of the newly established Navajo Community College to hear their ideas about priorities, resources, problems, and concerns. These meetings required traveling virtually the whole of the 26,000-square mile reservation.

Early in my stay at Navajo I learned that time for Navajos is more circular than it is linear, more of a *kairos* than a *kronos*. It was not unusual when asking a Navajo the time to hear the response, "Skin time or White Man's time?" So the last day of my week, I was not too surprised when I arrived for a morning meeting to find it was to take place in the afternoon. After the meeting I raced back to Window Rock in hopes of catching the Division of Education staff before they left at 5 pm. I was an hour and a half late. I assumed no one would be there when I returned, but I hoped the offices would not be locked; I had papers to pick up before leaving for Albuquerque to return to D.C.

When I entered the office, I was surprised to see three men sitting on small wooden straight-back chairs in a tiny room that served as an office for the three people who shared the one government-surplus desk. I knew one of the men, Ralph, fairly well. I had spent a good deal of time with him during my week at Navajo. "We've been waiting for you," he said. "We've been listening to you listen, and we think you can hear us. We have decided. We want you to come back." Indeed, I had been listening intently. It was my primary "activity" that first week at Navajo. But I was unaware that they had been listening to me listen. This was a new idea for me. "I would like to come back and work with you," I said. Thus began a five-year professional relationship with the Navajo Tribe. It was also the moment I began to learn the deeper meanings of *listening*. Over the next years I made many trips to Navajo, sometimes spending weeks at a time.

In 1972 I met Carl Gorman, a Navajo native, who was an artist and teacher of art and Navajo history, culture, and religion, and was a Navajo code talker during World War II. Carl was the founding director of the newly established Office of Native Healing Sciences. In that position he worked cooperatively with the Navajo Medicine Man Association, a recently formed consortium. At that time, Carl's office and the Association had surveyed the Navajo medicine men in practice and concluded that the *youngest* medicine man was somewhere between age 68 and 72, and that there were few, if any, younger Navajos in apprenticeship. It was obvious that, if something were not done quickly, Navajo religion and healing would die out completely within 15 to 20 years. Carl worked with the Medicine Man Association to recruit apprentices to work with individual medicine men to learn their specific healing ceremonies.

Through these contacts, I was exposed to Navajo religion and healing over the next several years. This had a profound effect on me. I began to have healing dreams that involved Navajo and sometimes Hopi healers/medicine men. At the time I had been in Jungian analysis for more than two years, and

I explored these dreams in my analysis. Over time, I realized that these dreams were leading me onto a new path: I was to become a Jungian analyst myself. In 1974 I was accepted into training at the C. G. Jung Institute in New York, from which I graduated in 1980.

One hot summer day in 1975 I was standing alone at the edge of a mesa at Old Oraibi on the Hopi Indian Reservation in Arizona. As I looked out at the vast expanse of desert below me, I imagined I could smell the ancient ocean that once covered the beauty that lay before me. To the west was the majesty of the still snow-capped San Francisco Peaks above Flagstaff. In the exquisite quiet of the moment I felt a presence. I looked up and saw two golden eagles flying toward me. They swooped down to within a few feet of my head, and, wings almost touching, flew together in a circle around me, as if they were doing a dance. They circled me three or four times, then flew off together to the west, disappearing into the brilliant horizon. I felt that their presence honored me, and that I had been brought there, to that place in that moment, to honor them. And in that moment I felt the mystery that was unfolding my life to me. I mused: "What is a fat little Jewish boy from southwest Washington D.C. doing at this ancient holy place at the edge of the world, immersed in Hopi and Navajo religion and healing?" And then I realized that one's personal mystery is not rational at all. I could not have conjured the events that had brought me to the edge of that mesa, yet I knew I could not be anywhere else. It was here that my path and the mystery of my self had taken me. As improbable as it seemed, it was indeed my path. It took another 20 years for me to transcend strong family, personal, and professional ties in the East and move to New Mexico. But when I did, I knew I was coming home.

Chapter 2

Living in the Borderland – The pathological and the sacred: Hannah

The noblest ministry of nature is to stand as the apparition of God. It is the organ through which the universal spirit speaks to the individual, and strives to lead back the individual to it.

Ralph Waldo Emerson

Over these last few years I've come to recognize that the very practice of psychotherapy in its traditional form can be dangerous to one's health, that a devotion to maintaining certain preconceived assumptions may actually prevent healing, for both therapist and client.[1]

The year was 1992 when I finally moved to New Mexico, establishing my analytic practice in Santa Fe. One year later a woman in her early 40s contacted me and asked for a consultation.

Hannah had already undergone at least 12 years of therapy with both male and female therapists. She had a history of sexual abuse. At the age of nine she was molested by a man at a sleep-away camp she attended. She also suspected sexual abuse by at least two family members, although her recall of specific events was vague and shadowy. Since the age of 20, she had suffered from recurring nightmares with graphic images of a murderer coming after her. She had made suicide attempts as a teenager. Her five siblings suffered severe and chronic depression as well, and all had been sexually abused at some point in their lives. During our initial session she indicated that she again felt suicidal; the only thing stopping her was her care for her dog, who was dependent on her. Her depression and despair were constant.

Hannah was an artist. She said of her painting: "I don't know how to bear the part of me that comes out." She painted animals almost exclusively. Sometimes she included human figures, but they were shadowy, usually considerably smaller than the animal figures. Her paintings were dark, the animals always in stages of stress, deprivation, mutilation, and torture. Hannah said that although these paintings did express suffering and pain, at the same time she had the hope that they expressed the possibility of transformation. She also stated: "I can't distinguish between my pain and the pain of other people. And it doesn't help when I do understand it."

Given Hannah's history, I began our work with a traditional approach. I explored her family experiences and pursued in depth the issues of substance abuse, sexual abuse, and parental neglect. I employed the whole repertoire of techniques involved in a good psychoanalytic-psychotherapeutic approach, as we call it. This was helpful to some extent. But always during our sessions, I had the feeling that something was missing, something was not happening – some part of her was absent.

When Hannah brought her paintings into the sessions, things livened up considerably. I wasn't sure if this was because her painting offered her a way of dealing with her depression, isolation, and despair, or if it was more than that. Yet, noticeably, we both sensed relief.

One day, a year or so into the work, she arrived at my office very distressed. Driving home from our previous session, she had found herself behind a truck carrying two cows. Her feeling was that the cows were being taken to slaughter. I pursued the standard approach of suggesting that she was projecting onto the cows, i.e. how she saw her life circumstance in the plight of these cows. She went along with me for a time. But then she protested in frustration: "But it's the *cows*!" I pointed out to her that her response was an identification with animals she experienced as abused. She acknowledged the truth of my interpretations. She began to talk about all the animals in the world that exist only as domesticated beings, and their sadness. And again she burst out: "But it's the *cows*!" After that last protest – by now at the end of the session – I became aware in *myself* of Hannah's distress and her identification with the plight of these cows. And I also became aware of a different feeling in the room. The feeling was attached to Hannah, yet it was separate from her. It seemed of a different dimension. It was a new experience for me.

Some weeks later, Hannah recounted how she had gone for a long walk in the country and was followed by some stray dogs. As she described the experience, the room filled with pain and remorse. I asked her what she was feeling. Again we had a go-round like the one with the cows. And again she acknowledged her projection onto the dogs. But this time, out of character for her, she became angry – so angry that she took her shoe in her hand and hit the floor with it. "You just don't get it!" she shouted, and slammed the floor again with her shoe. "It's the *dogs*!" It was as if she were saying the dogs were projecting something onto *her*. The urgency of her tone and her uncharacteristic anger jolted me into the realization that my standard interpretations were not enough and somehow off the mark. Something other was happening in the room.

The next week Hannah came to our session with a dream suggesting the threat of sexual violation by me. The dream jarred me, and I knew I had better *hear* her. I began to listen to her more closely and tried diligently to shut off my mind and training. I tried to listen as I sensed the medicine man listens.

Over the next months Hannah struggled to wrench out of her unconscious the words to talk to me. Clearly she was extremely intelligent, yet at times it seemed she was groping for a vocabulary that was beyond her reach – a vocabulary that perhaps didn't yet exist. Gradually, however, she did begin to communicate her feelings to me. And as she did, I was startled to realize that the things she was telling me I had heard once before.

During my analytical training I had also been learning from native elders and healers, particularly from my Navajo friend, Carl Gorman, from a Hopi elder whom I called Grandpa, and from a Hopi medicine man, Homer. These men were teaching me a new way of looking at life. I realized that here were people whose involvement with nature was completely different from the utilitarian, often adversarial if sometimes sentimental, attitude toward nature that had characterized the western mind for thousands of years. For the Navajo, religion and healing are the same. The psychic connection with nature is the source of – and at the same time is inseparable from – spiritual and physical health. Illness is a "disconnection" with one's psychic roots.

As I listened to Hannah struggle to articulate her emotions, I did "get it." It was indeed the cows. I realized that what Hannah was telling me was precisely the same message the native elders and healers were teaching me – and what my own unconscious was telling me through my dreams: Everything animate and inanimate has within it a spirit dimension and communicates *in that dimension* to those who can listen.

Darwin taught us that extinction occurs when a species becomes over-specialized and can no longer adapt to changing conditions. In my view, the most dramatic evidence of the western, overspecialized ego bringing our species to the edge of extinction is the game of Russian roulette we played with the former Soviet Union during the Cold War. This lasted for about 50 years from the post-World War II period until the early 1990s. As a consequence of this apocalyptic teetering on the brink of self-annihilation, the western ego became overspecialized and one sided. As a result, I believe we can see a massive compensatory shift to redress this imbalance, to reconnect with our split-off roots. This shift is not just – or even primarily – political and social. I believe it to be an evolutionary psychic shift. Navajo religion and healing – as do other paradigms – most poignantly represent a conscious conception of the world that is not separated from nature in all its forms, animate and inanimate. For non-Native people this is still a largely unconscious phenomenon. It is only recently liminally emergent in westerners such as Hannah, who experience this shift most intensely.

The psychic space where the hyper-developed and overly rational western ego is in the process of reconnecting with its split-off roots in nature is what I call the Borderland. Phrases such as "a reconnection to nature" can conjure up the idealized image of Native Americans as portrayed in the movies, or "New Age" ideas and movements, or vague allusions to ancient mysteries and the occult, many of which are perceived as "flaky" by the culture at large.

But it is my contention that these ideas are manifestations of the "Border-land" consciousness, indications of a "reconnection with nature" that is taking place in western culture. I am talking here of a profound, psychic process in which the very psychological nature and structure of the western ego is evolving through dramatic changes. It is becoming something more, and different from, what we have known in the past.

Hannah is a "Borderland personality." She *lives* in the Borderland. She embodies and reflects an evolving psyche that is not only new unto itself but one that in profound ways is strange and alien to her, as do many others. Such people are the frontline recipients of *new psychic forms* that are entering and impacting the western psyche. They experience the tension resulting from split-off psychic material reconnecting with an ego that resists and is threatened by it.

Borderland people *personally* experience, and must live out, the split from nature on which the western ego, as we know it, has been built. They feel (not feel *about*) the extinction of species; they feel (not feel about) the plight of animals that are no longer permitted to live by their own instincts, and which survive only in domesticated states to be used as pets or food. Such people are highly intuitive. Many, if not most, are psychic to some degree, whether they know it or not. They are deeply feeling, sometimes to such a degree that they find themselves in profound feeling states that seem irrational to them. Virtually all of them are highly sensitive on a bodily level. They experience the rape of the land in their bodies, they psychically, and sometimes physically, gasp at the poisoning of the atmosphere. Often they suffer from "environmental illness." This psychic identity with the animate and inanimate objects of nature is a phenomenon that anthropologist Lucien Levy-Bruhl recognized among native cultures, and which he called *participation mystique*.[2] It is a psychic identification from which, up until recently, westerners have been totally alienated. My experience working with Hannah brought into focus phenomena I had observed both inside and outside my practice over the past 20 years – phenomena that until now had made no sense.

The Borderland is a phenomenon of the collective unconscious. It is an evolutionary dynamic that is moving the western psyche to reconnect our overspecialized ego to its natural psychic roots. It is my view that we are all in the grip of this unfolding. Indeed, it is possible that our very survival as species *Homo sapiens* may depend on this shift that is taking place. The people I have dubbed Borderland personalities experience and *incarnate* these new psychic forms into their lives – and directly and indirectly into ours as members of the western cultural collective. In the case of Hannah, I felt I was observing the impact of this evolutionary process on a specific individual.

A difference between Borderland personalities and non-Borderland personalities is that the former might be thought of as being three or more standard deviations out from the psychic norm. The rest of us, being closer to the western rational norm at the center of the bell curve, still function in our preferred ignorance of Borderland phenomena. I say "preferred" ignorance because such phenomena do not readily fit our rational construct of the universe or of ourselves. Much of what might fall into the nonrational realm is perceived as irrational, that is, "counter-rational," and plays into a phobic abhorrence characteristic of the western ego. More often than not, Borderland phenomena, if experienced at all, are simply dismissed out of hand or labeled crazy.

In recent years, physicists have been developing "field theory," wherein interactions between bodies are seen as the result of changes in space surrounding the bodies, as distinct from a concept of space as a vacuum in which forces external to the space determine the behavior of bodies. The study of weather patterns (for example, El Niño, La Niña) now reveals that storms and other meteorological phenomena are known to constantly impact areas of the planet thousands of miles distant on a constant basis whether we perceive them or not. A popular conception of this phenomenon is the beating of a butterfly's wings that is said to impact a "field," however immeasurably, thousands of miles away.

Ironically, this new direction in science, through the ideas of David Bohm and others, seems to be approaching a kind of "Borderland realm" for the rational western mind. It is in the field of quantum physics that an interface between nonrational and rational phenomena of the *physical realm* is studied and accepted to an increasing degree. Quantum physics posits that form – and form alone – is itself matter.[3]

This world of quantum physics appears to be a strange "Borderland" world indeed. For the scientific mind confronted with such nonrational phenomena, the saving grace appears to be quantification, wherein the application of feeling-neutral mathematics is the ultimate accepted language. In this context, quantification provides a rational connection between the quasi-rational and the nonrational, and thus avoids a disquieting reaction on the part of the mind that studies them. However, when it comes to human *behavior* and *psychology* (fields of study that inevitably confront our feelings and emotions), the Borderland realm is not explored by most investigators. It is shunned because it thrusts the nonrational dimension under the nose of our obsessively rational ego. On a feeling and emotional level this is disequilibrating, often triggering a phobic reaction in those who are confronted with this dilemma.

Most of us in the psychological professions are trained in the mold of the medical model of healing, that is, a rational model where all phenomena are made to fit logical/rational theories of psychological health (of cells, organs, personalities, behavior). Those phenomena that do not fit our theories are ipso facto labeled "pathological." The term as used is not only descriptive of a psychodynamic process, it is also a judgment. That which is pathological is "bad" and therefore must be "cured" (fixed, gotten rid of, cut out.) What I learned from my work with Hannah – and subsequently with other patients – is that the Borderland phenomena they experience are *real*, however disquieting that notion may seem. Problems result from the fact that most often Borderland personalities themselves do not register their own experiences as real. They have been conditioned, like the rest of us with a western ego, to identify with the negative bias against the nonrational realm of phenomenology. Thus they see their own Borderland experiences as "crazy" – as pathological. And because they do, they become more neurotic than would otherwise be the case.

Many Borderland people I have encountered have experienced early childhood trauma, often sexual trauma. Like Hannah, they carry deep wounds and neuroses that *do* fit standard rational psychological theories of mental health and *do* fit the medical model of healing. Great personal suffering often occurs when nonpathological Borderland experiences become fused with personal traumatic experiences and the neurotic layers of personality structure. This in turn amplifies and reinforces a person's neurosis. Hence the experiences are then labeled as pathological either by the individuals themselves or by the healing practitioner, by the family, or by others around them. This fusion of the personal with the nonpersonal makes it difficult to sort out which is which, and precisely this was my problem in the first year or so of my work with Hannah.

Prior to our work together, Hannah could not distinguish between her own feelings and those of the earth and the animals. When I first encouraged her to talk about the animals, she was reticent. She feared, understandably, that I would label her "crazy." And for a while, until I "got it," my insistence on relating her feelings exclusively to her personal history confused and exacerbated the situation.

However, Hannah and I *were* able to sort out her pathology arising from her upbringing on the one hand and her nonpathological experiences arising from Borderland phenomena on the other. I was able to witness and authenticate her Borderland experiences as *objective nonpersonal, nonrational phenomena* occurring in the natural universe for which she was not responsible. And as she came to understand this, she felt more sane and whole, and became dramatically healthier and more functional. This has also been the case with increasing numbers of patients who come into my office.

I have referred to the Borderland phenomenon as "sacred." Much of it is. By sacred I mean that which is transpersonal, beyond rational experience, and which carries a feeling of numinosity. These phenomena are a mystery connected to the source of life itself – that is, to the godhead. Indeed, the word "god*head*" is a misnomer in that there is little of the rational mind that is connected with this dimension of the sacred. Here I am not talking about a personified god*head*, a god after whom we are supposedly fashioned, but of a dimension that preexisted any concept of personified deity. I am talking about that dimension of the sacred that resides – consciously for tribal cultures – in nature herself.

Navajo religion speaks to the source, the mystery from which life in all its forms emerges, by calling on the "Holy People." However, the Holy People are not so much personified *creators* as they are the purveyors of what *is* and what emerges from the Great Mystery. The various forms of the Holy People – Talking God, Calling God, First Man, First Woman, Changing Woman, Big Fly, Coyote, Wind, etc. – serve as mythological and symbolic messengers in a cosmology of all that is seen and unseen. They convey the knowledge of the way all things once were, and, in terms of basic order, the way that all things are *intended* to be. At the same time, each object, each symbol, each event has its own intrinsic spiritual form and purpose. We might take "wind" as one example as described in James K. McNeley's *Holy Wind in Navajo Philosophy*:

> It was seen that in the creation of the world on Earth's surface, the Holy People, existing as inner forms of natural phenomena of the cardinal directions, were given the means of communicating with others by means of Winds. These Winds could be sent as their "messengers," their "means of knowing things" and of providing guidance to Earth Surface People. The Wind within and about the developing individual consists in part, of such Messenger Winds conceived of as Little Winds or Wind's Child which exist within the Wind that is everywhere there is life. It is these Little Winds sent by the Holy Ones that are thought to provide the means of good Navajo thought and behavior.[4]

This dimension of the sacred, as it is expressed here in the Navajo religion, was *of necessity* sacrificed to the development of what we have come to know as western culture. It is to this dimension of the sacred that I believe evolution is now bringing us – to a reconnection in spite of our conscious intent. And it is a reconnection that is in process, a process that points forward, not backward, a process that is changing us profoundly. The nature of that change is the mystery that lies ahead.

I do not mean to idealize nature or the dynamic I have called the Borderland personality. The process of evolution accepts, modifies, or rejects the forms through which an organism has passed – it does not revert to them. Hence my term "a reconnection to nature" should not be confused with the idealized "back-to-nature" philosophy of Jean-Jacques Rousseau or of the later 19th-century writers and artists who followed him. Neither do I wish to idealize the suffering that Hannah and so many others experience; this would be cruel and completely miss the point. Environmental illness and dissociative states cannot be idealized.

Yet in many ways I do see Borderland personalities as heroic. In their struggles to survive and bring these sacred phenomena into our world – albeit in most cases unconsciously – they do work that benefits us all. Hannah does this through her painting, others write books; some do it in their consulting rooms, not only in the healing professions, but also even in the corporate world. Many, if not most, incarnate this sacred dimension in silent and unseen ways.

When I have the opportunity of working with Borderland personalities, I am moved not only by their struggle to do their personal work, but to do our work for us as well, that is, for those of us who are much less connected to and in touch with the Borderland. I see the deeper thrust of this new phase in our psychic evolution as *a pulling back from the brink of self-extinction*. It is in this sense that Borderland people are the unrecognized heroes and heroines of our collective evolution toward growth, consciousness, and individuation. Theirs is a large and sacred work. To the extent this is true, we all will stand or fall with the outcome.

When I attend the plaza dances at Hopi or at the Indian pueblos, particularly the Corn Dance at San Felipe Pueblo on their feast day, I am profoundly moved that this small band of people, which western civilization nearly exterminated, is doing sacred work for all of us, Indian and non-Indian alike. As I watch the barefoot dancers – men, women, and children – dance from sunrise to sunset, hour after hour after hour in the hot, shadeless plaza, I am moved by their gift to us. When I see one of the center men hold erect a huge ten- to 15-foot wooden pole and circumambulate the line of dancers, waving the pole back and forth, emulating a corn plant sprinkling its pollen in blessing over dancers and observers, I am thankful to him. I realize that these dancers and the headman with the pole are also emulating the earth rotating on its axis, maintaining the balance in nature necessary for the continuance of life in a sacred honoring and thanking of Mother Earth for her gifts to all of us. They are doing the work that we, as western civilized beings, no longer know how to do. And somewhere, deep down in my soul, perhaps in my Borderland place, I know that if they do not do our work for us as well as for their own, perhaps the earth in some sense *would* cease rotating on its axis.

And then there would be no one to sing the sacred songs.

I have presented the case of Hannah as a model for the ideas to follow. However, this case is only one of many Borderland personality types I have encountered in my clinical work. A number of them will be discussed in Part II of the book. I have chosen Hannah's case to open up discussion of this new dimension of consciousness, as well as a number of clinical considerations that ensue from it, in order to simplify the presentation for the reader. Throughout the book I use the case of Hannah for discussion purposes as representative of many cases. My theory is not based on a single case, but on the many cases discussed throughout the book.

The remaining chapters of Part I address the theoretical model that has emerged as I have struggled to explain the appearance of Borderland consciousness. The theoretical model presented in the following chapters is very much informed by my 30 years of clinical work; psychoanalytic theory, most particularly the psychology of Carl Jung; recent research in the neuropsychia-try of psychological development, as well as research in complexity theory and a number of other related areas of research reflected in the text. My work with Navajo medicine men, both as student and as patient, and the teachings of Hopi elders and a Hopi medicine man have been of immense importance in formulating this model. Individuals unknown to me other than through their correspondence have stepped forward and identified themselves as Borderland personalities (some of whose material appears in Part II with their permission). I am aware that theoretical models other than the one that follows might explain the phenomena that I describe as "Borderland." The theoretical model that I present, obviously, is the one that makes most sense to me.

Notes

1   Scott, 2000: 45.
2   Levy-Bruhl, 1966.
3   Peat, 1990.
4   McNeley, 1981: 36.

Chapter 3

Genesis: Birth of the western ego[1]

He [uncivilized man] does not dream of regarding himself as the lord of creation. His zoological classification does not culminate in *Homo sapiens* but in the elephant. Next comes the lion, then the python or crocodile, then man. It never occurs to him that he might be able to rule nature.[2]

[T]he essential biblical idea is that God is also beyond nature.[3]

You must forgive me, dear friend. I'm a lover of learning, and trees and open country won't teach me anything, whereas men in the town do.[4]

Throughout this book, I will be using the terms "psyche" and "ego." Psyche represents the *totality* of conscious and unconscious psychological life. This all-inclusive organ has many components: The unconscious, typological orientation (intuition, sensation, feeling, thinking, extroversion/introversion); constructs for apprehending subjective states and implicit memory; the sense of collective consciousness, and the motivations of unconscious cultural values and impulses. Dominant within the psyche, among what one might call these "background" psychic constructs, is the ego – the center of subjective being, the "I" of one's self. This ego is the *conscious* part of our psychic make-up, the mental tool we use to adapt to our personal experiences and perception of reality, and to our identity with the cultural and social groups through which we build our civilization.[5,6] Notwithstanding its one-sided dedication to consciousness and conscious process, it, the ego, is influenced by unconscious elements.

Psyche, and consequently ego, are inherently constructs of culture; hence the western *psyche* is the totality of those elements that throughout history have created a "western" psychic consciousness *and* unconsciousness. The western *ego* is the conscious personalization of European/American cultural constructs and the personal and collective experiences that are the motivations of behavior. At the same time, the western ego is influenced by unconscious elements.

There are two broad categories of unconscious psychic content. The first includes split-off repressed *personal* contents that have been experienced by the individual (or group) at one time or another and that, for various reasons, have been repressed, shoved back into the unconscious. An example might be a personal experience about which one feels guilty – a theft, for example – and which is subsequently repressed.

The second category of unconscious psychic content includes what Jung described as the *collective unconscious*. Although Jungian theory agrees with the concept of psyche as outlined above, Jung's concept of the Self extends the idea of "psyche" exponentially by the inclusion of the collective unconscious. In Jungian jargon, we use the term "the *Self*," to refer to those parts of our psychic structure that contain *both* individual and collective conscious and unconscious contents.[7] Without the latter, psyche is limited to *personalistic* contents, i.e. contents that, in one way or another, derive from the life experience of the individual. Jung's concept of the collective unconscious extends the idea of psyche to embrace transpersonal contents, i.e. spiritual, and other contents emerging from the collective unconscious, thus leading to the second category of unconscious content.

This second category refers to unconscious material that has never been manifest consciously. These latter unconscious contents can be both personal and collective. An example of *personal unconscious* contents emerging from the psyche might be that of a person who has always seen himself as an atheist who has begun to have a series of dreams involving emergent religious themes. An example of *collective unconscious* contents might be prophetic dreams,[8] transcultural myths, or the birth of new religions.[9] These could be said to have erupted out of the collective unconscious where, in the case of the new religions, they had lain as ungerminated psychic potential.

Throughout this book I will be using the term "psyche" in the sense that Jung formulated it to include his concept of the collective unconscious. I would like the reader not familiar with Jungian literature and concepts to know that it is not just his struggle to grasp some of these concepts. These concepts – and in particular Jung's concept of the Self – are difficult both to grasp and to put into words, as is witnessed by my own struggles to do so here and elsewhere in this book.

A rudimentary understanding of the concept of the collective unconscious and the theory of archetypes will assist the reader in understanding some of the material that follows. In his concept of the "collective unconscious" Jung asserted that mankind in general, and all cultures in particular, as well as individuals, are subject to nonpersonal unconscious contents that do not derive from personal experience and that are antecedent to personal and collective experience. These collective psychic forces are not directly knowable but are experienced through their manifestation in collective and individual behavior through universal psychic forms that he called "archetypes." Archetypes are also manifested symbolically through myths and fairy tales as well as through other modes of psychic expression such as dreams and imagination.[10]

In Jung's words:

> The other part of the unconscious [in addition to Freud's notion of the personal unconscious which contains personal material repressed by the individual] is what I call the impersonal or collective unconscious. As the name indicates, its contents are not personal but collective, that is, they do not belong to one individual alone but to a whole group of individuals, and generally to a whole nation, or even to the whole of mankind. These contents are not acquired during the individual's life-time but are products of innate forms and instincts. Although the child possesses no inborn ideas, it nevertheless has a highly developed brain, which functions in a quite definite way. This brain is inherited from its ancestors; it is the deposit of the psychic functioning of the whole human race. [Therefore it also brings with it the cumulative learned *capacities* (not content) that humans have acquired over the millennia: for example, the ready *capacity* to learn reading and math.] The child therefore brings with it an organ ready to function in the same way as it has functioned throughout human history. In the brain the instincts are preformed, and so are the primordial images [archetypes] which have always been the basis of man's thinking – the whole treasure house of mythological motifs."[11]

[Brackets added.]

I have described the "Borderland personality" as someone who psychically straddles the split between the developed, rational mind and nature in the western psyche, and one who holds and carries the tension of that split and an emergent reconciliation of that split at one and the same time. The Borderland is a recent evolutionary dynamic that appears to be rapidly gaining momentum and liminality in the western ego. It is manifested through the collective unconscious – a natural evolutionary dynamic – that is moving the western psyche to reconnect its present overspecialized ego to its natural roots. If we can entertain the idea of a Borderland dynamic that is reconnecting the western ego with nature, it would behoove us, then, to ask: Is the western ego an accident in history? Is it solely environmentally induced? Is it primarily a characteristic of geography or evolution? Does it have other source(s) for its development? Does it have other purpose(s) that reach beyond itself and that are not yet fully understood? And where is it headed as we proceed into the new millennium?

If we look at the evolution of western culture psychodynamically and archetypally, we see a process that has had as a primary goal the development of a highly specialized ego that would elevate rational process, i.e. *logos*,[12] above all other functions. Ultimately, the psychodynamic process giving rise to the specialized ego unique to the western psyche has yielded modern science and technology, democratic principles and government, and aggressive capitalism, among many other things. The fact that the roots of some of these ideas, philosophies, and technologies were appropriated from other cultures, e.g. China, the Jewish and Muslim Middle East, does not change the fact that it has been the western European ego, the American version in particular, that developed them to their "advanced" states that exist today. That the United States is the undisputed sole superpower in the world in the new millennium, and dominated the world technologically, economically, and politically throughout much of the 20th century, speaks for itself.

Genesis

The development of this highly specialized ego would appear to be the specific and primary mandate of the collective unconscious itself. I will argue below that this mandate is stated explicitly in Genesis, the first book of the Hebrew Bible, i.e. that man (through the instrument of his new ego), "shall rule over the fish of the sea, the birds of the sky, and over the animal, the whole earth, and every creeping thing that creeps upon the earth."[13] And we seem to be still in the throes of that directive, notwithstanding the passage of three and a half millennia since the writing of Genesis. The ego that was spawned through Genesis and that archaic Biblical imperative now threatens our very survival as a species.

But how is it that Genesis still has a hold on our lives in a culture that almost universally professes allegiance to evolutionary theory? Nearly half the peoples of the world observe a religious tradition that is identified as Judeo-Christian.[14] They all hold Genesis as sacred scripture. Genesis and evolutionary theory at cursory glance seem to contradict one another. So what is going on?

It is easy to slip by this question. We have been doing just that ever since Darwin formulated his theories in the mid-19th century, directly challenging both the timing and the nature of the "Creation" as set forth in Genesis. Although the scientific view of creation overwhelmingly holds to evolutionary theory, we wink at least one eye at the account of origins presented in Genesis. Virtually no one, scientists in particular, has challenged Genesis per se. Scientists readily assert the evolutionary view that existence far predates any interpretation of Genesis but, with very few exceptions, they do not directly challenge this Biblical chronology.

Why not, one might ask? Do they not see the contradiction between the chronology in Genesis, i.e. that the earth and humans were created in six days, and their own belief? Do they not care that they themselves – at least many of them – function in the face of a profound contradiction between their professed religious identification, which embraces Genesis, and what they do and believe professionally? Surely they do.

And what of the church? One would be pressed hard to find a nonfundamentalist minister/priest/rabbi who would subscribe to a literal translation of Genesis, particularly its chronology regarding human existence. Yet virtually all of them subscribe to the Hebrew Bible as scripture, sacred and revelatory, including Genesis, whether by the Christian calendar or the Hebrew calendar. At the same time one would be pressed even harder to find a minister/priest/rabbi who would openly assert that the Creation story in Genesis is *just* that, a "story." Despite the fact that virtually no one takes the chronology of Genesis seriously, the Creation as told in Genesis carries profound spiritual, religious, and archetypal weight. We don't believe it, literally, but we are very careful to not debunk it either. And those of us who do attend churches and synagogues still read Genesis *as if it were* sacred scripture.[15]

In other words, we consciously and unconsciously play both sides of the street when it comes to Genesis. The behavioral preference is to be silent on the "truth" or "falseness" of the Creation story/myth exactly because it *is* sacred. Factual truth has little, if anything, to do with sacred or divine truth. We might broadly define "sacred" and "divine" truth as truth revealed – truth derived from other than rational sources, i.e. revelation (from God), transpersonal, manifestation of the collective unconscious – a truth that is *transrational* and sanctioned by an accepted religious authority such as a tribal culture, an organized church, or other such institution. There is also a *personal* experience of divine truth. I will speak of this later. For our purposes here, I am speaking only of collective truth, i.e. collective shared belief. The Bible is a transrational document. The fact that it is no longer believed *literally*, does not diminish its contemporary mythic reality.

The sacred is always numinous, that is, it carries the aura of the divine.[16] But the numinous is seldom based on outer literal truth. Indeed, the "sacred" has more to do with inner psychological need and archetypal reality as it is reflected in, and emerges from, the collective unconscious. More often than not, the role of outer forces serves to induce a seeking for deeper meaning within the personal and collective unconscious. It is from the latter – from the source within – that the new truth is revealed. This is so on an individual level and particularly so on the collective level. Sometimes the new "revealed" truth is ego syntonic, i.e. consistent with the ego's sense of itself and its perceived needs; oftentimes it is not. And sometimes the new truth is paradoxically experienced as both syntonic and dystonic at the same time.[17]

"Truth," then, in ancient times, particularly on the collective level, had least to do with outer fact and most to do with inner need and reality and the flux and direction of the collective unconscious. Genesis and the other writings of the Hebrew Bible reflect the collective and archetypal reality of the time. They represent "revelation" on the part of the collective unconscious at a given psychological and temporal moment in history, in a given place, through a particular group or people.[18]

The Archetypal thrust of Genesis

Viewed symbolically and archetypally, the "creation" story of Genesis is not about the beginning beginning, i.e. the *first* beginning; it is about a *new* beginning in the midst of the beginning that *had already taken place*. And, as the story suggests, it is not only a new beginning for the human species but ultimately for all life.

Since one kind of day had already existed prior to Genesis, so had one kind of consciousness. And we know from scripture itself that the thrust of this new kind of consciousness was to subdue the earth, to conquer it; to be masters of the fish of the sea, the birds of heaven and all living animals on the earth. We also know that since Genesis announced this new mandate, western man has done just that; subdued the earth and established his dominion over every living thing that moves on the earth – plants as well as animals as well as the earth itself.

We can see this mandate as stated directly in scripture, specifically the first chapter of the Hebrew Bible (Jewish Publication Society edition):

> In the beginning God created the heaven and the earth –
> 2 the earth being unformed and void, with darkness over the surface of the deep and the Spirit of God sweeping over the water.
> 3 God said, "Let there be light"; and there was light.
> 4 God saw that the light was good, and God separated the light from the darkness.
> 5 God called the light Day, and the darkness He called Night. And there was evening and there was morning, a first day . . .
> 26 God said, "Let us make man in our image, after our likeness. They shall rule . . . the whole earth . . .
> 27 And God created man in His image, in the image of God He created him; male and female He created them.
> 28 God blessed them, and God said to them, "Be fertile and increase, fill the earth and *master it*; and rule the fish of the sea, the birds of the sky and all the living things that creep on earth."[19]

The King James version is more explicit:

> [A]nd subdue it: and have dominion over . . . every living thing that moveth upon the earth.[20]
>
> [Emphasis added.]

And the Jerusalem Bible puts it even more starkly:

> God blessed them [the male and female He created] saying to them, "Be fruitful, multiply, fill the earth and *conquer it*. Be masters of the

fish of the sea, the birds of heaven and all living animals on the earth."[21]
[Emphasis added.]

In this last version, the mandate is not only to rule over all living things that move on the earth, but to conquer earth itself.

Throughout recorded history, beginning with Greek civilization, but especially since the Middle Ages, western European culture has carried out this mandate. Europe, since the 16th century, through its colonial policies, and the United States in particular through its colonial policies of the 19th century and through its technological and economic dominance in the 20th century, have been the primary agents for the exercise of dominion over the earth. The Hebrew Bible, and its later archetypal manifestation in the form of the New Testament, became the underpinnings of the evolution of western civilization; the most prevalent characteristic of this civilization has been its highly developed and specialized ego complex.

One primary goal of the new consciousness commanded in Genesis was the development of a *new psychic construct in human evolution*. Pointedly, the goal was the development of this unique ego structure. "Dominion over the earth" was to be the means to that end. I am suggesting, however, that the underlying goal was *not* the simple control of the earth, but a *boundaried* and *contained* ego based on logic and the *logos* principle. *This* ego, unlike the ego merged-with-nature that preceded it, would elevate logic and left-brain thinking to the exclusion of the arational, the irrational, and the transrational, and right-brain functioning. It was to become an ego that would hold logic and rational process as superior and more real than feeling and intuition. It would consider any reality other than rationality as being inferior and less real.[22]

However, looking back on the 20th century in particular, it would appear – some would say obviously so – that the process went awry, and the "means," more than not, became the "end," i.e. an ego in service to the Biblical God's plan became an agency in service to itself. By the end of the 20th century the western ego had virtually deified itself and displaced Yahweh as the source of its own genesis. If we hold the view, as I do, that there was constructive evolutionary intent in the development of this new kind of consciousness, we have yet to discover the deeper meaning and mystery for which that new consciousness and a new kind of ego was commanded in Genesis. More on this later.

It is as if to say that in the course of human evolution the collective unconscious determined that there would be a new kind of consciousness – a *new kind* of day, a *reflective* consciousness. And this new, *self-reflective*, consciousness brought with it, for the first time, the idea of an unconscious, i.e. an awareness of one's *specific* unconscious*ness* in a given moment. Ultimately, through the discoveries of depth psychology in the 20th century, was the revelation that this personal unconscious *reflects on us*, even as we are unaware of its doing so – a discovery as radical as the theory of evolution itself.[23]

Role of the alphabet – the *aleph-bet*

As far as we know, "Genesis" was the first "creation" myth written in alphabetic language (as opposed to the hieroglyphic and other ideographic forms of writing that pre- or coexisted Genesis), thus making it the *first* creation myth that could be (and was) communicated across geographic boundaries and cultures throughout the world. Other creation myths such as the Egyptian one did exist in written form – hieroglyphic and later hieratic written form. Glyphic writing is a much more limited technology for communication than the alphabet. Thus other creation myths written in nonalphabetic language were limited in their comprehension and dissemination to the handful of scribes who could read that specific script language. Those written forms had no code associated with them (i.e. an alphabet) that would enable the reader to learn *how* to decipher the words. Leonard Shlain in his book, *The Alphabet versus the Goddess*, asserts in his discussion of Genesis:

> The key is that Yahweh expected all His chosen people to *read* what He had written. To mandate this new approach to religion, He forbade anyone from visualizing any feature of His person or from trying to imagine the form of another god [i.e. the First Commandment]. From Sinai forward, He proscribed the making of all images – He sanctioned only written words. It is not mere coincidence that the first book written in an alphabet is the Old Testament [The Hebrew Bible]. There is none earlier.[24]
> [Emphasis in original.]

This change from ideography to intellectual conception is discussed as well in *The Spell of the Sensuous: Perception and Language in a More-Than-Human World*, by David Abram. Abram makes a compelling case that the advent of "phonetic alphabetic writing," beginning with the Hebrews who developed the first alphabet around 1500 B.C.E. (as opposed to pictographic, ideographic, and rebus writing), which later was more fully developed by the Greeks, resulted in a technological "advance" that forever severed what was to become western culture from its (n)atural roots.[25,26]

Abram points out that alphabetic writing is one of a number of (evolutionary) dynamics and events that served to separate what was to become the western psyche from nature in the service of the development of the highly evolved rational ego that we take for granted today.[27]

Of particular importance as regards abstract thinking is the development of mathematics by the Egyptians (especially surveying and geometry) at a slightly earlier date, 2900 B.C.E., and higher forms of mathematics later in Mesopotamia.[28] Hence the development of the alphabet, along with mathematics, and out of the latter the roots of the sciences. Obviously all had their role in separating out what was to become the western ego construct from its natural roots in oral cultural forms. I suggest, as does Abram, that the development of alphabetic technology played a primary role in bringing about that evolutionary development. Shlain is even more emphatic about the primary role of the development of the first alphabet in this regard.[29] My emphasis is the ascendancy of left-brain *logos* thinking and its suppression of right-brain intuitive thinking that was dominant when psyche remained unsplit from nature. It is this development that, ultimately, has led to what I call an overspecialized ego that has come to threaten life as we know it. The alphabet has played a crucial role in this process.

I have "dated" the "annunciation" of this new kind of consciousness to 1900–1500 B.C.E. Of course, no one knows exactly when the Hebrew scriptures were written.[30] Their contents most likely first existed as separate oral stories of the Creation for quite some time before being written down.[31] And that "annunciation" was not so much a pronouncement at a fixed point in linear time, as a subliminal archetypal awareness reaching conscious threshold over time through the telling and retelling of those stories of the era, each storyteller adding his twist to a story that had endured over generations and centuries, to the point when their thematic substance became "fixed" in the collective "truth" of the time. Edward C. Whitmont points out that the mythological phase of consciousness is a bridge from magical to mental functioning. He says: "As the hot lava of the magical level is touched by the first, cold air of the discerning mind, it gels into forms. These are the mythological images."[32] Alphabetic technology and the capacity for *universal writing* that it made available became the superstructure for that bridge.[33]

An anthropomorphized ego cleaved from nature

As one reads Hebrew Biblical scripture, it is clear that Yahweh did not need "dominion" since He already had it. This is a crucial point, since western culture *behaves* as if the goal of the new awareness heralded by the new creation myth of Genesis was dominion over the earth, with the ego complex as the means towards that goal. Hence our ecological and spiritual crisis as western civilization ends the 20th century and enters a new millennium. Pointedly, the perception that humans in general, and European Americans in particular, *should* exercise dominion over the earth and all that moves on the surface cannot be sustained if we value continued existence of our species. Along ecological lines alone, we have become a major threat to our own survival.

But there is more to this story. So let us return to the Hebrew Bible, this time to Exodus:

13 Moses said to God, "When I come to the Israelites and say to them

'The God of your fathers has sent me to you,' and they ask me, 'What is His name?' what shall I say to them?"

14 And God said to Moses, "Ehyeh – Asher – Ehyeh." [Translated: *I AM THAT I AM*] He continued, "Thus shall you say to the Israelites, '*I AM* has sent me to you.'"

15 And God said further to Moses, "Thus shall you speak to the Israelites: The Lord [*YHWH*], the God of your fathers, the God of Abraham, the God of Isaac, and the God of Jacob, has sent me to you:

This shall be My name forever,

This My appellation for all eternity."[34]

[Brackets added.]

"I AM THAT I AM," is the name of the new God heralded by the Hebrew Bible – the God who cannot be seen except by the signs He chooses to give, the God who is everywhere and nowhere, the God who, whether summoned or not is present, the God who will have no graven images, who cannot be represented through any image, and who can be represented only by His word; He is the God who above all else is mystery, the God, who, if we are to come to know His nature, requires that we explore His mystery and therein our own, since we are made in His image. This is a God who demands to be heard, a God who requires understanding, a God who demands obedience and who chose a people who, like Moses, dialogues with God. This is a God who demands love and who gives love, a God who feels repeatedly wounded by His chosen people, a God with emotions, a hurting God, a needy God, a raging God, a repentant God. This is a God who, despite His claims of omnipotence and His peoples' belief in His omnipotence, permits His weakness to be known to those who would see. He is a lonely God in need of His people at every turn,[35] a God who is different from all other gods who have preceded Him. This is a God who requires a new kind of ego for *relating* to God – an ego that is not just subservient to the godhead, despite His demands that it be so, but at the same time independent of it and thus capable of reflecting the godhead and reflecting on the godhead. This is a God, as Martin Buber would say, in need of an *I–Thou* relationship.

Relationship requires an ego that is separate, that has the capacity for reflection – of self and other. *And* this ego, so demands Genesis, must separate itself from merged unconsciousness and partial awareness – from the "old" consciousness that preceded Genesis – in order to reflect a new manifestation of the godhead and to be available to form a relationship with it.

This *initial* separation, psychodynamically speaking, required a stance of dominion over the earth, i.e. a conscious *and directed* power drive in service to an identified goal. Without that capacity for "dominion" over all things, post-Genesis man could not separate himself sufficiently from being merged in a state of union with nature[36] to be available to *interactively* relate to the new godhead.[37] Heretofore, pre-Genesis, the godhead was synonymous with some aspect of nature. But as we are told in Genesis, "God created man in His *own* image, in the image of God created He him" (emphasis added). So if man is the image of God, then the godhead can no longer be falcons, or cows, or serpents, or crocodiles, or fire, or trees, or any other aspect of nature. From Genesis forward, God was to be experienced in anthropomorphic terms, unknown and mysterious, *but forever distinct from nature.*

As Jung says:

> The further we go back into history, the more we see personality disappearing beneath the wrappings of collectivity. And if we go right back to [tribal/oral] psychology, we find absolutely no trace of the concept of an individual. Instead of individuality we find only collective relationship or what Levy-Bruhl calls *participation mystique.* The collective attitude hinders the recognition and evaluation of a psychology different from the subject's, because the mind that is collectively oriented is . . . incapable of thinking . . . in any other way than by projection. What we understand by the concept of 'individual' is a relatively recent acquisition in the history of the human mind and human culture.[38]

Thus, "dominion," i.e. separation from nature in Genesis terms, was aimed at generating a new kind of ego that could receive a new kind of God whose principal characteristic was His need for interaction and relationship with His people who were "chosen" for that purpose.[39] This new archetypal incarnation was not initially aimed at the development of an ego of which a power drive in service to itself was a characteristic. The power drive that did emerge with this new ego was aimed at separating man from nature. Only in its later manifestations, after the advent in the 5th century B.C.E. of the "Golden Age" of Greece, did an *independent* power drive in service to the ego itself, separate from the new godhead, begin to take root in a major way on a collective level. That independent power drive was fed by a new psychic construct, i.e. intellect. This new construct needed nothing outside itself.

Abram writes:

> [I]t was only then, under the slowly spreading influence of alphabetic technology, that "language" was beginning to separate itself from animate flux of the world, and so becoming a ponderable presence in its own right. The scribe, or author, could now begin to dialogue with his own visible inscriptions, viewing and responding to his own words even as he wrote them down. *A new power of reflexivity was thus coming into existence, borne by the relation between the scribe and his scripted text.*[40]

Thus the basis was laid for perception and awareness itself to be withdrawn from the numinosity engendered in a *participation mystique* with nature, in order for the development of that new ego complex, ordained in Genesis and demanded by Yahweh in Exodus through his commandments given on Mount Sinai, to take place.

It took a mere 1,000 years or so for the rudimentary Hebraic alphabetic structure to spread to Greece and become adapted into a new, more sophisticated alphabetic literacy that became the germ of what was to become western culture as we know it today.[41] That technological "advance" with its inexorable commitment to the development of left-brain functioning at the expense of the then prevalent right-brain functioning, gave rise to abstract thinking and to a science of philosophy, which, along with mathematics, became the basis for most of the other sciences that are foundational in the evolution of western civilization.[42,43] With this new ego construct, one was now capable of dialoging with one's own words and one's own concepts, and, psychologically speaking, with one's own (s)elf, as well as with others.

Abram notes that Socrates developed a new term for this reflective awareness, "*psyché*":[44]

> For Plato, as for Socrates, the *psyché* is now that aspect of oneself that is refined and strengthened by turning away from the ordinary sensory world in order to contemplate the intelligible Ideas, the pure and eternal forms that alone, truly exist. The Socratic-Platonic *psyché*, in other words, is none other than the literate intellect, that part of the self that is born and strengthened in relation to the written letters.[45,46]

Indeed, this transition from one awareness/consciousness to the other was so rapid that Socrates, Plato's teacher, in accompanying Phaedrus on a walk into the countryside is quoted in the *Phaedrus* as saying:

> You must forgive me, dear friend. I'm a lover of learning, and trees and open country won't teach me anything, whereas men in the town do.[47]

If we can imagine the broad sweep of this development, in less than 1,000 years, the numinous has moved from outer to inner, from trees to ideas and from nature to *psyché*. Even Plato's use of the word *psyché* itself has been distorted from its original Homeric meaning in which the word contained numinosity in its essential definition. As used in the Socratic-Platonic sense, it is "the invisible breath that animates the living body and that remains as a kind of wraith or ghost, after the body's death."[48] And once the ego began the slide into an independent power drive *in service to itself*, it began arrogating to itself the powers of the godhead. This became profoundly evident during the Enlightenment (17th and 18th centuries), reaching its zenith in the second half of the 20th century where it became the particular and manifest drama of western culture.

It does not take much imagination to hear God's declaration in Exodus, "I AM THAT I AM," echoed millennia later in 1629 by Descartes' supreme declaration of ego: "*I* think, therefore I am"[49] not, "*God* thinks of me, therefore I am," which had been the ruling psychological principal operating in (western) humankind prior to the Enlightenment. With regard to the latter statement, according to Genesis, man and woman were literally thoughts in God's mind and that is how they/we did come into being. The incarnation of man and woman into flesh and blood was a "higher" incarnation of God's thought. Unlike when Adam and Eve were "mere" thoughts in God's mind, their incarnation made possible God's interaction with them and their interaction with Him, ending – as far as we know – God's isolation and loneliness.[50] And, for at least three millennia we remained there, with the roots of our existence in God's mind, by God's grace, not our own. Thus Descartes' statement can be taken as the articulated demarcation point of western man's arrogation of the powers of the godhead unto himself. Man no longer needed God to think of him in order to be. Now, from 1629 forward, man had only to hold himself in his own thoughts in order to be. And God? God became a belief, not a fact – a belief that one could *choose* to accept or reject. God now needed to be held in man's mind in order to be. Man could believe in Him or not.

An ego wrenched from nature

I have suggested above that the advent of Genesis announced the beginning of the development of a new kind of ego as a new psychic construct in human evolution. Characteristic of this ego was its allegiance to a deity that was more like humans than like nature – *I* AM THAT *I* AM. The new ego was to sacrifice a quasi-merged state of awareness *with* nature, a *participation mystique*, to use Levy-Bruhl's term, for a more reflective and mentalized consciousness *separate from* nature. And this separation was to be absolute – if that ego was to develop. One could not be in a state of *participation mystique with* nature and be optimally *self*-reflective. And to be self-reflective requires the development of a highly individualized and personalized ego. A state of fusion with nature holds one more than not to a group identity, and inhibits individualized identity.[51]

I am distinguishing "consciousness" as characteristic of self-reflective, (alphabetic) cultures from "awareness" characteristic of (oral) cultures, which are more functional participants in nature. Although cultural "consciousness" develops later, this does not mean it is superior to cultural "awareness." Indeed, a central theme of this chapter is how that "higher" ego form has become overspecialized and therefore poorly adaptive for its own survival. By any definition, such an ego would not be "better," although later I do argue that, notwithstanding its threat to our very survival, its development was inevitable (not "better").

Abram describes this "awareness" of oral societies prior to the introduction of alphabetic writing as being on a magical plane in a semi-merged state with nature. He states: "That which is regarded with the greatest awe and wonder by indigenous, oral cultures is . . . none other than what we view as nature itself." And again, "in tribal cultures, that which we call 'magic' takes its meaning from the fact that humans, in an indigenous and oral context, experience their own consciousness as simply one form of awareness among many others."[52] Today, we tend to think of contemporary tribal cultures as usually darker skinned, "aboriginal" groups. It is important here to remember that the societies living in the area of what later became Palestine were all indigenous tribal and oral societies 3,500 years ago.[53] The roots of all humanity trace back ultimately to one tribal group or another. Abram goes on to say:

> Magic, then, in its perhaps most primordial sense, is the experience of existing in a world made up of multiple intelligences, the intuition that everyone perceives – from the swallow swooping overhead to the fly on a blade of grass, and indeed the blade of grass itself – is an *experiencing* form, an entity with its own predilections and sensations . . .
>
> [I]n genuinely oral, indigenous cultures, the sensuous world itself [i.e. nature] remains the dwelling place of the gods, of the numinous powers that can either sustain or extinguish human life.[54]

What is described here is a world, a psychic reality, which we, with our western egos, can understand only as an *idea*, not as a *knowing*. We are on the other side of the mirror. However hard we may strive to perceive – know – this other reality, we are separated from it by three and a half millennia. For the most part, we have relegated this magical world of reality – the *only* reality prior to the advent of alphabetic technology – to such two-dimensional terms as "animism," "magic," and "primitive," most of which carry pejorative connotations.

This new (evolved) *psyché* struck the death knell for oral tradition and all that it represents as the carrier of a particular kind of magic and numinosity no longer known, for the most part, in western culture. Lost were not only stories about the history of now-forgotten cultures but so were certain techniques and ways of healing based on magic, and along with them certain types of psychic/mental *processes*, psychic/mental ways of *being*.[55] Different forms of intuition and the conscious use of body awareness for apprehending information in the environment as well as communication between individuals and groups and with animals are unknown to most of us today.[56] Subtly, we substituted hearing for *listening*, the latter determined as much by that which is listened *to*, as by the one listening. This new *psyché* also made it possible for us to mentalize spirituality through an intellectualized focus on words of prayer and (written) song. What was lost was a direct experience of the numinous conveyed through the power of oral imaginal drama by a wise person in a setting both conjured up by story and reflective of it, where the listener is both receptacle for, and amplifier of, the transpersonal. *Here*, as subtle as it is, is the difference between *knowing* and understanding, between *knowing* and believing, between being *touched* and remembering.

I would further refine Abram's definition of magic as being the ability of the individual to suspend reason and to invoke the *inherent* power of nature to bring itself to bear in a given context. In this definition the major work is, *at first*, to get the reasoning mind out of the way so that the fullest power of nature can be brought to bear. This is clearly evident in what the Navajo medicine man does and, for that matter, any tribal healer. Of course, the question naturally does arise as to what would happen if *both* reason and nature could be brought to bear in a situation where each *enhanced* the other, rather than conflicted with the other? Is such an idea imaginable? Is there something indispensable that the western ego can bring *to* nature itself?

Notes

1 Throughout the theory chapters in Part I, I will not be *directly* discussing the Borderland. These chapters will be focused on my theory which underlies the concept of the Borderland which will be further discussed in Parts II and III.
2 Jung, 1931: para. 134.
3 Gafni, 2003: 52.
4 Plato, 1961: 479 *Phaedrus*, 230d.
5 The *Psychiatric Dictionary* defines "ego" as:

> [T]hat part of the psychic apparatus [the psyche] that is the mediator between the person and reality. Its prime function is the perception of reality and adaptation to it. The ego is the executive organ of the reality principle ... The various tasks of the ego include perception ... and self-awareness; motor control; adaptation to reality ... affects, thinking, and a general synthetic function manifested in assimilation of external and internal elements."
>
> (1988: 232)

6 Jung, 1945: para. 204.
7 The *Self*, in Jungian terms, is the all-inclusive organ of human psychic being. The ego construct emerges out of the Self. Therefore, the concept of the Self includes the ego, while going beyond it. This will be discussed in greater depth in Chapter 7.
8 See the dreams of "John Doe" and "Justin" in Chapter 16.
9 Mormonism, founded in the early 19th century by Joseph Smith, and the Baha'i religion, which was founded in the late 19th century by Baha'u'llah, based on the prophecy of Mirza Ali Muhammah (the Bab), are two such examples.
10 Bernstein, 1989: 5–6.
11 Jung, 1972: 310–311.
12 The *Chambers English Dictionary* defines *logos* as: "The active principle living in and determining the world: the Word of God incarnate." *Logos* derives from Greek, meaning, "word" (1988: 841). It is the principle of reasoning and logical analysis.
13 (1996) Genesis 1:26: 5.
14 *The World Almanac*, 2002: 684.
15 I am aware that there are mystical and esoteric beliefs and literature in both the

Jewish and Christian traditions that give a more symbolic interpretation and meaning to the "stories" of the Hebrew and Christian Bibles. However, these traditions, like the Kaballah, come much later than the actual scriptures themselves and most importantly, it is the scriptures – the literal scriptures – that have guided scholars and rulers since the decalogue was given to Moses over 3,000 years ago. Only a handful of people are familiar with these mystical and esoteric texts and traditions. The question is not which are more or less valid, but, rather, which have had the greatest influence on the evolution of western culture. Scripture, unquestionably, has continuously had the greater impact.

16 See Otto, 1923.

17 For example, "chosenness" on the part of the Jews has been a mixed blessing at best – both ego syntonic and ego dystonic, given the enigma of "chosenness" as the primary target of the Holocaust.

On a somewhat lighter side, there is that wonderful moment in the movie, *Fiddler on the Roof*, where Tevya, after having endured one hardship and catastrophe after the other, looks up to the heavens and pleads to God, "Why don't you 'choose' someone else for a while!" Chosenness, for him, as well as for virtually all the Jews in his village, was far from a universal blessing, if not experienced as a curse.

18 Interestingly, Daniel J. Siegel suggests a neurobiological dimension to these psychic and archetypal "truths" when he observes, "[T]he genetic determination of mental processes may be in the direction of adaptations to past environments, not necessarily to our current ones" (Siegel, 1999: 31).

19 The Tanach, 1988 [5748 – Hebrew Calendar]: 3–4.

20 (1987) Gideons International Bible: 1.

21 (1966) Jerusalem Bible: 16.

22 Verse 6 of Chapter 11 of the Book of Isaiah in the (1966) Hebrew Bible says: "The wolf will live with the sheep and the leopard will lie down with the kid; and a calf, a lion whelp and a fatling [will walk] together, and a young child will lead them." Verse 9 says: "They will neither injure nor destroy in all of my sacred mountain; for the earth will be as filled with knowledge of Hashem as water covering the sea bed." A note to these verses by the biblical commentator/translator states: "The prophecy applies to *Eretz Yisrael* [The Land of Israel], *where the righteous people will be protected from the violence of nature*: 972–973. [Emphasis added.]

23 Jung introduced the notion that this unconscious Self that reflects on us without our knowing it also informs us about contents we have pushed back into the unconscious. In addition, it also informs us about parts of ourselves (and even about life itself) that we have never known or experienced. As Jung puts it: "We have obviously been so busy with the question of what *we* think that we entirely forget what the unconscious psyche thinks about us" (Jung, 1961: para. 606).

24 Shlain, 1998: 71.

25 Anyone interested in a more in depth exposition of the dynamics of the development of alphabetic phonetic language and its impact in severing western culture from nature is referred to Chapter 4 in *The Spell of the Sensuous* (Abram, 1996).

26 It is stressed that throughout this book I am attempting to *describe* the evolution of the psyche, the western psyche in particular. I am endeavoring to make no value judgments in any of the descriptions set forth. Evolution is what it is and does what it does – certain aspects seem to be more complex and "difficult" than others. However, even those "difficult" aspects I see as only that – "difficult", *not* "good" or "bad." They are what they are and we have to live with them and deal with them. Thus when I use terms such as "advance," I am speaking in evolutionary neutral terms.

At the same time, I am aware that I am writing (with this alphabetic technology) and through the lens of my personal western ego. Thus some bias must seep through. Therefore I would request the reader's indulgence as to my *intent* and *meaning* above and beyond the limitations of my ego to get outside itself.

27 Abram, 1996; 263–265.
28 (1992) *Encyclopedia Britannica* vol. 23: 562 ff.
29 Shlain, 1998: 7, 119.
30 The works of Shlain and Abram would appear to support this "dating" (Abram, 1996: 100–109; Shlain, 1998: 7, 119).
31 Some take their roots from Sumer around 4000 B.C.E.
32 Whitmont, 1982: 49–50.
33 *The New York Times*, in an article on the discovery of the oldest known alphabet writing in Egypt, observed: "Evidence at the discovery site supports the idea of the alphabet as an invention by workaday people that simplified and democratized writing, freeing it from the elite hands of official scribes. As such, alphabetic writing was revolutionary in a sense comparable to the invention of the printing press much later" (Wilford, 1999: 1).
34 1988 [5748 – Hebrew Calendar], Exodus, Chapter 3: 88.
35 See Jung (1952) for a penetrating elucidation of this point.
36 A state of *participation mystique*. (See Chapter 2.)
37 This is movingly reflected in Yahweh's pleadings with his chosen people as reflected in the Book of Hosea. See particularly the Jerusalem Bible, Chapter 14.
38 Jung, 1921: para. 12.
39 A prayer said on the Jewish New Year (Rosh Hashanah): "Despite all our frailty, we are Your people, bound to Your covenant, and *called* to Your Service." (Emphasis added.) (Synagogues, 5738 B.C.E.; 1978 C.E.: 89.)
40 Abram, Ibid.: 107.
41 Durant, 1966, vol. I: 106, 295, 343; vol. 2: 667–668, 671.
42 (1992) *Encyclopedia Britannica*, vol. 16: 425–428. Durant, 1966: 667–668.
43 Durant, vol. II: 667–668.
44 *Psyché*, as the word is used by Plato and Socrates, refers to the original genesis of the word and the concept. The definition quoted below is different from how the term "psyche" is used in modern English to connote the mental being in all its psychological as well as its rational aspects (as apart from somatic being).
45 *Psyché*, according to the *New Shorter Oxford English Dictionary* (1966), is from the Greek meaning, "breath, life, soul, mind . . . The mind, especially in its spiritual, emotional, and motivational aspects; the collective mental characteristics of a . . . people".
46 Abram, Ibid.: 113.
47 *Phaedrus*, 230d.
48 *Ibid.*: 113.
49 Descartes, 1934.
50 This point is dramatically, even passionately, reflected in Chapter 6 of the Book of Hosea:

> This love of yours is like a morning cloud,
> like the dew that quickly disappears.
> This is why I have torn them to pieces by the prophets,
> why I slaughtered them with the words from my mouth,
> *since what I want is love, not sacrifice;*
> *Knowledge of God, not holocausts.* [Emphasis added.]
> (1966: 1458)

51 Levy-Bruhl, 1966.
52 Abram, 1996: 9.
53 "Early" Palestine encompassed much more territory than the modern state of Israel.
54 Abram, 1996: 9–10.
55 In the book and TV drama *Roots*, based on fact, Alex Haley would not have been able to trace his ancestor, Kunta Kinte, and his tribal roots in Africa, had that oral tradition been lost totally.
56 See Chapter 2: "It's the *cows*!", pp. 6–8.

Chapter 4

Make-up of this psyche split-off from nature

> We have assumed that our lives need to have no real connection to the natural world, that our minds are separate from our bodies, and that as dismembered intellects we can manipulate the world in any way we choose. Precisely because we feel no connection to the physical world, we trivialize the consequences of our actions.[1]

> This ever-present "neurotic" dissociative tendency ... seems to consist in a basic resistance of the conscious mind to anything unconscious and unknown.[2]

As we have observed, characteristic of the western ego is a consciousness not merged with nature, but wholly cleaved from it.[3] Therefore it is not a diffuse consciousness, but rather a primarily "solar" consciousness: Intensely focused, highly mental, abstract, categorical, mathematical, mechanical, and wedded to linear time. This consciousness is more comfortable with hearing than listening, more focused on the head (literally) than the body, primarily left-brain dominant; it is heroic and preferring abstraction to directness and metaphor, complexity to simplicity.

Because of its separateness from nature and its weddedness to ideas, this ego demonstrates a high capacity to reflect on and interact with its own mental abstractions and to interact as a separate entity with objects around it. On an interpersonal level, it can reflect on others and reflect others to themselves as a mirror. This ego has spawned all that we have come to associate with western civilization: The sciences and the technologies, particularly economics, political science, medicine, psychology, and engineering; a formalized system of mathematics; the many worlds of the arts, including forms of music made possible by the ability to write music and to formalize music theory (and theories); an untold wealth of literature; the capacity to feed more and more peoples of the world; the building of wondrously engineered cities; the extension of length and quality of human life, and so on.

An ego cut off from a relationship with nature tends to be left with its own reflections on itself, unmediated by the transpersonal[4] dimension, and readily trapped in its own mentalisms. Thus it is more prone to power inflations. It tends to be addicted to power and materialism, and thus has also spawned modern warfare with the capacity to eliminate life as we know it: Over-population; runaway greed; a century (the 20th) that, despite its "advances", has seen the worst carnage in human history; human and cultural genocide without precedent; a violent assault on the ecology that the species may not survive; and a fear/panic of the realm of magic, and the rich and complex spirituality associated with it.

Konrad Lorenz, as noted by Jungian analyst Helene Shulman in her book, *Living at the Edge of Chaos: Complex Systems in Culture and Psyche*, says that: "The mind can become the enemy of the soul."[5] Shulman goes on to say of the western ego:

> In the educated sectors of western countries, the ego process may have fallen into a rigid development, losing contact with an unconscious ratiomorphic Self in an extreme and stressful state of vigilance. Many of us have lost access to a ritualized "world center" where deep healing and rejuvenation can occur . . . our prophets speak from television sets. We require our children to stay in school from age five [or before] to twenty-five or thirty if they get professional degrees, but rarely in this education do we make room for the integration of psyche in ritual. In many school systems in the United States, no money is made available for art, music, theater, or any other creative activity. The majority of people in the United States pay no attention at all to their dreams, and most children have thousands of dreams throughout their childhood that they never tell to anyone because no one listens or asks. The end product can be a dissociated adult who has been taught more about correct behavior, competition, and conformity than about inner wholeness.[6]

Western ego's fear of fragmentation

As western European man became increasingly separated from his own tribal roots, and as he developed his rational function in the name of ego development, that same rational function took over the process of separating him increasingly from the transrational dimension, becoming an end unto itself. There are two salient hallmarks of this ego complex that are pertinent here:

1. *Psychic inertia*, wherein the ego resists, powerfully, anything that aims at changing its self-definition and outward orientation.
2. *Abhorrence of the irrational, transrational,[7] and the unconscious*, particularly nature and the collective unconscious, which are perceived to be anathema to its very being.

Over time, virtually all that was nonrational to this ego complex became associated with and eventually viewed as synonymous with "magic" and nature – those dimensions that by definition, through regressive forces, were *perceived* as standing in the way of and preventing its development. Thus nature, herself, became the force to overcome – the enemy. Nature was to be "dealt with" as that ego deals with other objects – as a denuminized object to be exploited. Any suggestion that the numinous *within* and *characteristic of* nature could or should be related to *on nature's own terms* would immediately invoke intense unconscious fear.[8]

Vine Deloria, noted Native American writer, says this well:

> I think the primary difference between [the western and indigenous ways of life] is that Indians experience and relate to a living universe, whereas western people – especially scientists – reduce all things, living or not, to objects. The implications of this are immense. If you see the world around you as a collection of objects for you to manipulate and exploit, you will inevitably destroy the world while attempting to control it. Not only that, but by perceiving the world as lifeless you rob yourself of the richness, beauty, and wisdom to be found by participating in its larger design.
>
> In order to maintain the fiction that the world is dead – and that those who believe it to be alive have succumbed to primitive superstition – science must reject any interpretation of the natural world that implies sentience or an ability to communicate on the part of nonhumans. Science insists, at a great price in understanding, that the observer be as detached as possible from the event he or she is observing. Contrast that with the attitude of indigenous people, who recognize that humans must participate in events, not isolate themselves . . .
>
> Respect for other life-forms filters into our every action, as does its opposite: perceiving the world as lifeless. If you objectify other living things, then you are committing yourself to a totally materialistic universe – which is not even consistent with the findings of modern physics.[9]

As we have seen in the discussion of Genesis, initially the call to develop this highly functioning ego emerged *from* the collective unconscious itself. Paradoxically, the collective unconscious, unknowable in its essence, was and still is perceived by the ego that emerged from it as irrational and therefore threatening. Once a certain threshold of left-brain consciousness was reached by European man, the repression of the nonrational dimension became a defining characteristic, if not an obsession, of ego self-preservation. This split became absolute and total – a living, magical, numinous nature could not be tolerated as a reality just as potent as the rational ego. It could only be tolerated in a desacralized state, as something to be used, not related to, subject to the "dominion" of the rational ego, but not as equivalently potent. On an unconscious level, this may have influenced the genocidal assault on indigenous peoples and culture by western civilization and its armies more than conscious dynamics.

Fragmentation complex

Ultimately, the abhorrence of nature as *the* enemy became a characteristic of the western ego and of western culture itself, resulting in what I have come to call a "fragmentation complex." Characteristically, a fragmentation complex leaves one with a feeling of disintegration or ego fragmentation in the face of powerful irrational forces that cannot be explained, psychologically split off, or rationalized away. The very existence of such phenomena is perceived and experienced as a threat to ego survival – a threat to the very survival of the individual him/herself. It is a feeling that can leave one in abject terror, a feeling that can be experienced as even more frightening than a perceived physical threat to one's life. Physical threat can be understood; the transrational is usually beyond the ken of this kind of ego.

A fragmentation complex can be experienced as a collective phenomenon as well as on an individual one. On a collective level, we can see this phenomenon manifested in the burning of heretics during the Inquisition and the witch trials in the Middle Ages and the early years of the colonial history of the United States. The crime of those "witches" was the use of "magic"– irrational by definition, and, communion with nature, i.e. the "devil." Forces that cannot be dealt with by the ego must be destroyed lest the ego itself be destroyed.

Certainly any discussion of the *inherent* qualities and characteristics of nature that did not fit existing definitions/"rational" explanation, was ruthlessly put down, as Copernicus, Galileo, and others learned at their great peril. In more recent history, subtle manifestations of a fragmentation complex might be the wholesale dismissal of so-called alternative forms of medicine, many of them ancient, such as homeopathy, kinesiology, natural remedies (plants and herbs), acupuncture, etc. These "healing" modalities do not operate on the same principles and laws as do allopathic, i.e. modern western, medicine. Their function often seems to be based more on magic than on "rational" law.

Psychic phenomena such as prophetic dreams, intuitive cognition, various phenomena related to outer space, astrology, precognition, etc., typically have been dismissed out of hand, no matter what supportive data or other verification might be produced, and even though many, if not most people have had some personal experience of these phenomena. The United States elected a president – Jimmy Carter – *after* he had acknowledged his conviction that he personally had seen an unidentified flying object (UFO).[10] At the same time, neither he nor anyone else discussed his experience publicly after he became president. It also came to light that Nancy, wife of President Reagan, regularly used astrological charting of the President's planned activities to determine when they should or should not take place, or if they should take place at all – particularly after the near fatal attempt on the life of the president in his second year in office. For a while, use of astrological charting in the White House was scandalous. In the long run, it served to open a narrow window on an issue heretofore considered to be taboo, even, by some, blasphemous. But not for long. The use of astrology, as most such arenas, was quickly split off and repressed, and a few months after the revelation, not another word was said by anyone – not by the White House, the Congress, the media, or even the astrological community. Both of these events were treated as if they had never happened. It wasn't that the public felt these issues were not important. Rather, I believe they were – in their full import – too frightening to look at. They set off our culture's fragmentation complex.

It is well known and documented that throughout the Cold War the United States and the Soviet Union resorted to the services of psychics to aid in their respective espionage work. Millions of dollars were spent on the use of such resources; millions more are still being spent in this arena by the Central Intelligence Agency, the National Security Agency, and the Federal Bureau of Investigation. At the same time, such operations are kept under wraps – as much for their efficacy as for their failure. Again, any opportunity to subject these technologies to rational analysis is lost – even in the face of knowledge that some of these techniques succeeded where rational process failed. I believe that the deeper reason for keeping these activities hidden is less the anticipated controversy – the Nancy Reagan episode lasted only a few months with no serious political repercussions – but more because of the fragmentation complex characteristic of the western ego. Most of this kind of information that does manage to leak out is quickly split off and repressed. Such events simply "didn't happen," i.e. there is nothing to talk about. Or in other words, it is too frightening to talk about or even think about.

And, as I will discuss in the next chapter, the most salient characteristic of this western ego complex split-off from nature is its tendency toward suicide.

Notes

1 Gore, 2000: Chapter 7.
2 Jung, 1961: para. 434.
3 Here I am referring primarily to literate individuals. Members of the culture who are not literate reflect a somewhat different profile that will not be discussed here. Theirs is not the psyche that rules.
4 The *Chambers English Dictionary* (1988: 1560) defines "transpersonal" as: "Going beyond, transcending, the individual personality: denoting a form of psychology . . . that utilizes mystical, psychical or spiritual *experience* as a means of increasing human potential." The *New Shorter Oxford English Dictionary* (1996) defines it as: "Designating a form of psychology . . . which seeks to explore transcendental *experiences and states of consciousness* that go beyond normal personal identity and desires." [Emphasis added in both definitions.] It should be noted that both definitions distinguish between different states of *experience* and *consciousness*

versus *ideas*. The latter refers to cognitive constructs, mentalisms; the former refer to states of being and experience which often go beyond the ability of cognition to define.

5　Shulman, 1997: 172.
6　Shulman, 1997: 173.
7　"Supernatural" is the wrong term for nonrational experiences. The term "supernatural" is spurred by the fragmentation complex of the western ego. It is fear driven. *Transrational* is the more accurate term.
8　Jung, 1972: para. 415.
9　Deloria, 2000: 6.
10　This would imply at least an unconscious tolerance for the transrational on the part of the American cultural collective.

Chapter 5

Darwin and overspecialization

But with man we can see no definite limit to the continued development of the brain and mental faculties, as far as advantage is concerned.[1]

Our intellect has created a new world that dominates nature, and has populated it with monstrous machines . . . Man is bound to follow the exploits of his scientific and inventive mind and to admire himself for his splendid achievements. At the same time, he cannot help admitting that his genius shows an uncanny tendency to invent things that become more and more dangerous, because they represent better and better means for wholesale suicide . . . In spite of our proud domination of nature . . . [we] have not learnt to control our own nature, which slowly and inevitably courts disaster.[2]

For the most part we tend to think of evolution primarily in physical terms. However, the human psyche is as evolutionary in character as our biological selves. I am not using the term "psyche" as synonymous with the brain. The brain is the organ where the psyche resides just as a radio is the conduit for the transmission of radio waves that can carry the human voice. The radio is not the voice, it is a transmitter. Notwithstanding strong conviction in some quarters[3] that psyche and brain are one and the same, there is as yet no evidence to prove one conviction over the other.

The "psyche" as I define it here is the totality of the nonphysical being of the individual – what Jung called "the Self" – in its known and unknown manifestations, including the whole of its conscious (the ego), and its unconscious being, as well as its spiritual and transpersonal essence. Conceptually, physical evolution without psychic evolution makes no sense. The separation of *psyche* and *soma*, i.e. mind and body, is dualistic, an artificial dichotomy that arose with the influence on Christianity of the Greeks[4] and particularly since Descartes' "cogito ergo sum," has become a fixed tenet of western thinking. This split is seen in the bias toward physiology within evolutionary theory.

Much has been written about the history and development of the human psyche; however, little has been written of the evolution of that psyche, notwithstanding the body of research and literature on developmental psychology and psychosomatic medicine.[5] Yet, I would postulate that the human psyche in general and the western ego, in particular, represent the most rapidly evolving phenomena known to humankind.[6]

The threat of species suicide

In *The Origin of Species*, Charles Darwin, in discussing "natural selection," asserts:

> Can we doubt (remembering that many more individuals are born than can possibly survive) that individuals having any advantage, however slight, over others, would have the best chance of surviving and of procreating their kind? On the other hand, we may feel that any variation in the least degree injurious would be rigidly destroyed. This preservation of favourable individual differences and variations, and the destruction of those which are injurious, I have called Natural Selection, or the Survival of the Fittest.[7]

And later, in discussing natural selection in the case of the larva of an insect, he points out that:

> Natural selection may adapt [the organism] to a score of contingencies . . . but in all cases natural selection will ensure that they shall not be injurious: for if they were so, the species would become extinct.[8]

He goes on to demonstrate regarding the specialization of organs (e.g. the thumb, tail, mouth):

> All physiologists admit that the specialization of organs, *inasmuch as in this state they perform their functions better*, is an advantage to each being . . . On the other hand, we can see . . . that it is quite possible for natural selection gradually to fit a being to a situation in which several organs would be superfluous or useless: in such case there would be retrogression.[9]
>
> [Emphasis added.]

In other words, specialized organs had better adapt their "specialization" to changing conditions along the way, or they will become vestigial and in some cases, the species itself will become extinct.

Survival through "specialization" has its advantages but also its drawbacks. Should the environment change suddenly, those who have gambled on specialization may lose, while those who have retained a generalized form and remained adaptable can adjust to the new situation and survive. Because of a highly developed brain and, ultimately, the tool of language, humans and their ancestors have retained an evolutionary flexibility that has enabled them to respond to change when it has arisen.[10]

In *The Descent of Man*, Darwin, in 1871, sees the extinction of races as being limited primarily to what he called "savage tribes," "barbarians," and "wilder races of men," among other appellations.[11] Notwithstanding his extraordinary breadth of intelligence and exceptional scientific rigor, particularly given the times in which he lived, the cultural prejudices of white western culture clearly show through with the use of such phrases and references with which his works are replete. With regard to western civilization, he makes some extraordinary statements – not necessarily so in 1871, but extraordinary in the present context. He clearly sees western civilization as being superior to "noncivilized" groups *in every way*.[12]

He also makes some astonishing assertions regarding specialization in humans, seeming to challenge his own theory of natural selection and survival of the fittest. The seeming contradiction results from his apparent perception that man's brain – particularly the brain of western European man – has no negative limits to its advantageous adaption and specialization. *Other* organs can jeopardize man's survival through overspecialization, but not the human brain. In arguing that since "man" should not be classified separately from his animal/primate forebears, he says:

> We can . . . see why a great amount of modification in some one character ought not to lead us to separate widely any two organisms. A part which already differs much from the same part in other allied forms has already, according to the theory of evolution, varied much; consequently it would (as long as the organism remained exposed to the same exciting conditions) be liable to further variations of the same kind; and these, if beneficial, would be preserved, and thus be continually augmented. In many cases the continued development of a part, for instance, of the beak of a bird, or of the teeth of a mammal would not aid the species in gaining its food, or for any other object; *but with man we can see no definite limit to the continued development of the brain and mental faculties, as far as advantage is concerned*.[13]
>
> [Emphases added.]

But Darwin also points out that natural selection acts only tentatively:

> Individuals and races may have acquired certain indisputable advantages, and yet have perished from failing in other characters. The western nations of Europe [in 1871] . . . stand at the summit of civilization [and] owe little or none of their superiority to direct inheritance from the old Greeks, *though they owe much to the written works of that wonderful people*.[14]
>
> [Emphasis added.]

The Greeks, he says, may have "retrograded from a want of coherence between the many small states, from the small size of . . . their country, from the practice of slavery, or from extreme sensuality." These "enervated" that civilization and corrupted it to its "very core." But the threat here is to specific nation-states, societies, and races – not to species *Homo sapiens* itself. Darwin seems convinced that the (western) human brain, with all its wondrous developments and adaptations, is the one organ that will escape the negative possibilities of overspecialization.

In 1871, the height of the Industrial Revolution, Darwin could not imagine, literally, "disadvantage" to the "mental faculties" of humans in the context of his theory of evolution and survival of the fittest. Although he could imagine humans, particularly non-western, non-European groups, being negatively impacted by environmental and other factors other than their "mental faculties," the (western) human brain would not become overspecialized and a threat to the survival of the species. The western ego was to be the one exception with regard to his theory of natural selection and (over)specialization. Apparently he saw human intelligence, particularly the western ego – *the American version specifically* – as superior in every way and without limit. This, plus his cultural bias, led to an idealized fascination with the western ego's accomplishments in the United States:

> There is apparently much truth in the belief that the wonderful progress of the United States, as well as the character of the people, are the results of natural selection; for the more energetic restless, and courageous men from all parts of Europe have emigrated during the last ten or twelve generations to that great country, and have there succeeded best. Looking to the distant future, I do not think that the Rev. Mr. Zincke takes an exaggerated view when he says: "All other series of events – as that which resulted in the culture of mind in Greece, and that which resulted in the empire of Rome – only appear to have purpose and value when viewed in connection with, or rather as subsidiary to . . . the great stream of Anglo-Saxon emigration to the west."[15] Obscure as is the problem of the advance of civilization, we can at least see that a nation which produced during a lengthened period the greatest number of highly intellectual, energetic, brave, patriotic, and benevolent men, would generally prevail over less favoured nations.[16]

Of course, some of these "highly intellectual, energetic, brave, patriotic and benevolent men" referred to above were engaged in those very acts that Darwin earlier attributed disparagingly to "savage tribes": Torturing their enemies, remorseless infanticide, mistreating their wives, and gross superstitiousness.[17] But unlike some of those "savages," they, and their government, were also guilty of *intentional* genocide.

In one sense, one can understand Darwin's near intoxication with the experiment in natural selection that was taking place, virtually before his eyes, in the United States. The period from 1868 forward was indeed an astonishing period, not only in that nation's history, but in the history of any that had gone before. The Civil War had been fought and the losers were being readmitted as equals under the law to the nation from which they had defected – an astonishing display of democracy and forgiveness in its day.[18] The first transcontinental railroad had been completed in 1869; the Industrial Revolution had really demonstrated its capacity during the Civil War with the development of the ironclads, the *Monitor* and the *Merrimack*. Indeed, it was its industrial might, perhaps more than anything else, which had won the war for the North. Foreigners (at least initially) were being welcomed in droves to the shores of the United States to tend and feed the developing industries; large cities of unprecedented scale, including the first "high rises," were under construction, and there was an excitement in the air that brooked no obstacle. Hence one can understand Darwin's fascination with natural selection as it played out in the United States of his day.

In my view, western man still carries Darwin's 19th-century myopia and bias. Because Darwin had faith in the ultimate "advantage" of, and the absence of limits to, the continued development of the human brain and *mental faculties*, his vision was profoundly limited. What he did not anticipate was that when the western ego displaced God and assumed those powers previously attributed to God, the resulting hubris would bring us to the edge of extinction.

I have asserted earlier my belief that we, species *Homo sapiens*, if not all life forms on this planet, are threatened with species extinction due to our over-specialized western ego. Certainly this is a shocking assertion, and I do not make it lightly. It alarms me and frightens me to even consider the thought.

I believe that we are today exactly at the point of a *feeling* realization of the disadvantageous limits of western man's "mental faculties" and that, under the threat of self-extinction, we are under the greatest pressure to adapt the western ego to the actual reality(ies) that we have created. Ironically, the primary threat to our survival is not external to that ego; the primary source of that threat is the ego itself. That is the good news as well as the terrifying news. This *feeling* realization is just becoming conscious. The events of 9/11 have seen to that, with all of the graphic drama that was needed to pierce our unconsciousness as we watched the collapse of the Twin Towers of the World Trade Center in New York City.

I stress that it is a "feeling realization" because mental or *logos* realizations are too easy to rationalize, abstract, deny, split off, or just numb out. Feeling realizations bring with them a somatic embodiment of emotion. We have not learned – yet – to shut down our body sensations the way we have learned to shut down our thinking and rational process. And for increasing numbers of us, when we do try to shut down our body processes to avoid frightening truths, we become ill – literally – with everything from depression to psychosomatic disorders to environmental illness. So, from whence does this notion of self-extinction derive?

Since the time of ancient Greece, western culture has pursued a near obsessive preoccupation with expansion of civilization and culture building. Beginning around the 15th century alchemy sparked a pursuit of a science that would ultimately become the Industrial Revolution of the 19th century and the technological revolution of the 20th, particularly its second half. By the end of the 20th century, the western ego had extended its dominion over virtually all that "moveth" on the face of the earth. And, paradoxically, man himself had become one of the things that "moveth" that was becoming subjugated to the products of his own ego.[19]

With the advent of modern warfare in the 20th century, man began to rely increasingly on his technology for waging war, more than on numbers of troops and "blood." Increasingly, war became more detached from feeling and human connection between the combatants. Importantly, wars were fought over ideologies or *ego ideas* (e.g. capitalism vs communism) as much as over things and greed (territory, minerals, the "Seven Cities of Gold" etc.). Or, another way of putting it, ideology and technology have enabled modern man, through rationalization and sublimation, to distance himself from a *feeling realization* of his own power complex and greed and, above all else, from the destruction and terrorization of individual human life and *personal* human tragedy that had been associated with war from the beginning of time. World War I was "the war to end all wars," and fewer than 21 years later, the world fought a larger war dubbed "the last just war" to defeat evil (fascism) "once and for all."

Since World War II, we have become increasingly aware of the fact that wars are fought more for collective *psychological* reasons, i.e. shadow projection.[20] This is relevant because it reflects a subtle, but rapid, psychodynamic shift on the part of the collective western ego. Although one would certainly wish for a better way, one can view the unprecedented carnage of the 20th century as forcing major and rapid (in evolutionary terms) ego awareness about our own violent and self-destructive nature. Ultimately, as we now proceed into the 21st century, this consciousness has brought us to the threshold of an awareness that we are in danger of wiping out the whole of our species, if not all life on this planet.

The conflict with the former Soviet Union represented a different kind of phenomenon from all previous conflicts and wars between nations throughout human history. Whatever the ideological points of the conflict, technology, i.e. the atomic/thermonuclear warhead and the intercontinental missile, made grand scale warfare between technological superpowers untenable. For the first time in history western science's technological "advances" produced weapons of war that were so awesome in their destructiveness that they dare not be used. This was the first manifestation of a subliminal realization that humankind had reached a point where it *felt* itself in danger of the consequences of overspecialization in the Darwinian sense and thus in danger of species (self-)annihilation. Importantly, in the context of the Cold War, the governments, i.e. the collective ego construct, of the Soviet Union and the United States were able to contain their suicidal impulses. Somehow, we managed not to go to war with each other. That choice, that decision-making apparatus, that capacity, has been seriously limited and exacerbated on the governmental level with the advent of the post-9/11 world and the new age of international terrorism. The suicidal tools of man's inventiveness – the weapons of terrorism, from anthrax, small pox, the commercial airplane, the "dirty" nuclear device that can be contained in a suitcase, the long range missile developed by "third world" economically prostrate states such as North Korea – are now accessible to *individuals*, not just governments. These are sufficiently cheap and easy to make as to pose an ever-present threat that holds little potential for defeat or collapse as did the Cold War. The Cold War did demonstrate and provide the first "hard data" that the western ego has become overspecialized and must adapt, and do so quickly, to changing times and the monsters of its own creation. From the collapse of the Soviet Union in 1991 up until 9/11 in 2001, we have been too afraid – too terrified – to look deeply at how close we did come to species suicide during the Cold War. However, terror is no longer an abstraction or something that happens "over there." In terms of feeling realization, 9/11 has upped the ante on our terror of looking at our suicidal impulses.

In a far-reaching overview of the crisis we are in, William Van Dusen Wishard of WorldTrends Research, discusses what some scientific intellectuals call the "Post-human Age," where "medical science, neuroscience, computer science, genetics, biology – separately and together, seem to be on the verge of abandoning the human realm altogether . . . [and] it grows harder to imagine human beings remaining at the center of the process of science. Instead, science appears to be in charge of its own process, probing and changing people in order to further its own course, independent of human agency."[21] Wishard reminds us of Einstein's charge to science that concern for "the *fate* of man must be at the heart of our technical endeavors and that this requires moral imagination," and of Jacob Bronowski's assertion that we "have to cure ourselves of the itch for absolute knowledge and power."

In his summary of the shadow of "scientific culture," Wishard sums up the characteristics of what I have been referring to as the overspecialization of the (western) ego:

In the long sweep of time, it appears we have created a scientific culture that is an immense complex of technique and specialization without the guiding moral framework to which Einstein and Bronowski referred. The highest standard is efficiency. The defining ethic is the pragmatist's's dictum: "If it can be done, it will be done." It is as Kevin Kelly suggests, "We have become as gods, and we might as well get good at it." But we may be closer to being "good at it" than Kelly knows. Bernard Knox has a view of what it means to be a "god" with which Kelly might agree. In the Introduction to the Penguin Classic edition of the *Illiad*, Knox says: "To be a god is to be totally absorbed in the exercise of one's own power, the fulfillment of one's own nature, unchecked by any thought of others except as obstacles to be overcome; it is to be incapable of self-questioning or self-criticism. But there are human beings who are like this. Pre-eminent in their particular sphere of power, they impose their will on others with the confidence, the unquestioning certainty of their own right and worth that is characteristic of gods."[22]

We have spent a great deal of the entire period since Genesis developing and being dominated by an ego-derived power drive that has become captive of its own technological prowess. It is an ego that appears to be out of control much of the time. At the same time we have come out of the Cold War with some consciousness of how close we came to self-annihilation, and with a quasi-conscious commitment in the face of a still powerful and regressive power drive to avoid repeating that drama. The Cold War and its demise confront humankind with *both* of its ego extremes: Its capacity and *willingness*, at some level, to accept self-annihilation and at the same time its ability to hold back from the brink – if only by a thread.

Up until now our well-being has relied, more than not, on the extraordinary inventive genius of our "western ego." Its influence and impact has come to dominate the whole of life on this planet. But, as we also learned during the Cold War, we can no longer afford to trust a primary reliance on it for adaptation for survival, since it, itself, has become the paramount threat to life.

So, the question poses itself: What kind of adaptation is called for to reorient our overspecialized western ego to make it more functionally adaptive in support of continued species survival? And, further, are there indications that such an adaptation is possible?

Notes

1 Darwin, 1871: 543.
2 Jung, 1961: para. 597.
3 Medicine and the biological sciences, for example.
4 Abram, 1996: 94–95, 121–123.
5 These two fields, in my judgment, provide the most accessible observation on the evolution of the human psyche.
   The field of psychosomatic medicine remains in the medical "camp" that pioneered its research, i.e. it remains caught in the split between psyche and soma notwithstanding the obvious bridge reached for between the two. The one-sided medical bias over the psychological, has been due as much or more to the field of psychology and even psychiatry than to allopathic medicine. It would appear that the brain research in the past decade or so which is bridging the gap between

medicine and psychology/psychoanalysis also will be the bridge to a more prominent role for psychology and psychoanalytic theory in the field of psychosomatic
medicine.

 6 Whitmont, 1982: 39–40.
 7 Darwin, 1859: 63–64.
 8 Darwin, 1859: 67.
 9 Darwin, 1859: 94.
10 (1992) *Encyclopedia Britannica*.
11 Darwin, 1871: 497, 542–550.
12 Darwin, 1871: 543.
13 Darwin, 1871: 514.
14 Darwin, 1871: 507.
15 Rev. Mr. Zincke published an article in 1868, which Darwin read, entitled, "Last
     Winter in the United States."
16 Darwin, 1871: 508.
17 Darwin, 1871: 919–920.
18 This was a magnanimous gesture *under the law*. Lincoln's Second Inaugural
     Address is a model of forgiveness and magnanimity. Of course, Reconstruction, as
     it was practiced, was harsh and punishing and far from magnanimous.
19 The primary theme of the 1999 film, *The Matrix*, is of a world where virtual
     reality, a product of man's "ingenuity" and technology, threatens to become the
     primary, if not the only, reality, subordinating "objective reality," one might even
     say, "human reality," to itself, i.e. to virtual reality.
       In the 2003 movie *The Core*, as the result of a seismic underground weapon, the
     core of the earth is damaged and the earth just stops spinning. This threatens the
     survival of humankind due to natural disasters, including runaway global heating,
     which will "fry" the planet.
20 This was most easily seen in the mutual projection of "enemy" shadow elements
     onto each other by the Soviet Union and the United States. In this context psycho-
     logically, the *projection*, rather than the particulars of their contents, was the key
     dynamic that held the two psychologically bound to one another throughout the
     Cold War (e.g. Reagan's "Evil Empire." George W. Bush's "Axis of Evil" is a
     contemporary version of the same dynamic). See Bernstein, 1989: Chapter 3.
       It is not that wars were not fought for these reasons prior to the 20th century.
     The point is that psychology as a consciousness-raising technology – particularly
     until the advent of Jung's psychology – was inadequate to enable us to *become*
     aware of the underlying archetypal dynamics of warfare. We simply didn't have
     the technological tools to analyze the collective and archetypal dynamics that
     unconsciously predispose civilization to warfare. For a detailed analysis of those
     dynamics, see *Power and Politics* (Bernstein, 1989).
21 Jaron Lanier as quoted in, "Understanding Our Moment in History," by William
     Van Dusen Wishard (2003).
22 Wishard, 2003.

Chapter 6

Beyond Darwin and Newton: Complex adaptive systems

> What we witness in the fossil record of earthly life is the gradual accumulation of various types of simpler evolutions into the organic whole we now call evolution. Evolution is a conglomeration of many processes which form a society of evolutions. As evolution has evolved over time, *evolution itself has increased in diversity and complexity and evolvability. Change changes itself.*[1]

The relatively new field of complexity theory offers a view of the world that includes, but goes beyond, the linear cause and effect model of Newtonian physics and its Darwinian counterpart in the biological sciences, including modern medicine and psychology. Complexity theory holds that at the root of all complex systems, from the behavior of molecules to the actions of nation-states to the balancings in nature, lies a set of dynamic principles that when identified, will yield a grand unification of the life sciences. It maintains that order emerges spontaneously from complex, dynamical systems inherent in the organism. Jungian analyst Helene Shulman, author of *Living at the Edge of Chaos*, asks: "What if we were to think about human consciousness, mental illness, and health without the local cause paradigm?" A fascinating question. In exploring the building of this biological evolutionary bridge to human consciousness, Shulman says:

> Western scientific models have tended to think of the development of biological organisms as dominated by a kind of central control mechanism, usually the genetic code, which allows occasional random mutations.
> In the new model, many biological processes are understood through the model of parallel rather than linear computer programs. In parallel processing, each node in a network responds simultaneously to others which are responding to it. The nodes can have many or few connections, yielding many different types of behavior in the system. It is impossible to predict what will happen in a large network because there would never be time to compute all the possibilities. On the other hand, surprisingly,

parallel processing systems can produce order on their own. The grammar of this order can be studied, even if no state of any particular network can be predicted. The study of this grammar has come to be called "complexity theory," because it is about the behavior of complex systems. *A subset of these systems are "self-organizing," in that order evolves as the system "learns" to regulate itself through positive feedback during its ongoing encounter with its internal environment.*[2]

[Emphasis added.]

These "self-organizing systems" have come to be known in the field as "complex adaptive systems (CASs).

Stuart Kauffman, in his book, *The Origins of Order*, addresses a problem that has gnawed at biologists for many years: In Darwinian theory, complex adaptive life forms arose merely through random trial and error, without some principle of internal organization. In effect, the existence of many of the complex life forms that we have come to see and know about were the result of a kind of genetic table of random numbers – a biological crap shoot. The intuition of many biologists was that there had to be something more, a missing piece in the puzzle of the development of complex life forms. As Shulman puts it: "There had to be other undiscovered sources of order, which Einstein had called 'secrets of the Old One'."[3]

Kauffman postulates that although the genetic *details* of an organism would result from random mutations and natural selection, *the organization of life itself*, **the order**, would derive purely from the *structure* of the network, not the details. This notion is consistent with chaos theory, one of the theoretical roots of modern-day complexity theory. In short, order is given and spontaneous, and appears to be one of the "secrets of the Old One."[4]

Perhaps Darwin himself had intuited this inherent "order," above and beyond the "details" of natural selection – at least in the case of the western human brain – when he implied that it alone of biological organs might have no negative limits to its advantageous adaption and specialization. He seemed to be arguing that, somehow, this unique organ might be able to sidestep the perils of overspecialization. Perhaps he was also intuiting what Kauffman has referred to as the "inattention of contemporary evolutionary theory to the contribution of the organism toward its own evolution."[5] This concept would later come to be known as "self-organization" – the organism itself becomes a partner in its own evolutionary process. This concept of self-organizing systems is central in new models of the origins of life that are currently being explored in complexity theory and in biology. These new theories integrate Darwin's principles of random mutation and natural selection in combination with self-organizing features inherent in the natural world.

"Coevolution," as traditionally used in biology, refers to a reciprocally induced evolutionary change between two or more species or populations; a change in the genetic composition of one species (or group) in response to a genetic change in another. An example would be the long neck of the giraffe, which evolved to access vegetation from the higher elevation of trees when there was sparse vegetation on the ground *and* the reciprocal response of trees, which grew higher to protect the leaves essential for their own health and survival. These definitions relate to biological evolution. In this chapter I am addressing *psychic evolution* where the western ego construct[6] is one coevolutionary partner with nature (physical and psychical) as the other partner in a coevolving reciprocal process.

However, to the extent that consciousness is a major player and major self-organizing dynamic in the coevolution of humankind, for now the consciousness demonstrated by the western ego more than not appears to be caught in a major power complex[7] – it has no check other than itself on its obsession with power and control. Thus, it is a threat to its continued health and survival as such – to its own evolutionary process.

Evidently, this new dimension of evolutionary theory is not limited to the biological dimension. Ervin Lazlo, founder of the General Evolution Research group of the United Nations, says that we can understand all structure in the world as self-organizing. He says that historically social scientists studied "statistics instead of dynamics; structures and states instead of processes and functions; self-correcting mechanisms instead of self-organizing systems; conditions of equilibrium instead of dynamic balances in regions of distinct disequilibrium." He proposes what he calls a "Grand Evolutionary Synthesis," based on the notion that evolution is singularly consistent: "It brings forth the same basic kind of entity in all its domains." This grand evolutionary synthesis comprises many CASs.[8]

This aspect of complexity theory holds that life forms of any type live close to an "edge of chaos" both individually and as a group. For the most part, they are more or less stable in a subcritical state at the edge of chaos, and perform a more integrative function. Or natural selection may favor others that sometimes cross over that edge of chaos *in order to go through a creative reordering phase*. If they go too far, so to speak, no learning can occur and chaos or even self-destruction may ensue. I believe that this is what happened during the Cold War and why no one understood/understands *why* what happened did happen.[9] The progressive upping of the ante of the build-up of nuclear missiles brought the world to the edge of chaos. The height of the nuclear build-up crossed that subcritical state at the edge of chaos and a "creative reordering phase" – what Jung called the "transcendent function" – was triggered.[10] This came from within the complex system of the Cold War itself. The role of the policy planners and "operators" of the Cold War, on both sides, served as a catalyst to bring the drama to the edge of chaos. The reordering process, i.e. the end of the Cold War and the collapse of the Soviet Union, *came from within the system itself*.

This is the good news. The difficult question is this: To what extent did western consciousness learn the lessons to be learned from that encounter with the edge of chaos? On the surface, one might be optimistic. The teetering back and forth and self-correcting of our struggles have had clearly positive results: Certainly there has been a sharp reduction in nuclear warheads and the missiles to deliver them since the end of the Cold War; the ecology movement has sunk definite roots in western culture. But is the number of missiles and intensity of greenhouse gasses the symptom or the problem? Or is the problem more the power complex of the western ego itself? Could it be that the western ego's efforts at self-*correction*, i.e. reducing nuclear missiles, is a "cover" by its own power complex to avoid *reordering* of its basic frame of reference, which could threaten the ego's power and control? Is this not perhaps the deeper meaning and message of 9/11? Seemingly, the only political response to 9/11 by the United States is the assertion and protection of its power complex. And to the extent that this is true and remains unseen as the *source* of symptoms such as nuclear missiles and biochemical and other forms of terrorism, then to what extent is the process of coevolution in this regard seriously, even potentially fatally, compromised? We know quite well from medicine and psychology that a pathological condition treated only symptomatically will erupt somewhere else, and oftentimes with deadlier results.

Perhaps the immanence of calamity for species *Homo sapiens*, "wise man," is what must be risked by going to the edge of chaos in order to obtain the necessary reordering for the growth and relative stability of civilization. Perhaps that is the choice (not choices) given us by natural law. But what if that natural law and its inherent self-organizing/ordering principles *intend* that humans consciously be a major player in the coevolution of life? Then it would behoove us to ask the questions:

- What is the nature of that consciousness?
- Can we trust it?

As Shulman describes the process:

> Ecosystems that have achieved some control over their interactions and evolvability would best be able to "ride" changes in the environment and adapt to them. *They can evolve their evolvability . . . the human body is such a* coevolving ecosystem, with some systems – breathing, heartbeat, – controlled by more or less frozen structures, while other systems – immune reactions, dreams, thinking – are free to continue evolving . . . there would be a kind of tacking back and forth between too much order and rigidity, and too little. These adjustments could then feed back into the system, altering its structure and causing emergent patterns.[11]
>
> [Emphasis added.]

In this schema of "natural selection," some conditions would favor organisms with an integrative (adaptive) function that would essentially hold in a fixed state its existing structure; others would favor allowing other features to coevolve to the edge of chaos, where new possibilities of creativity are maximized.

Regarding fixed states: A hubristic western ego that does not see itself as a part of a codependent system coevolving with the rest of the ecosystem, and sees itself instead as controlling the entire process, is caught in a power complex. It is unconscious of seeing itself as a superior operator not beholden to the same natural laws as a coevolutionary partner – at its own peril. This superior attitude leads to such outcomes as an overuse of antibiotics and the resultant return of new diseases (skin-eating diseases, Group A Streptococcus (GAS) disease – necrotizing fascitis) and even more virulent strains of disease e.g. tuberculosis (TB) previously cured and now resistant to all known drugs. The one-sided approach to 9/11 of overpowering the problem of terrorism without addressing its psychopolitical etiology is as blind as it is dangerous.

Chaos theory and the Borderland

This scheme describes the dynamics of what I believe takes place in the Borderland. As described in Chapter 2, when I was able to intuit that a new approach was needed to work more effectively with Hannah, that approach consisted of sorting those aspects of her inner "chaos," which needed to remain fixed, i.e. her basic ego structure and reality adaptation, from the material in her outer chaos that did not fit the former. By taking seriously her insistence that "It's the *cows!*" and by listening to her and realizing that she was reporting her experience of a relationship between herself and nature (i.e. the cows), we both entered the marginal realm of chaos where those two possibilities existed simultaneously: The notion that she could feel (not feel about) the drama of these animals was crazy (did not fit her or my existing mental structures), and one where perhaps there was something here to be listened to, i.e. one of the "secrets of the Old One." In this vis-à-vis between Hannah and the cows and between Hannah and myself, *and our willingness to linger in that very uncomfortable liminal space*, we both went to the edge of chaos where the experience did not fit the existing structure, but where we went through a "creative reordering phase" where perhaps it could fit after all – and did. I can't explain what makes the difference here, between what ultimately sounds crazy (i.e. fixed and not fitting the existing structure), and a phase change, a creative reordering phase (a *kairos*, a magic, a synchronicity, an incidence of grace, a miracle). I can't explain why and when the one happens and the other doesn't. But I *know* that it had to do with "listening" and I *know* it had to do with the relationship between Hannah and me; I *know* that it had to do with our willingness to accept that our experience could be crazy; and I *know* that it had to do with the call of the cows to be listened to.

I don't believe that the same experience would have happened had either of us been alone.

I also know that this liminal space at the edge of chaos that is so uncomfortable – most often terrifying – is one that many people experience as they transition from profane to sacred space. Those who have participated in peyote ceremonies, for example, know this terror, many of them reporting their most fervent oaths to God – to all the gods – that they will never *ever* take peyote again, if only they can survive this one terrifying moment. But they do participate again, swearing the same oaths even more fervently the next time around. It is a terror that some people describe in their first encounter(s) with the unconscious, not as an abstract idea, but as an experience at the deepest levels in the very cells of their psyche and soma, to the core of their soul. I have experienced it in the dark of a bitter cold winter night while waiting to descend the ladder into a kiva to partake of the ceremonial mysteries that lie within. Those who have experienced this terror know it as one born out of awe, less than out of fear. They also know that when, once again, they have survived the transrational terror of that threshold at the edge of chaos and are graced with entry into sacred space, most often, but not always, terror transforms into the most humbling and peaceful awe.

John Holland, a computer scientist and complexity researcher, asserts that: "All complex adaptive systems – economies, minds, organisms – build models that allow them to anticipate the world."[12] They are "feedforward" (as well as feedback) systems. Shulman interprets his meaning as reaching for some aspects of what I have referred to as "transrational" experience and the transrational healing dimension. She says: "What Holland is looking at could be described as a preconscious, prenervous system, self-organizing tendency at a somatic level in biological organisms." She points out:

> [P]aramecia and amoebae, which do not have nervous systems, are immobilized by anesthetics just as humans are. Based on a schema of some sort of quantum coherence phenomena in the microtubule structure of living beings, there would be "know" in every cell of our bodies. This would be the basis for an "Old One" which has been in the process of learning for billions of years. Animals, the human body, and consciousness would be her offspring, and she would be like the Great Goddess of ancient myth who created the world through her dance.[13]

It does not take a giant leap from this notion to connect with Jung's concepts of the collective unconscious and archetypes. These concepts could be seen as the psychic constructs of that "knowing" in every somatic and psychic cell of our bodies of which she speaks.

Jung postulated that the Self is the integrating, self-regulating organ of the human psyche operating on a compensatory principle in the name of preserving the health and well-being of the individual. I would say that the

Self is also the vehicle through which there is an interplay between the individual and groups and the cultural collective, i.e. civilization.[14] Therein, it is part of the evolutionary schema as a self-organizing system maintaining the integrity of the complex system of individual(s), group(s), culture(s), and species *Homo sapiens*.

But then there is still the dilemma of the western ego. What therapists know from clinical work is that the Self primarily *informs* the ego – for the most part, it does not *rule* the ego.[15] The ego, in most instances, has the power of choice regarding human decision making. So the Self can inform the ego that it is headed for trouble, but the ego makes the final decision regarding what action it chooses to take. That ego, as observed above, is caught in a negative power complex that threatens the survival of us all. In fact, it did so in almost every conceivable way during the height of the Cold War, choosing to pursue a suicidal course not withstanding its own analyses of the immanence of nuclear self-annihilation. (Thank goodness for "creative reordering phases" at the edge of chaos! I believe that is why we are still here.) To the consternation of us all, the post-9/11 world confronts us once again with the question of survival and the paradoxical role played by our ego complex.

The obvious question is: Is there anywhere to go from here? Is there anything that could mitigate the western ego's hubris and power complex and its resulting inability to cooperate with and benefit from the self-correcting/reorganizing dynamics inherent in the Self?

Notes

1 Kevin Kelly, *Out of Control*, as reported in Shulman, 1997: 238. (Emphasis in original.)
2 Shulman, 1997: 102–103.
3 Shulman, 1997: 107.
4 Waldrop, 1992, as reported in Shulman, 1997: 107.
5 Shulman, 1997: 109.
6 Particularly its defining characteristic of self-reflecting consciousness, which makes conscious choice possible.
7 Jung defined the psychological dynamic of a "complex" as a "feeling-toned idea with an archetypal core." Bearing in mind that feelings have more potency, particularly on an unconscious level, than thoughts or ideas in governing human behavior, a complex is an *unconscious* psychological dynamic in an individual or group that determines a behavior that is not willed by the ego. It usually overrules behavior intended by the ego. A "complex" operating in an individual or group would behave as if it were a separate, *autonomous*, part of the individual or group. In the example of the Cold War, *obviously* the ego's intent would be its own survival. However, its *behavior*, governed by an unconscious power complex, was optimally threatening to its survival.
8 Shulman, 1997: 110.
9 Gaddis, 1992/93.
10 See *Power and Politics*, 93–94.
11 Shulman, 1997: 114–115.

12 As reported in Shulman, Ibid.: 119.
13 Ibid.: 141.
14 Despite our narcissistic need to see ourselves as above the kind of differentiation/ specialization of function reflected in all species, we too, as individuals and as groups, have specific functions that we are "assigned" by the Self, and through it, by the archetypes of the collective unconscious, as part of our cultural group and for civilization as a whole similar, for example, to bees. In the case of bees, they are called "drones," "workers," and "queen" bees. The differentiation of function in bees is determined by genetic structure. Specialized function in humans is determined more by the archetypal dynamics as well as genetic structure – one might look at archetypal energy as a kind of psychic genome – impinging on given individuals. These "psychic genomes" of humans manifest as those of scientist, therapist, engineer, warrior, priest, lawyer, street cleaner, computer specialist, etc.
15 When it does so, the result is usually psychosis.

Chapter 7

A coevolutionary partner

On the way back home from the moon, as I was gazing out the window at mother earth, the awe-inspiring beauty of the cosmos suddenly overcame me. While still aware of the separateness of my existence, my mind was flooded with an intuitive knowing that everything is interconnected – that this magnificent universe is a harmonious, directed, purposeful whole. And that we humans, both as individuals and as a species, are an integral part of the ongoing process of creation.[1]

[T]he attainment of consciousness was the most precious fruit of the tree of knowledge, the magical weapon which gave man victory over the earth, and which we hope will give him a still greater victory over himself.[2]

The integrating function of the Self is outside of consciousness, a "counterpole of the world."[3]

We ended the last chapter with a rhetorical question: Is there anything that could mitigate the western ego's hubris and power complex and its resulting inability to more fully cooperate with and benefit from the self-correcting/reorganizing dynamics inherent in the Self?

The western ego, as it stands now, is in need of the following:

- being boundaried and contained; being taught the limits of its capacities, and the consequences that could ensue from not recognizing and integrating limits
- an appreciation for the wondrousness of its own solar/left-brain consciousness, and its accomplishments – as *one* of a number of consciousnesses, each informing, appreciating, and reflecting the other
- a consciousness informed by feeling and intuition as much, if not more than, by ideas
- a consciousness mediated by a transpersonal dimension on an experiential level not under its control, where "belief" becomes equivalent (not superior) to an appreciation of what is experienced and what is "known"

- a compelling coevolutionary partner to give it dimensionality outside itself and one which leaves it feeling both humble and cared for in terms of its own well-being.

Figures 7.1, 7.2, and 7.3 present a schema of the development of the western ego, the primary organ for consciousness, and the ego's relationship to the Self. They also depict post-Genesis consciousness and the emergent Border-land consciousness which I have proposed is a by-product of the prevailing evolutionary process of which we are now in the midst. In essence, they summarize the theoretical framework of Part I of this book and provide a context for the clinical presentations in Part II.

Figure 7.1 presents a schema of ego development from birth to adulthood.[4] We can see a progressive emergence of the ego from containment within the Self. Edward Edinger, a Jungian analyst and major interpreter and proponent of Jung's theories, observes of this relationship:

> Jung's most basic and far-reaching discovery is the collective unconscious or archetypal psyche. Through his researches, we now know that the individual psyche is not just a project of personal experience. It also has a pre-personal or transpersonal dimension which is manifested in universal patterns and images . . . it was Jung's further discovery that the archetypal psyche has a structuring or ordering principle which unifies the various archetypal contents. This is the central archetype or archetype of wholeness which Jung has termed the Self.
>
> The Self is the ordering and unifying center of the total psyche (conscious and unconscious) just as the ego is the center of the conscious personality. Or, put in other words, the ego is the seat of *subjective* identity while the Self is the seat of *objective* identity.[5]

As is apparent from the discussion in the previous chapter, the above definition of the Self – particularly Edinger's references to Jung's "ordering principle" – is reflected in the more recent theories of evolution emerging from the field of complexity.

The ego–Self axis, a construct identified by Jung, refers to the conscious awareness and "dialogue" that can take place between the ego and the Self. It is important to remember that the Self is the nexus of connection *directly* with the transpersonal/archetypal dimension and with nature in all its numinosity.

This means that the Self can inform the ego of realities *that have never been part of conscious reality*. Thus, for example, in the case of an individual who has been struck with a life-threatening illness, and whose conscious attitude toward the illness might be despair and hopelessness, it is the Self that can constellate the archetype of healing in the individual and that may unleash a flood of dreams, some of which may point directly towards specific healing approaches above and beyond those being employed. In some cases, the Self

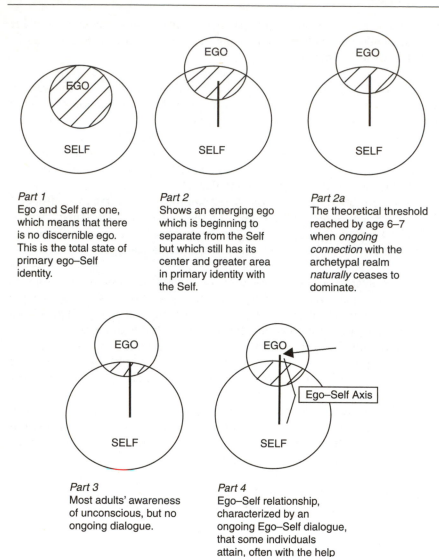

Part 1
Ego and Self are one, which means that there is no discernible ego. This is the total state of primary ego–Self identity.

Part 2
Shows an emerging ego which is beginning to separate from the Self but which still has its center and greater area in primary identity with the Self.

Part 2a
The theoretical threshold reached by age 6–7 when *ongoing connection* with the archetypal realm *naturally* ceases to dominate.

Part 3
Most adults' awareness of unconscious, but no ongoing dialogue.

Part 4
Ego–Self relationship, characterized by an ongoing Ego–Self dialogue, that some individuals attain, often with the help of psychoanalysis.

Figure 7.1 Ego–Self relationship during course of normal psychic development.
Source: Parts 1, 2, 3, and 4, Fordham (1957).

appears to stimulate the self-healing dynamics of the body's autoimmune system.[6]

The vertical line in the figures represents the ego–Self axis – the essential link between the ego and the Self. It is through this link, for example, that the Self "sends" dreams to the ego. The "bit" of ego–Self axis in the conscious awareness of the ego[7] (as depicted in Figure 7.1, Part 4) provides an *opportunity* for a *two-way* dialogue between the ego and the Self.[8] In cases where the individual is conscious of, and respectful towards, the role that the Self can play as a guide, even a protector, in the individual's life, some dramatic and "non-ordinary" experiences can and do take place. A notable example is the author Robert Louis Stevenson, who had a "strong sense of man's double being." He had searched for years for a story that would fit this theme, when, suddenly, the plot of *Dr. Jekyll and Mr. Hyde* came to him in a dream.[9] Another is the chemist, F. A. Kekulé von Stradonitz, to whom the image of the construction of the benzene molecule, the "benzene ring," came as a spontaneous vision from the unconscious.[10] There are numerous other recorded examples of this phenomenon. As we shall see later, the Self *can be* a literal source of life-saving information for the individual.

Edinger points out that the ego–Self axis (which, in Figure 7.1, Parts 2 and 3 is completely unconscious and therefore indistinguishable from ego–Self identity) has become partly conscious in Part 4.[11] But there is a catch: All the oracles, dreams, warnings, and interventions by the Self are of little or no value *if the ego does not heed the information*. The *dialogue* between ego and Self in a given individual represented in Part 4, typically is initiated by a shock to the system – a particularly startling, frightening dream, for example. Prior to some kind of dramatic opening of such a dialogue, the level of awareness of its presence is typically not sufficient for it to remain as an ongoing process that the individual substantially integrates into everyday awareness. Thus, when that dialogue does become integrated as part of an individual's ongoing life experience, it is usually the result of focused work. This "work" may take many forms such as maintaining a personal journal, recording one's dreams, artistic expression that is then reflected on and analyzed by the individual, a dramatic life crisis, or engagement in a formal psychoanalytic process, among others. Notably, in all these examples, there is an *accepted* engagement of the rational (the ego) by the transrational (the Self).

However, what *has* taken place for 2,500 years or so since the birth of the western ego, particularly on a collective level, is an ever-increasing separation of ego from Self. *But* in the last 50 years, on a collective level, there has been a proportionate *lessening*, not an increase, in the ego–Self *dialogue* as Edinger suggests (see Figure 7.2, Part 5).[12] The Self has endeavored to compensate for the ego's inflation, but, its capacity to restrain the ego, up until now, has been limited by the degree to which the ego has heeded its warnings.

In other words, the "dialogue" – a two way communicative *exchange* – has been less a dialogue than the Self pushing at the margins of an increasingly inflated ego resistant to any change that would inhibit its grandiosity and sense of power. It is important here not to confuse the ego's expansion of its own conscious awareness of the object (outer) world, which it seeks to dominate through its mastery of technology as a primary instrument in that endeavor, with a consciousness that is mediated by transpersonal elements. The latter, by definition, as a power dimension *outside the domain of the*

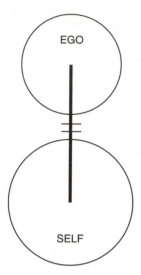

Part 5
Dissociation
The inflated overspecialized ego
behaves *as if* it has no connection
to the Self

Figure 7.2 Dissociated ego–Self relationship resulting in an ego that has become over-inflated and suicidal.

ego, brings a dimension of reality that at one and the same time is beyond the rational ken of the ego and is essentially humbling.

As we observed in earlier chapters, the mandate of a self-reflective ego commanded in Genesis[13] set up a paradox: Separation from nature also meant the ego's alienation from the Self – too close a relationship to the Self risked regression into *participation mystique* with nature and loss of individual identity, and a triggering of the ego's fragmentation complex.[14] We might say that up until now, although the Self has done its job of pressing for ego–Self dialogue, the western ego felt it could not afford to listen to the compensating voices of the Self – a kind of psychic standoff. Western culture itself has evolved so as to prevent that very dialogue from happening. At the same time a progressively autonomous ego became increasingly inflated with its own power and in danger of becoming an overspecialized organ of the psyche, threatening its own survival. (See Figure 7.2, Part 5. Note the increase in size of the ego relative to the Self, as compared to Figure 7.1, Parts 1–4.)

Fortunately, something else has been taking place as well. The "tacking" back and forth between the ego and Self at the edge of chaos has at one and the same time threatened the survival of our species *and* strengthened the *capacity* of the ego to *consciously* (re)connect with nature while withstanding

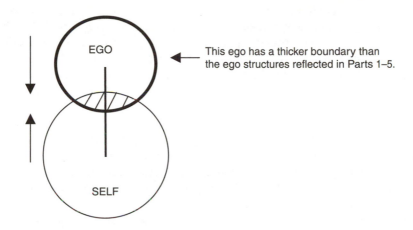

Part 6
Borderland Consciousness

Figure 7.3 Emergent ego–Self relationship resulting from the ego's reconnection with nature: Borderland consciousness.

its fragmentation complex, which it developed over the last three millennia.[15,16] (See Figure 7.3, Part 6.)

Thus, as we near the end of the fourth millennium since the advent of Genesis, we can now get a glimpse of the higher goal that the collective unconscious mandated in Genesis may have intended. While we cannot know, it is likely that prior to Genesis, no highly developed self-reflective, *logos*-based ego or intellect existed *or could have existed* since the western ego, as we know it, was a nascent germ existing as a potential contained within the Self. (See Figure 7.1, Parts 1 and 2) That potential could not be realized while the psyche was in a merged state of *participation mystique* with nature. An "absolute" separation from nature was essential for that ego germ to emerge from the Self and to become realized. The cost of that process of ego development has been living at the edge of chaos with increasing risk (Figure 7.2, Part 5).

I propose that we are arriving at a point in the history of humankind where the western ego (as depicted in Figure 7.3, Part 6) and the Self are struggling/ learning to function as coevolutionary partners. This dynamic is *in process* and therefore the outcome is not yet certain. The risks are still precarious. I have called this threshold in the evolutionary process the "Borderland." The challenge for the western ego at this time is to (uncharacteristically) struggle with its own inflation and power complex in order to work *with* the Self as a coevolutionary participant in the evolution of a new psychic paradigm and a new, transcendent, consciousness.

As I see it, since the ego cannot be trusted to curtail its own inflation and sense of omnipotence, we remain in danger of species extinction. It is far from certain that consciousness raising in which Jung and others (including myself) have placed so much confidence *alone can* curtail the suicidal tendencies of our species – particularly given that the ego itself is the organ of consciousness. The problem is that we inflate and idealize consciousness. We don't see its shadow side which is not unconsciousness, but hubris – consciousness split off from ethics, split off from an informing transpersonal link.

Although consciousness raising is our most powerful and hopeful technology, at the same time it cannot be entrusted as the sole carrier of life's holy mission. I continue to invest in consciousness raising because I can offer no better alternative – and, it is a wondrous adventure. At the same time my hope in the sustainability of life and our species is bolstered and supported by my faith in *un*conscious process as well.

The unconscious has been the source of powerful body blows to the spirit of humankind over the millennia. Sometimes – in the wake of the Holocaust, for example – it is difficult to think of it as an ally. And yet, life itself, consciousness itself, was born of the unconscious.[17] And in spite of itself – and its recent progeny the (western) ego construct that threatens our survival – life has managed to be sustained and grow into wondrous expressions over the millennia. So I will continue to invest in consciousness raising but all the while counting on the (collective) unconscious and evolutionary process to hold the organ of consciousness in containment, nudging it like a sheepdog towards the realization of life's most wondrous potential and mystery – and its own self-preservation and self-realization. As I see it, this new relationship will be reciprocal in nature. One where nature counterbalances and brings humility to the hubris of the ego complex, one where a resultant increasingly self-reflective ego, resistant to its own fragmentation complex, consciously integrates its deepening connection with a growing sense of moral consciousness. Richard C. Lewontin, Alexander Agassiz Research Professor, Museum of Comparative Zoology at Harvard University, addresses the reciprocal nature of (co)evolutionary process when he observes:

> The usual view of evolution is that organisms are "adapted" to their environments by natural selection. This view assumes that the environment of an organism preexists and organisms are molded to fit into this already existent ecological "niche." In fact, organisms select, reorganize, alter and destroy their environments as they evolve so that the environment and the organism are a coevolving pair in which both are equally the causes and the effects of the evolutionary process.[18]

This would apply no less in the case of evolution of the psyche and its relationship to nature, as it does between biological species and the physical environment in which they coexist.

What I am proposing is not a positivist "solution" to the suicidal tendencies of our species. The self, like nature, has a negative pole as well as a positive pole. The Self cannot be *fully* trusted either.[19] But life has survived and flourished over the past two million years since the human's presence on this planet. Given those negative poles as well as the increasingly self-destructive nature of civilization over the millennia, there would appear to be an inductive case that, *so far*, the unconscious and evolutionary forces reflect a kind of bias towards the preservation of life over the destruction of life. Complexity theorists talk about a self-organizing principle in the context of evolution. One might ask the "final cause," i.e. self-organizing *for what*? I would suggest a self-organizing principle in the name of the preservation of life, perhaps even, *self-reflective conscious life*. Is that perhaps what is suggested in Genesis when Yahweh Himself reflects, "God saw that the light was good?"[20]

It is my thesis that prior to the advent of Genesis and the development of the western ego construct, life more or less was self-contained, and the life-sustaining and life-destructive elements were more or less in a natural functional balance, with the life-sustaining elements having a slight edge. It is that "edge" that holds the threads of our potential survival as a species.

What holds hope for our species is a containing dynamic *outside* the ego. Reconnection with nature offers that, since it does connect the ego – *in spite of itself* – to the transpersonal dimension. This has nothing to do with either choice or belief. The evolutionary thrust is to have a containing/constraining dynamic outside of the ego that can contain its inflation, arrogance, and hubris. This has nothing to do with religion or philosophy of any sort. It has to do with the kind of dynamic that gripped Nikita Khrushchev during the Cuban Missile Crisis of 1962, and which moved him to back down in the face of imminent nuclear mutual annihilation by the United States and the Soviet Union. He was undoubtedly well aware that it would likely cost him his political life, if not his physical survival. In essence, he placed the highest value on the preservation of life above and beyond the value placed on (geopolitical) power. I call this dynamic that gripped Khrushchev in that moment, "moral consciousness."[21] Not morality. Morality is dependent on philosophy, codes, and ideas, a product of left-brain *logos*.

Moral consciousness, rather, is a dynamic in service to the life principle itself, the life instinct, as Freud put it. It therefore transcends ideas and codes. We cannot choose or unchoose it. We can choose to behave consonant with it or counter to it. To act counter to it can leave one with intense conflict or profound dread, since the values it brings are experienced as coming from within and are profoundly compelling. To violate them is seemingly to violate one's deepest truth. In that sense, moral consciousness chooses us more than we choose it. In the end, this is no guarantee, since the power drive is up to the contest. Minimally, the power drive will have been confronted by something equally, if not always, more powerful. At the very least, we will not be able to act *as if* our choices were without suicidal risk. We would *know* that we were going against our own moral consciousness – as Khrushchev ruefully discovered – and the act would be experienced, internally, as a "sin."[22]

William Van Dusen Wishard, in discussing various assessments that humankind may not survive "post-human technological scenarios," points out that the western psyche has focused on the destructive aspect of the Apocalypse, virtually ignoring the renewal that is to follow. He goes on to observe:

> A critical factor appears to be left out of all such discussion, and that is the whole realm of the unconscious domain. In recent decades, psychology has made great gains in understanding the conscious functioning of the brain. Less attention, however, has been given to the dynamics of the unconscious. While certain groundbreaking work has been done, no one of the stature of Jung or Freud has been able to take their investigation of the unconscious to a significantly new level. Indeed, with notable exceptions, the implications of Jung's exploration into the collective unconscious – that foundational layer of unconsciousness common to all humanity – are blithely dismissed by some, and generally ignored by others in the scientific community. By definition we know far more about our conscious life than the unconscious, even though the salient features of consciousness remain unknown. *Yet the unconscious may well determine* [positively or negatively] *far more of our collective activity than does the conscious.*[23]
>
> [Emphasis added.]

He also reminds us that myths are more than fanciful stories left over from the childhood of man:

> [Myths] emanate from the unconscious level of the psyche, that level which connects us to whatever transcendent wisdom may exist. It's a level at which, as quantum physics suggests, there may exist some relationship between the human psyche and external matter. Mind and matter may be but two dimensions of some larger reality, some fundamental pattern of life common to both that is operating outside the understanding of contemporary science . . . [W]e may be fooling around with phenomena that are, in fact, beyond the ability of humans to comprehend . . . a great mystery that does not yield to rational interpretation . . . *The mystery is the giver of these gifts*, and we only lose the gifts when we grasp at the mystery itself. Nature will not permit arrogant man to defy that mystery, that transcendent wisdom. In the end, nature's going to win out.[24]
>
> [Emphasis added.]

Notes

1 Edgar Mitchell, US astronaut and founder of the Institute of Noetic Sciences (IONS)
2 Jung, 1933: para. 289.
3 In Shulman, 1997: 128.
4 Edinger, 1972: 3.
5 Ibid.: 3.
6 This impression derives from my clinical experience over three decades. Psychoanalysis and psychoanalytic/psychotherapy, particularly those that are Jungian based, are treatment modalities that establish an ego–Self dialogue. See below and Edinger, 1972: 1–7. Often it is through this "dialogue" that the archetype of healing is constellated. At the same time it is not possible to isolate the "archetype of healing" under a microscope. Research on "spontaneous remission" offers the best inductive data that suggest a stimulation of the autoimmune system by some internal psychic/psychosomatic process which I refer to as the "archetype of healing" (O'Regan, 1993).
7 This level of awareness of the role that the unconscious endeavors to play in our lives is about as far as most individuals reach, developmentally, in the modern context. There are notable exceptions such as Swiss psychoanalyst Carl Jung, physicist Wolfgang Pauli, author Hermann Hesse, Shakespeare, and others.
8 Dreams represent a oneway communication from the Self of the individual to his ego.
9 Carl G. Jung and M.-L. von Franz, 1964: 38.
10 Ibid. Jung, 1954: para. 143; Jung, 1954: para. 353; 1955 and 1956: para. 88.
11 Edinger, 1972: 6.
12 Dialogue implies a more or less open exchange of "views." The ego's hubris since the dawn of the atomic age has made it progressively resistant to "exchange." Laurens van der Post puts it thus: "Western civilization has progressively failed itself. That is, it's become lopsided. Instead of broadening the basis of consciousness, it has narrowed the basis of consciousness" (Ryley, 1998: 24).
13 See Chapter 3.
14 This could also lead to psychosis in a given individual.
15 Kauffman, 1993: 234–235, 280–281.
16 Shulman, 1997: 102–122.
17 See Figure 7.1.
18 Lewontin, 2003.
19 Jung, 1934–1939: 432–433.
20 The Tanach, 1988 [5748 – Hebrew Calendar]: 3–4.
21 Bernstein, 1993.
22 The sin would not be against God so much as it would be felt as a sin against the Self.
23 Wishard, 2003.
24 Wishard, 2003.

Part II

Chapter 8

Introduction to Part II: Psychological and clinical implications

Psychotherapy represents the recreation of an optimal interpersonal environment which facilitates the growth of psychic structures that store and process social and affective information. Early forming representations of the self-interacting-with-a-misattuned-dysregulating other become unconscious internalized object relations that mediate psychiatric psychopathology. Such representations are imprinted predominantly with painful primitive affect, which the developmentally impaired personality can not intrapersonally nor interpersonally regulate. Certain forms of external and internal affective input are therefore selectively excluded from conscious process. These strategies of affect regulation must be recognized and addressed in the dyadic psychotherapeutic treatment of developmental disorders.[1]

I don't think I had been meditating very long when two beings of light appeared to me and began speaking. They told me about my connection with the nonphysical world, the world of energy and vibration. They reminded me of the way I lived in fuller consciousness as a small child and suggested it was time to live that way again. They did not remind me of all my childhood experiences, but opened the door for me to begin my own process. While there are several things about this experience that were very profound for me, what was perhaps the most profound was that I did not question what had occurred. It felt "normal" and as if the rest of the life I had been living was out of sync with the authentic "me." A Borderland personality.[2]

It seems to me that what I have identified as Borderland consciousness is the most evident manifestation of that mystery in the liminal realm between the collective unconscious and collective consciousness. Its primary goal appears to be the reconnection of the western ego construct with nature in the name of the preservation of life and our species, as well as to serve as a constructive partner in the next phase of life's evolution. At the same time, the reconnection of psyche with nature means that more *and different* primitive levels of the psyche and emotional states will be released than those with which we have become familiar and (more or less) comfortable. A major thesis of this book is that many of those different primitive levels and emotional states, while being transrational, are not pathological. The challenge is to learn to differentiate between those that are and those that aren't. Doing so clarifies both dimensions – the pathological and the sacred – and the process contributes to healing and wholeness.

The Borderland has many implications for every aspect of human existence, from science to economics, to psychology. In Part II of this book, we will be looking at some of its psychological and clinical implications.

Notes

1 Schore, 1994: 472–473.
2 The quote is from a spontaneous correspondence I received via email from someone who had read the chapter on Hannah in *The Salt Journal*. I have never met this individual. She is describing part of an event that took place at age 32, which stimulated her to reopen her Borderland connection after having shut it down at age 7.

Chapter 9

A Great Grief

Man feels isolated in the cosmos because he is no longer involved in nature.[1]

What is needed now . . . is to find a way to restore a sense of the sacred to science and to the world – to embody mind and to "enmind" matter. Getting there will involve a radical approach to studying consciousness, where the researcher (scientist or philosopher) may be profoundly changed in the process of exploring his or her own consciousness.[2]

In his passionate essay, "Healing the Split," written shortly before his death in 1961, Jung puts most of his reliance on dreams for the "recovery" of humanity's previous connection with "natural symbols" (as opposed to cultural symbols) that have been repressed into the deepest layers of the psyche. He does not distinguish between "natural *symbols*" and nature as a living, breathing organism. With regard to the western ego's reconnection with lost symbolic contents from "nature," he goes on to say that, "It is the single individual who will undergo it and carry it through."[3,4]

On the one hand, this is obviously true since we all have our individual psyches and egos. On the other hand, it is increasingly evident that as an *evolutionary* phenomenon, the reconnection of the western psyche with its roots in nature – not just as "natural *symbol*" – is also a collective phenomenon taking place both externally as well as internally within the single individual.[5] It would appear that Jung did not foresee what I am proposing is happening at this very moment: That the *collective unconscious* itself would be working to bring about a "healing of the split," and that such a reconnection would not depend solely on the personal work of each individual to reintegrate repressed unconscious contents.[6] For Jung the individual psyche is the "patient." I am proposing that, along with the individual psyche as patient, the western ego itself is the designated patient that is presently involved in a healing process. The healing agent, as I discussed in Chapters 6 and 7, is the evolutionary process as reframed through the lens of complexity theory in a reciprocal coevolutionary relationship with the western psyche.

In a letter dated February 9, 1960, to A. D. Cornell of Cambridge University, Jung writes, "As far as we can see, the collective unconscious is identical with nature to the extent that nature herself, including matter, is unknown to us . . . the collective unconscious is simply nature."[7] There is much about this statement that seems right to me. But there is much about it that does not, and that is even more unsettling.

Arguably, the concept of the "collective unconscious" is perhaps Jung's most brilliant contribution to the field of psychology. Certainly it is on the order of the discovery of the personal unconscious by Freud. At the same time it does not suffice in addressing this evolutionary dynamic that is unfolding in our midst. Indeed, in many ways it detracts from it. The major problem is that the concept of the "collective unconscious" is just that – a concept. As a cogni-centric[8] concept, it is a by-product of that *logos*-based rational ego that I have identified as *the* problem that today most threatens the survival of our species. For all of Jung's effort and intention,[9] at this point in our psychic evolution the notion that the collective unconscious is synonymous with nature is a detraction. It pulls us back into that post-Genesis ego and a cogni-centric view of nature. In this view we *perceive* nature from the outside as a thing – inanimate, objectified, dynamic, soulless. We have enormous difficulty *experiencing* nature as living, and the very source of our being, the *prima materia*, the primordial ooze out of which we emerged, including our soul(s).

I cannot define nature. It seems to me that every attempt to do so – to circumscribe nature by rational limits and definition – runs counter to the very essence of nature. I could say that nature is beauty, ugliness, mystery, laws, chaos, gentle, violent, monstrous, knowable, unknowable, . . . and go on at some length giving two-dimensional words to what we experience as nature.

In *Man and his Symbols*, Jung wrote:

> Man feels isolated in the cosmos because he is no longer involved in nature. Natural phenomena have lost their symbolic implications. Thunder is no longer the voice of an angry god, nor is lightning his avenging missile. No river contains a spirit, no tree is the life principle of a man . . . No voices now speak to man from stones, plants and animals, nor does he speak to them believing they can hear. His contact with nature is gone, and with it the profound emotional energy this symbolic connection supplied.[10]

It is important to note that in the above quote regarding "man's" costly loss of his connection with nature, Jung writes from his perch as a Euro-centric, cogni-centric scientist, albeit one whose eyes were dramatically opened in his travels through New Mexico, Washington D.C., Africa, and India 40 years previously. His use of the universal "man" as if it referred to all (western) humanity belies the cultural prejudices of his day. It also fails to openly recognize that there is still a *direct* source for that (re)connection in those very cultures that he visited – though diminished by their having been assaulted by western civilization – that can enlighten, even heal western civilization itself.

For those of us not born into tribal cultures, it is true that we are "stuck" with our cogni-centric center. But we can strive to *know* our dilemma and behave in a manner that contains it, rather than in a manner that identifies with it. Here again I will call on my experience with Borderland patients to illustrate this drive to know, to understand the meaning of this dilemma.

During one analytic session, one man in his 30s talked about his struggles to pull his outer life together – where to live, what kind of work/career he should be pursuing, etc. He stopped talking mid-sentence, and there was a long silence. Then he said:

> I carry a Great Grief. I feel it deep inside (points to his heart). It's never not there. I feel its presence. It is never far from me. In Montana I felt connected. (He had just returned from a trip there.) Here I'm disconnected – in my car, living on top of the land. I'm part of the land; that's my home. But I'm a product of my culture and therefore cut off from my home. I felt expanded there; I feel contracted here. When I was at the gathering in Montana (a wilderness experience) I was part of a community. When I was there a voice kept saying, "Teaching kids about nature may be one of the most important things you do."

This particular young man – I shall call him Allan – was familiar with the concept of the collective unconscious. But I knew that in the moment when he named and revealed a deeply intimate part of himself – his Great Grief – for me to mention the "collective unconscious," or any other rational construct as a definer or container for what he was sharing in that moment would be to profane the moment and leave him feeling profoundly unseen and unheard. I had no impulse to do so, having been taught by Hannah that many experiences of nature can be related to only on their own experiential terms.

And even here I need to be careful. It is tempting to use phrases like "feeling" versus "thinking," *logos* versus sensation, to use metaphor – "It's as if . . ." These would be better than the heavy "collective unconscious," but still inadequate, a profanation to the individual – and to nature herself.

The challenge is to not interpret at all – certainly not in the moment – to hold an experience that can feel *between language*, that can leave one with the tension of holding one's intellectual and rational breath for far longer than any of us can imagine doing. To not seek the comfort of rational understanding, but to come to some kind of knowing through a holding and a wonderment.

Interestingly, not many weeks after Allan revealed his Great Grief, his long-standing "stuckness" regarding his need to negotiate more functionally the mundane world loosened, and he found it possible to focus on claiming the greater fullness of his life. It was as if he had to have a place to put his secret, his Great Grief. Not to get rid of it, but to lay it in a safe place after having it consciously witnessed in order to move forward. Allan began to explore career options and to consider earning money, which he had always disdained as being *the* source of the world's troubles. He became committed to a relationship, and even considered the previously unspeakable subjects of marriage and family, commitments he had never perceived as possible before. But in his sessions, he would periodically remind me that his Great Grief was "in there," and truth be told, some part of him felt that it's too late: "We blew it, and we humans probably won't survive." For Allan, the word "probably" was new. Ironically, it became part of his personal statement after our focusing on the concept of Borderland phenomena and the idea that the mourning he felt was not of him, but *by him*, in response to a "Great Grief" that he felt in and for nature and the human dilemma.

The word "probably" resulted also from our discussion of my notion of a new evolutionary phenomenon that was reconnecting the western ego with nature. "Probably," which for Allan was a euphemism for "hope," entered in because now he could separate his despair about where we have come as the human race and our (self-)destructive inclinations. He could conceive a new departure point, the Borderland, which points to a new evolutionary unfolding and possibility. It was freeing him to recognize that he was grieving *something out there*, and that the source of his grief was not "just" his depressive nature. (Although he experienced painful events in his life that were depressing, I don't think he has a depressive "nature.")

This same "Great Grief" is manifest in a dream reported by a man in his 60s:

> I was in south Florida, near Miami. The area was quite developed – "modernized." Lots of people, hotels, high-rise apartment buildings, long walkways near the ocean. I was there on business. I was near the hotel I was staying in. As I walked along the winding concrete walkway near the beach, it was as if the walkway divided the "civilized" part of the world from the "nature" part of the world, although there was only a narrow, serpentine path separating the two. There was a thin stand of "jungle" on one side, and concrete and development on the other. The "civilized" part seemed to go on for miles and miles. I noticed that on the "nature" side of the path, there were some kids playing. I saw a large frog sitting on the ground quite still – presumably in a hyper-vigilant defensive mode. Nearby was a snake, coiled, also quite still, in a similar defensive stance. Between the two was a little girl with a stick, trying to shove the snake towards the frog and vice versa. She was obviously looking for some "action," trying to get the snake to attack the frog. She hadn't noticed that the snake was much too small to eat the frog, or do much else with it. I don't think the snake was poisonous. The girl didn't get it and kept trying to bring about an attack. It seemed to me that the frog and the snake were more afraid of her than anything else. Neither moved. It seemed a pitiful sight.

I did get to my hotel room. I don't know what my work was there. But I found the place depressing. It seemed to me a microcosm of where the world is today – sad and depressed and split in the midst of its new millennium and prosperity. Here was nature, tired, oppressed, with even its instinct depressed. And here was a young girl, cut off herself from her own instinct, her own connection with nature, with life, witlessly trying to prod instinct into these near lifeless-seeming, very sad forms.

The dreamer commented that this was one of his saddest and most profound dreams, unlike any he had ever dreamt. There was something about it that was even more compelling than the more dramatic nightmares and monster dreams that he had experienced over the years. The most prevalent feelings associated with this dream were depression and despair. If this is the state of our world, what does all the rest of it mean – all that technology and "progress"? The dream lingered with him for weeks, even months, and seemed to haunt his very breath. The world is dying, he felt, and our souls with it. And the world is too busy to even note it. How can we let this happen? This feeling left the dreamer in a state of grief and mourning. He said it left him with the refrain of a Tom Waits song going through his head for days. The title of the song is "The Earth Died Screaming".

One of the more disturbing images for him in the dream was that of the little girl. She was about 8 years old. Where was her mother, he wondered. Why was she out there by herself on the Borderland between the industrialized world and what was left of nature? Were her parents not aware that she was depressed, that the little bit of instinct or earthly connection left in her was seeking in her own feeble, naive way to spark life into dying nature? Why was she left alone with this dilemma? Didn't they know that her soul was depressed?

Neither did the dreamer miss the message about himself. For he knew that his dream represented his own psychic landscape, that the little girl represented his own depressed soul, and that his critical judgments of her parents were judgments that were also aimed at him. What was *he* going to do about it?

Perhaps most important to him was that he was not able to repress it and make himself feel better by watching his net worth grow on his computer screen. This dream impacted his life, and he began to process how he might make some difference, what of value he might do in this drama unfolding in our midst. One thing he did immediately was to take seriously the subject of the earth's dying. When colleagues and acquaintances gave the usual verbal nod to the daily blurb in the newspaper about global warming or other forms of ecological deterioration, he would insist on discussing the implications. He was not satisfied with perfunctory exchanges on the subject.

Mostly, however, he wondered about the spiritual implications of the earth dying. Where was God? Did God not care?

During the course of reading Susan Griffin's book, *What Her Body*

Thought: A Journey into the Shadows, I was startled to come across a dream she reports while she was in Germany, one which mirrors both the symbolic content and the import of the dream reported above. She introduces her dream as follows:

> While I was still in Germany, just after my collapse [from Chronic Fatigue Syndrome – CFIDS], the newspapers were preoccupied with a mysterious illness that was killing seals in the North Sea. Their bodies, lifeless or nearly dead, were washing up by the hundreds on the beaches of northern Europe. The papers suggested that something was injuring the immune systems of these animals. One photograph run on the front page of a German newspaper showed a pile of dead seals, just at the end of the sea, rising higher than six feet.

> *The dream*:
> I dreamed I was on a beach. In their swimsuits, wearing sunglasses and cotton hats, children beside them digging sand with small shovels, several bathers lay on blankets, taking in the sun. They acted as if they were completely unaware of the dead animals all around them. In my dream, I was the only witness. Standing in front of the stacked-up bodies of seals, I began to plead with [the people]. *Don't you know*, I called out to them, *unless you do something now, what is happening to these seals will happen to you too.*[11]

When dreams of a number of dreamers, like the two preceding ones, have such strikingly similar symbolic images and themes, it suggests that there is a message from the collective unconscious, in addition to the one from the individual personal unconscious. It is as if the collective unconscious were speaking to western culture through the medium of these two dreamers with the message that civilization's impact on nature is degrading the natural world in which we live and that degradation threatens our own survival as a culture, if not as a species.[12]

Another man, Rich, in his late 30s was engaged in a scientific project. He spontaneously offered the following concerns in a session:

> The earth is sterilized by our expansion. Where will you find a wolf that is actually dangerous? Or an elk that is alive not merely because of a game preserve? There is no wilderness to die in. Once when I was hiking, a shy bighorn sheep came right up to me and wanted me to feed it some sun screen I was putting on. It makes me feel conflicted. There's no "outside" any more.

> I'm afraid of the wilderness – it's dangerous. But that's what's wonderful about it. I don't know what I'm talking about, but it sits in me like a rock sometimes. The good thing about science and technology is

making way for people. But we've won over nature, you know. It's fear more than sadness. Fear about it: I'm afraid that everything – the people and places I love – will be crushed. For every effort you undertake to save them – people and places – it's part of what destroys them. The plans one makes are corrupt. Your soul is weeping. I feel petrified with pain and fear about it, and I don't have a clue as to what could be done about it. I felt that for a long time. I feared it would turn into cancer or some other autoimmune disorder. It's like a big black hole (he points to his chest). The nature and instinct that's destroyed . . . I feel conflicted when I'm designing things, rational structures in my job. There are people – activists – running around throwing their mourning in my face. They're too busy to have a center, too busy trying to change/fix it, instead of living a process, digesting what is happening. You can't mourn enough. You somehow have to digest it, absorb it, you can't just burn it up right away.[13]

At this point in the session I asked him "What value does your mourning have?" He answered, "My mourning is my own problem." To which I responded, "It matters. It matters because your mourning appreciates them – the people and places you love, the wolf, the elk, the choking earth – and thanks them for their being. It matters." So much of human despair derives from the sense that what one feels most deeply does not matter.

Rich's concern for the animals and his despair of the choking-off of instinct reminded me of a session with Hannah late in our work. (At this point Hannah would ask for a session as she felt a need.) She complained that she had lost her footing and was experiencing some depression and friction with her husband. She blamed him for her malaise, while knowing that he was not a major contributor to her current upset. She presented a dream in which a dark male figure was pursuing her and threatening her. She was frightened and felt cornered in the dream. She had no idea what this male figure repre-sented in her psyche. At my suggestion that she do an active imagination with the dream character, the dialogue revealed that he felt isolated and in despair. His despair was paramount. When asked about the nature of his despair, he said that he was despondent about the state of the world, the destruction of the earth, the dying of the species. He could not bear it.

I recalled a session earlier in our work. At that time Hannah said that "Nothing can make-up for this world that has been lost. Nothing. Nothing. It's all gone." I felt that the voice that spoke those words within her un-conscious a year or two previously were his, those of the current dream figure. In that earlier session I said, "But there are animals and trees here now. Will you abandon them?" She replied, "I am angry that everything is not des-troyed so there will be nothing new born to suffer." I suggested to her that because the despairing male figure in her dream was left alone with his despair about the plight of nature and the human dilemma, he had no alter-native but to attack her to get her attention. Ironically, this dynamic in her dream was, to a significant degree, the result of her healing, both in her inner life and outer life (she had begun to refer to herself as "happy") over the past couple of years. "He" felt left behind. And he had begun to pull her back into that old despair as a way of getting her attention.

Hannah and I (and in the back of my mind, "he") spent the rest of that session talking about what was shifting toward the positive, toward the pre-servation of nature, and particularly about the shift taking place in human consciousness. It was my thought that her despairing inner masculine figure did not know that hope was possible, that a shift in consciousness was occur-ring that was more focused on preservation of life than on its destruction. We talked specifics: The move toward socially responsible investing and effective corporate governance in the financial and corporate worlds; a heightening consciousness in politics regarding preservation of the ecology.

She reported a few weeks later that her depression had lifted – within a day of the session – and that she had stopped attacking her husband and was able to resume her work. It seemed that she ("he") had connected with the spirit of hope inherent in the life instinct. She did not ask for another session.

I could go on with more examples – there are many. However, the point is that although for all these individuals their despair does connect with and par-tially derive from personal emotional and psychological antecedents, their "Great Grief" derives from their connection to nature herself – not as neur-osis, but as *objective, nonpersonal, nonrational phenomena occurring in the natural universe*. These are individuals, as I described in Chapter 2, who have one or both feet in the Borderland. Their psyches are connected to and respond to nature as living essence – not in an *as if* context of symbolic meaning only, but as ongoing feeling *connection*.

Our culture has become so dissociated, that in its one-sidedness and its own dissociation neurosis it communicates profound distress coupled with dire warnings about the future of our ecology and our way of life, indeed our very survival. And yet it condemns those who take these warnings to heart and are emotionally distressed by them. It is acceptable to address these warnings rationally as *thoughts* and *ideas*, to engage in the pros and cons of given political positions and possible actions. But those who take them to heart – and to soul – are often seen as extremist, one sided, and neurotic. To point out the contradictions emerging from within the scientific and political spheres is to point out that the emperor has no clothes.

Unfortunately, this prejudice and cultural dissociation often is reflected in a one-sidedness of psychotherapy in all its forms when it pathologizes behaviors and emotions that do not fit its preexisting definitions and categor-ies of rationality and normative behavior. This prejudice within psychology is so prevalent and unrelenting that it is a major contributor to the suffering and pain of many patients seen in hospitals and private consulting rooms.

I have come to the conclusion over the past 15 years that the collective unconscious has tapped certain individuals within the culture to be carriers of personal and collective mourning for the profound assault and wounds to nature wrought, predominantly, by western civilization and the modern technological society. Globalization has only accentuated the speed and intensity of this process. I am seeing more and more individuals like Allan, Hannah, and Rich who are gripped by a mourning that is both personal and outside themselves. On the collective level, they are not unlike the "professional" mourners described by Nikos Kazantzakis in *Zorba the Greek*, whose job it is to mourn loudly for those who had just died and to wail at their funerals. These professional mourners chose their work and were paid money for their services. The Allans, Hannahs, and Riches – and there are many of them in our culture – were chosen unasked. Often they pay dearly in emotional terms for their sensitivity as Borderland personalities. My clinical work with each of them as individuals consisted in learning to sort out my own cogni-centric and cultural prejudices from what appeared to be their legitimate experience, and assisting them in learning to discriminate their experience of the sacred from what they perceived as pathological.[14]

As the following chapters will reveal, some of the individuals who might be seen as Borderland personalities are quite worldly and secure in the outer world. Some, contrariwise, might be seen as "old souls," with a sensitivity that makes it painful for them to have too much commerce with the mundane world. Their connection to nature and Borderland reality leaves them with both a shyness and sensitivity to living in an industrial world. I remember one individual for whom living in an apartment with a refrigerator became oppressive because the sound of the refrigerator when it came on and shut off was like fingernails on a blackboard to him. Although this is an extreme example, there are many versions of what feels like oppression by a world caught in technological madness. The following poem, in my view, reflects the sensitivity of these gentle souls:

There Are Men Too Gentle to Live Among Wolves

There are men too gentle to live among wolves
Who prey upon them with IBM eyes
And sell their hearts and guts for martinis at noon.
There are men too gentle for a savage world
Who dream instead of snow and children and Halloween
And wonder if the leaves will change their color soon.
There are men too gentle to live among wolves
Who anoint them for burial with greedy claws
And murder them for a merchant's profit and gain.
There are men too gentle for a corporate world
Who dream instead of candied apples and ferris wheels
And pause to hear the distant whistle of a train.

There are men too gentle to live among wolves
Who devour them with eager appetite and search
For other men to prey upon and suck their childhood dry.
There are men too gentle for an accountant's world
Who dream instead of Easter eggs and fragrant grass
And search for beauty in the mystery of the sky.
There are men too gentle to live among wolves
Who toss them like a lost and wounded dove.
Such gentle men are lonely in a merchant's world,
Unless they have a gentle one to love.[15]

Notes

1 Carl G. Jung and after his death M.-L. von Franz, l964: 95.
2 Quincey, 2002: 11.
3 Although Jung is speaking implicitly of the western ego when he uses the term "ego," he never explicitly states so.
4 Jung, 1961: 261.
5 Jungian analyst, Marie-Louise von Franz, seemed to be reaching for a related notion in her discussion of "reciprocal individuation." In Edinger, 1999: 24–25.
6 My contention that Jung did not foresee this psychodynamic role of the collective unconscious was reinforced in a personal conversation in 1989 with Jung's son, Franz Jung.
7 Jung, 1960: 540.
8 A term coined by the modern authority on shamanism, Michael Harner.
9 That is, between 1911 when he wrote his essay, "Two Kinds of Thinking," and 1961 when he died. The overspecialization of the western ego became dramatically identifiable around the time of Jung's death and has increased exponentially in its threat to species survival since then.
10 Jung, 1964: 95.
11 Griffin, 1999: 97.
12 The personal content of these dreams are manifest as reported above. In the case of the man in his 60s, I am familiar with the personal import of his dream since we have a relationship. I have had no contact with Susan Griffin, and her dream as reported stands for both the personal message about her life and health and the broader more collective message that it reflects. It is clear from her book that she took the import of her dream on both the personal and collective levels.
13 This echoes Jung's assertion that, "It is the single individual who will undergo a reconnection with the lost symbolic contents of nature and carry it through."
14 A brief glance back to the 16th-century Inquisition of the Catholic Church and the lives of Galileo Galilei and Nicolas Copernicus displays the profound confusion of western civilization regarding what was perceived as pathological and what was perceived as sacred. That confusion has evolved as western civilization has evolved. Although today we are more sophisticated, and the "punishments" less severe than in the 16th century, this confusion remains with us still.
15 Kavanaugh, 1991.

Chapter 10

Portals to the Borderland

A purely personalistic psychology . . . does not capture the true mystery of that *coming into being* of the personal spirit in the face of trauma . . . This is because it leaves out the transpersonal element or it interprets the transpersonal element as infantile omnipotence and neglects the primacy of the numinosum in human experiences.[1]

In terms of personal psychology, it would appear that there are three portals[2] to the Borderland:

1 evolution
2 personality structure (i.e. the type of psyche we are born with)
3 trauma.

Evolution portal

In the preceding chapters I made the case for a compensatory evolutionary shift wherein the western psyche is in the process of being reconnected to nature from which it began its psychic split over 3,000 years ago. In essence, the western ego is being pushed into that reconnection with nature by an evolutionary process in the name of species preservation – if not the preservation of all of life as we know it.

This "reconnection" is not a regression. Rather it is a reconnection to nature as a *dimension of existence*, as a *life form*, as a *reality principle*, different from that to which we have accustomed ourselves, integrating with it. The major impact of this reconnection on the western ego is psychological and spiritual. It is compelling an awareness of nonrational reality and experience on which this ego progressively turned its back millennia ago. In the post-Enlightenment world, we have behaved as if those dimensions of reality simply ceased to exist. But they have remained what they were and what they are, and we are being pushed to reconnect with those dimensions of reality – like it or not.[3]

Evolution is predominantly a biological term. The "collective unconscious" is the concept formulated by Jung to describe the dynamic through which unconscious contents heretofore unknown and unrealized emerge into human awareness – a kind of psychic evolution. The western ego itself is one such psychic evolutionary construct. While the impetus for evolutionary change is unknown and essentially unknowable, we can infer deductively and inductively the *probable* telos – or final cause, of a given evolutionary process.[4] This is no less true in the case of psychic evolution as it is of biological evolution. Most biologists/scientists would argue that there is no telos, there is simply the structure and order that we see, the source of that order and organization is beyond our capacity to know and therefore is not addressed *in the data*. But too often the telos is very much experienced by many biologists in their *subjective feeling reaction* to the numinosity of the beauty of the order we do find in life. The data, in this context, are their awe – and ours as well. And, as was suggested in the introduction, science, and the mathematics that supports scientific endeavor, is not the only universal language. Neither is it a language of objectivity "purified" of subjective, i.e. human, influence.[5] Subjective feeling reaction – "knowing" – is a universal language too. The latter conveys an *experience* of truth, however well or poorly we may be able to express it verbally. The Borderland, as I have described it in Part I, is the by-product of that evolutionary process, the "space," the nexus, the threshold whereby the western ego is being thrust into reconnection with transrational dimensions of reality.

It is important here to distinguish between the imaginal world, the source of which is internal to the individual, and the Borderland. Borderland experiences are not imaginal – although these two realms often inform, stimulate, and feed each other. They are not experiences secondary to fantasy. They are direct experiences of transrational reality. In one sense, this is not a new phenomenon in terms of psychic experience. There have been isolated *individuals* for whom these experiences have been known and commonplace. And, historically, we know about some of them. Some individuals once burned as witches, might today be seen as Borderland personalities. Others have been the wise people who, over the centuries, were consulted about the health and welfare of the people and their animals. Yet others have been dowsers. And, of course, some – many – have been branded as "looney" and shunned from the community.

What is new is that reconnection with these nonrational dimensions of reality is taking place rapidly on a collective level within western culture and is beginning to affect many individuals at all levels of society. And if indeed this phenomenon is happening as a function of evolutionary process, then it portends to affect tens of thousands of individuals and the culture as a whole – I would say, in the short span of the current century.[6]

In the case of children who experience Borderland phenomena as a natural part of their childhood, these experiences should not be particularly stressful since they naturally have one foot in the archetypal realm as their young egos gradually develop.[7] It *can* become stressful for children if they develop in a family and/or cultural context that is hostile to what they experience as "natural." Where this evolutionary dynamic typically has stressful impact is in the case of individuals who begin their lives where the magical level of consciousness is suppressed in their early developmental years – before age 7 – or whose initial conscious experience of Borderland phenomena comes either later in childhood (after age 7) or as adults in their 20s or 30s for whom this dimension has newly opened. There appears to be a correlation between the age of initial conscious experience of Borderland phenomena and the potential for disturbing psychic and emotional impact on the ego: The older the individual the greater potential for deleterious impact. Some individuals become highly inflated and pursue grandiose goals. In this instance, some go over the edge in pursuit of self-destructive, unrealizable ventures and relationships. In other instances, this grandiosity leads to highly creative processes and successful artistic careers of one sort or another. I have seen individuals in clinical practice who came into therapy because the Borderland dimension had opened up to them, either frightening them or because they were intrigued to explore the mystery of this dimension in themselves in greater breadth and depth.

Personality structure portal

Jung's concept of the Self holds that each individual comes into this world at birth with an innate character structure/personality type. Included in that character structure are a number of personality traits, such as introversion/extroversion, artistic traits, native intelligence, and, through the Self, the degree and nature of connection to the transpersonal dimension. Some individuals fit the Borderland personality type, that is, they have a more *natural* connection to the transpersonal dimension than do others. Another way of saying this is that their psyches have not fully adapted to the absolute psychic split from nature that is apparent in the mainstream of western culture. Sometimes a genetic or personality link to parents or grandparents appears to be evident with regard to these traits.[8] Sometimes not. When there is a link, there has tended to be less stress connected with being a Borderland personality.

Historically there have been isolated *categories* of individuals such as artists and highly intuitive people who are naturally more prone to experiencing Borderland phenomena than others. The very nature of their personality structure has "several toes," if not a whole foot, in the nonrational realm of psychic experience. Most of us have heard or read about creative individuals whose inspiration, if not the work itself, *came to* the individual from some transpersonal source through the artist's unconscious. We talk of creative "gifts," as if they come from a source outside the personal ego. In the case of many artistic personality types, these individuals have developed with an *ongoing relationship* to the transrational realm. That does not mean that many of them have not had a difficult time – in some cases an extremely difficult time – bridging the rational world of everyday life with their subjective experience of the transrational dimension. But, they grew up being *used to* living with their transrational experience and, often, of being out of step with the rational world in which they live. Developmentally speaking, the transrational dimension of experience has never been alien to them.

Subjectively, the experience of the artistic personality is significantly different from that of many Borderland personalities whose connection to the transrational (magical) dimension of experience ended developmentally, for the most part, between ages 6 and 7.[9] For these Borderland individuals, being thrust into reconnection with transrational reality later in life can be quite unsettling. In addition to the emotional discomfort of not knowing what is happening to them, many may come to wonder if something is not "wrong" with them. Often this unspoken self-doubt *is* reflected back to them by loved ones, friends, and co-workers, who increasingly find them to be "weird." Many have difficulty adjusting to the demands of outer life. And many who seek therapy have their worst fears ratified by being told that something is "wrong." A diagnosis of pathology (often "Borderline personality disorder") gives rise to even greater anxiety and can become part of a self-fulfilling prophecy.

The second chapter of this book, which discusses the case of Hannah, was published independently in *The Salt Journal*[10] and in the *IONS Noetic Sciences Review* in 2000.[11] As a result of those articles I received a number of communications from individuals who read the piece and who identified themselves as "Borderland personalities." A number coined the term, "Borderlander." Several said that the article was the first time their life experience had been put into words. Several offered descriptions of their "Borderland" experience. As a result of these communications, I developed an informal questionnaire (see Appendix), which I sent to 20 individuals, mostly via email. Some of the responses I received are contained in this and the next chapter with permission of the individuals.

One respondent reported:

> I was sort of born with an inclination toward the Borderland and had semi-Borderland experiences throughout my youth . . . I trusted my Borderland experiences from the beginning . . . I shared them with peers, former professors from college, fellow evangelical Christians, anyone who would listen, because I felt my experiences to be important. I received two main types of reactions. Either blank stares, or (more often) stern, defensive opposition.

A 46-year-old woman identified herself in a letter as a "Borderland person." She said of herself:

> My sensitivities to all things animate and inanimate were with me from my earliest memories. I would touch my bedroom door and it would "tell" me about the forest it came from. Though we had no pets, dogs and cats would show up at our front door – I had invited them to come over. The dog next door was my best friend, literally.
>
> Everything I came in contact with had something to tell me. It was not a problem until I realized that no one else heard what I heard or felt what I felt. I kept waiting, hoping, to find other people like me. There is nothing worse for a child than to be different. I was different from everyone, my own family included. Interestingly my older brother and sister made up a story that I had been dropped on the door step by an Indian. I was only about three years old when they told me this story, but I remember being so happy to hear that I did have a "real" family and that maybe they would come back for me. I used to watch out the front door, looking for an Indian.
>
> As a small child (2 to 5 years old) I was very tuned in to both the animate and inanimate world. I remember my mother trying to explain death to me. She said that when an animal dies, it stops eating, breathing, and becomes like a rock. I told her, well then it is still alive, because for me rocks were very alive.

This woman intentionally shut down the Borderland dimension of her life at about age 8. It was too lonely and frightening for her to live in that realm with no validation or support. Although "I had lost conscious memory of most of my Borderland existence, I had been a spiritual seeker for several years and practiced meditation." Through some synchronous connections at age 32, she consciously chose to reconnect to the Borderland.

Psychic personalities

It is easy to confuse "psychic" individuals with Borderland personalities. A few of the individuals who have contacted me and who have identified themselves as Borderland personalities, when asked, stated that these two dimensions were one and the same. Certainly for some individuals, there is indeed an overlapping of psychic and Borderland personality characteristics. However, to my mind it is important to distinguish between the two.

Psychic personalities typically pick up bits and pieces of information, i.e. psychic data, not unlike the far distant radio stations one can sometimes pick up late at night that are not detectable during daytime hours. The source of this information is other than the life experience of the psychic individual. That information can be about people, things, or events, and, as anyone who has had a relationship with a psychic individual knows, can be shockingly accurate. Some psychic individuals can hone in, focus, on specific subjects or issues. And sometimes, because of that focusing ability, they are consultants to police departments, the FBI, and various agencies of the intelligence community.

Psychics sometimes have difficulty discerning what is psychic information – information coming to them from a source outside themselves – from their own intuition. They often have difficulty discerning whether the information they pick up has to do with some aspect of their own lives, or whether it is about someone else's life. I have more than once had a client innocently bring in a dream that, in graphic detail, was about some current aspect or sensitive issue of my life. Indeed, sometimes these psychic intrusions can be quite disconcerting. Unless one is used to such events, one can find oneself suddenly enraged being psychically violated, as if one has discovered a Peeping Tom looking through the window. In my experience, not only do the individuals with the psychic dream or "intuition" present this information in innocence, but they often suffer emotional consequences from the fear they have left the other person feeling violated. They sometimes know that the material is not theirs but often they have no idea to whom it is connected. That is part of the reason they bring the material into therapy – to try to make some sense of it and to see what relevance it may have for their own process. It takes a great deal of sensitivity on the part of the therapist to be able to identify and discern psychic material when the client doesn't realize that they have picked up personal or sensitive material about the therapist. Sometimes it is necessary to set boundaries around what will and will not be pursued in therapy: The therapist's personal relationship with his or her spouse, for example. The client will also need help in learning how to manage material that he does withhold in the name of respecting boundaries. And, above all else, it takes a great deal of self-control on the part of the therapist to not *react* on a personal level when such a violation does take place. Such a reaction can be quite wounding to the client, even traumatizing, and in extreme cases, can result in the client hiding this dimension of his/her life so as to not incur the wrath of the therapist, thus compromising the whole of the therapeutic work.

Some psychic individuals are tormented by information they pick up when the content is emotionally upsetting. They have no idea to whom or to what it is connected, why they have the information, or what to do with it. And, of course, there are times when such psychic information can be enormously comforting and helpful, even life saving.

Borderland personalities, contrariwise, may or may not have their own psychic experiences. However, whether or not they do, they all have an *ongoing relationship* with transrational reality. Their connection with that dimension is not random, and is usually based in a *feeling dialogue* which, depending on the content of that dialogue, can either be comforting or – as we saw in the case of Hannah and the cows – discomforting or worse.

After reading my article on the Borderland and discussing this aspect of her life with her oldest son, one mother said that he offered some "additional insights into my gifts. The most obvious and yet profound is that I always was able to differentiate my thoughts and feelings from those of the objects and animals around me. I could be overwhelmed by the thought forms but I always knew that they didn't originate with me."

Another person wrote:

> I believe that I was born with the ability to enter liminal psychological space . . . I also believe it came as a gift to show me that this is not the only world. When I have been receptive to my Borderland experiences, I have been less attached to what is going on in the world. I feel now that I have a perspective that allows me to process events differently. I also attribute my art to my encounters with Borderland entities.
>
> I did not discover my Borderland connection in therapy. Rather I came to love myself and my Borderland ways . . . I would choose to be the way I am all over again and I continue to do so today.

And, of course, there are many Borderland personalities who do not realize this dimension of their lives – at least not fully. Although they register Borderland phenomena they do not know how to relate to some of them because of prejudice in the dominant culture against transrational experience. This can be quite damaging to the individual. This will be discussed in greater depth in the next chapter.

In my experience it is much more common for Borderland personalities to have psychic experiences than for psychic personalities to live in the Borderland. Clinically, if one is used to working with individuals considered to be Borderland personalities, it is not difficult to differentiate one personality type from the other.

Children's personalities

Another type of personality structure that functions as a portal to the Borderland is that of the young child. Unless they are shamed or cognitively yanked out of it, most children under the ages of 6 or 7 experience the Borderland as a "natural" mode of experience. If we return to Figure 7.1, we can see in Part 1 a schematic description of the psychic structure of an infant child whose ego sense of subjective identity, rests totally as a psychic *potential*, yet to emerge from total containment within the self of the individual and its mother.[12] At an *ego level*, the child lives more than not in the unconscious realm with no self-identity, no sense of an *I*. Psychologically speaking, she/he swims in a kind of archetypal soup. By "archetypal soup," I hope to create a *feeling* metaphor for something that in fact is unknowable to us as adults because we are too separated from it by our highly developed cognitive structures. We can only fantasize what that realm must be like subjectively (when literally there is no subject "self") for the infant and for the very young child. My fantasy is one of swimming through myriad body sensations, one flowing/slopping over into the other and back again, having *all* experience mediated on a body level (including, particularly, the eyes and skin), and being constantly flooded with archetypal "material" (a meaningless phrase in this context – but we only have words here), with no sense of control or input over what comes and goes and what impacts the child.

If we move on to Figure 7.1, Part 2, we see a schematic description of the psychic structure of a child somewhere between ages 4 and 6 or 7. Here we see an ego structure, a subjective sense of *I* that has begun to emerge from total containment in the unconscious archetypal soup. Children in this age range are still at the mercy of the archetypal ebb and flow (we are no longer using the word "soup") through their psyches, most particularly at night.[13] This latter psychodynamic fact is reflected in the cross-hatched section of Figure 7.1, Part 2, where more of the child's ego lives in the unconscious realm – the Self – than it does in the mundane world of day-to-day organized life. And, for those of us who are parents, most of us know the night terrors that our children have experienced with "bad dreams," "monster dreams," that seem to come up from below to terrify them. This is the archetypal realm flowing into, out of, and through our little ones. For the most part, we are helpless to control these comings and goings because they are autonomous within the psyche of the child. By the time the child is 3 or 4, we can begin to talk about these terrors because they now have shape and form, i.e. "monsters," in the language of our children. But inexorably they will come back to terrify our children until an ego structure has developed that functions more outside the unconscious realm than in it.[14] With language comes the capacity to symbolize. So what had been an archetypal soup is now (at age 3–4) transformed into symbolic forms – monsters, dragons, princesses, fairies – some positive and some negative. Because of their archetypal nature, even the positive symbols carry overwhelming numinosity for their little egos.

There is a positive side to this dual life in the archetypal and mundane worlds: The child *naturally* experiences the magical level of consciousness, and, along with it, the Borderland realm. Indeed, the latter is a natural state of being for most children between 4 and 6 or 7 – *depending on the degree of cognicization imposed on the child by its parents and other caretakers.*[15] Some parents do not permit their child to live inside and to live out their magical worlds – worlds that are quite real to him or her. Indeed, American culture in particular is often hostile to this dimension of a child's reality. That hostility is expressed in dramatic and subtle ways. Although the psychological result of spoiling – and even in extreme cases killing off – the magical dimension of consciousness for many of our children is unconscious, this drive in our culture is inexorable and, even traumatizing in and of itself.

As has been observed, some children before age 7 lose their Borderland sensitivities and connections, others don't. The culture at large and specifically TV are so contaminating and destructive of the child's natural internal imaginal realm, that unless these little psyches are consciously protected from these forces that surround them in everyday life, there is a constant erosion of their *natural* healthy relationship to the Borderland dimension.[16]

For a very long time Disney productions so sanitized fairytales and myths in their films, that they came close to portraying life without a dark side, or, at best, one so weak that it had no real potency.[17] At the same time, children in their connection to the archetypal realm *know* there is a dark side to life because they experience it in their fantasies (the ghost/monster under the bed) and in their night terrors and dreams. And indeed, this is the true significance of fairytales: To stimulate an inner psychic struggle on the part of the child that will compel him or her to learn to manage the tension between those opposites, i.e. the light and dark sides of life, *and to prepare him to face the outer world and its formidable challenges into which he will emerge full time with decreasing parental protection*. This is why the fairytales are often so dark and grim(m).

One of the main attractions at Disney World is MGM Studios, visited by over one million children every year, a large proportion under age 7. This "attraction" proudly presents the technology behind the magical effects in films and other entertainment arenas. The subtle, but quite effective, message behind these "entertainments" is that there is no real magic, there is no real magical realm, and that the things to be ogled are the worldly wonders of technology. On an even more subtle level the message to the child is that you should not be in the imaginal world in your mind, you should *know* that cognition, not imagination, produces the *simulation* of magic. Subtly, the awe of the magical realm that children *know* because it is *natural* in the psychic realm in which they live, is debunked as fake. In its place is offered the "awe" of technological prowess. Typically for children, this technological prowess "impresses," but it does not *awe* because it is devoid of "magic." So much for some of our future artists, architects, musicians, writers, etc. – the impact can be that profound!

With the damaging/killing of awe comes the damaging/killing of spirit in our little ones. It is their connection to spirit (*not* religion per se, but *spirit*), their relationship to the transpersonal realm that protects and guides them, *and is essential for the formulation of **functional** defenses* to events that otherwise can be quite traumatic in their lives. Because they *are* little people, the conflict between the dark and light forces that they experience intrapsychically in their pre-school years calls forth their connection with positive transpersonal forces of the spirit dimension far more powerful than their little egos. Their egos cannot be given the full burden of constructing (rational) ego defenses of sufficient power to withstand such archetypal onslaughts. They need to *feel* their little egos backed up by spiritual powers greater than their own egos *and their own understanding*. This is why, all too often, when parents use rational explanations alone to help a child cope with night terrors ("it's *only* a dream;" "there's nothing there;" "it went away"), either they don't work, or worse, the child is subtly coerced into agreeing that what she/he is experiencing is not real when it feels profoundly otherwise. Oftentimes, the presence or absence of this connection with the spirit dimension makes the difference between whether or not a child emerges into the mundane world with a legacy of an ability to symbolize, imaginal richness or creativity, or even emotional trauma. When I speak of children's connection to the spirit realm, I am aware that I am attempting to describe something that is their own *unique* relationship to that dimension, i.e. something that is different from our adult concept of "spirit" and for which I do not have adequate language. (One difference between their relationship to the spirit dimension and ours that I do know is that theirs is not split off from nature.)[18] This connection to the magical realm, then, is all important in determining whether children experience trauma in the manner Donald Kalsched so well describes and documents in his book, *The Inner World of Trauma*. Or whether "the gods" and "good fairies" will protect them as they traverse that awesomely scary land between the pre-egoic self and the post-magical ego world where the outer world must be engaged without those *natural* protections.

Many TV programs, video tapes, and DVDs now feature "Behind the Making of . . ." commentaries on, for example, *Star Wars* or *Lord of the Rings* or *Harry Potter* – films with a lot of fantastic imagery and depictions of what could be called Borderland reality. These add-ons to the actual movie focus on the technology involved in making the various films. So the message is that holding our collective breath in the suspense of wondering whether Luke Skywalker can permit himself to follow The Force in combating Darth Vader (the Dark Side) is not really warranted. The various airplanes and the battles were just miniature wooden and plastic figures manipulated for effect. The imaginal and Borderland linking world of the right brain is subtly overpowered by left-brain smartness and the science of digital technology.

I once took my 4-year-old son to a puppet show put on by the brilliant and magical Jim Henson. When we emerged from the theater into the lobby, I was astonished to see none other than Jim Henson displaying how the puppets and the mechanics of the set "worked" to this crowd of children, many of whom were 7 or under. We did not stay for the demonstration.[19]

Lest the reader think that I am hostile to technology per se, I am not. Indeed, I find wonder in much of technology. "Neutral" technology is not the culprit. The damage to children results from the way in which technology and rationality are used to co-opt and/or supplant the *natural* internal relationship of children to their imaginal and Borderland realms.

I specifically mention the ages 6 to 7 because it is somewhere in that period, in the more or less healthy psychological development of the child, that there is a bit more of that child's ego that is outside of containment in the self than there is in it. (See Figure 7.1, Part 2a.) This is a process that continues in the life of the individual to about age 7 as illustrated in Part 2 and Part 3 – see

Part 2a. The essential point here is that when that theoretical threshold is reached by ages 6 to 7, the child's *ongoing connection* with the archetypal realm *naturally* ceases to dominate. The monster dreams stop, more or less, and the child's connection with the imaginal realm takes a back seat to cognitive development. Of course, all of this is reinforced by the facts of rapid socialization and of formal education with their near exclusive emphasis on cognitive development to the exclusion of the imaginal, magical, archetypal and other "right-brain" dimensions of psychic existence.

Trauma portal

In his eloquently penetrating work, *The Inner World of Trauma*, Jungian psychoanalyst Donald Kalsched, discusses "trauma" in children as "any experience that causes the child unbearable psychic pain or anxiety."[20] He goes on to say that "unbearable experiences" are those that "overwhelm the usual defensive measures" and that the distinguishing feature of such trauma is what Heinz Kohut calls a "disintegration anxiety," an unnameable dread associated with the threatened dissolution of a coherent self."[21] Kalsched describes the alternative inner world opened by the archetypal defenses that rescue the personality when trauma strikes. The result is what he calls a "self-care system" peopled by the "mythopoetic" or "daimonic" denizens of the collective psyche. The alternative world he describes bears a marked similarity to what I am delineating as the Borderland, although Kalsched focuses on the *inner* world and not on the connection to nature, which so frequently characterizes the "Borderland personality."

I do not intend here to discuss in depth the nature of trauma or its treatment. Rather my focus will be on the role of trauma – of those "unbearable experiences" – in opening a portal to the Borderland world and the complications and implications that ensue. As we saw in the previous section, trauma can be especially unbearable to the psyche of the child. But it is not a necessary precondition for entrance into the Borderland. The child's natural sense of magic is all the preconditioning necessary. But the implications of trauma for opening consciousness of the Borderland is not limited to the psyches of children.

One woman who contacted me after reading the "Hannah" chapter in the *IONS Noetic Sciences Review* and who was traumatized in first grade by a too early and too deep confrontation of her Borderland/magical existence by the left brain cogni-centric approach to life, wrote the following:

> There was not one event that I can point to with certainty and say, that was it. What happened was that from the time I was three until I was around eight years old a series of events and processes took place that forced my abandoning of my special world [the Borderland].
>
> First grade was a huge turning point . . . I had a first grade teacher who

was an amateur naturalist. We spent a great deal of time learning about the animal world. I should have been very happy. Unfortunately for me, most of the animals that came into class were stuffed and mounted. It bothered me a great deal. What really disturbed me to the point of trauma was the "sleeping" jar. My teacher encouraged the children to bring into class unusual insect specimens, preferably alive. She would then put them in the "sleeping" jar, which I believe had an ether soaked rag in the bottom of it. After they went "to sleep," she would take them out of the jar and mount them on a large cork board.

No one else in the class had any problem with this almost daily scenario. I found it to be torture. I could hear the bugs dying. Some were very quiet about it; most made gasping and moaning sounds as the air in the jar was replaced with unbreathable fumes. The butterflies screamed. It was a high pitched staccato sound. I could not stand it, and it was very obvious that no one else in the room heard it. I asked to be excused, went into the bathroom, turned on the water, to drown out the screams, put my hands over my ears. I did not hear the teacher knocking on the door. When she opened the door and saw me standing with my hands over my ears, crouched down in the corner she must have thought I was mentally ill. The teacher called my parents. They were upset with me, told me that there was nothing wrong with the "sleeping jar" and I had to get over it. Soon after this I began getting sick quite often. I had severe upper respiratory infections. At seven years old I developed pneumonia.

While I was home sick I had an out of body experience. I went to what I call my real home. It was the place I lived before I came into this body. There I was greeted by my real parents. They were very happy to see me. I was beyond joyous to see them. They explained to me that I had been getting sick because I was thinking about leaving this body. They assured me that was ok, but if I did leave now there were some things that I had come into the body to do that wouldn't get done, so I would be needing to come back soon to complete those things. I remember them showing me what I can only describe as a book with moving pictures of what was to be parts of my life. I cannot remember anything in particular of what I saw. Just the feeling of wanting to complete my tasks now, and not wait for another lifetime. I do remember asking them if I could keep coming to visit them. They told me no, that if I decided to stay in my body I could not come to visit them again for a very long time. That was the beginning of my loss of contact with the Borderland. [She did not permit herself to reconnect to the Borderland realm again until her adult years.][22]

This kind of cultural and pedagogical assault on a sensitive psyche is often overlooked as a source of early trauma in children. The fact that this woman's trauma was experienced in the classroom is instructive. The left-brain bias of education in this country may be a more significant source of trauma in young children than we might imagine. I do not suggest that development of left-brain skills is the problem here – certainly that dimension of education is beneficial and essential. It is the left-brain *bias*, the insensitivity to, and de-legitimation of right-brain sensitivities of many children that can be damaging or even traumatizing, as in the above example.[23]

If the rapid evolutionary reconnection of the western ego with nature is taking place as I have described above, then this sharp delineation between the magical realm of consciousness before ages 6 to 7, which is shut down after this age in favor of cognitive (left-brain) development, will become less absolute. In its place there will be more of an integration collectively of the two, which can then be carried forward developmentally in individuals.[24] The individuals I have identified, and who identify themselves as being Borderland personalities[25] have access to both the cognitive and magical realms. But the extent and the manner in which they have integrated both remains an individual matter. Contrary to the projection of many, not all Borderland personalities live in a kind of mental ether. A number are quite grounded in both left-brain and right-brain functioning. One respondent quoted in this book is the former head of a state bar association.

One woman who stated that she experienced "extreme physical and verbal abuse" her entire childhood into her teenage years, wrote the following:

> What I am thinking is that therapy has really helped me cope with the real world much better in terms of the conflict and day-to-day stresses of living. HOWEVER, I can still inhabit the other world as well. It is sort of like being able to love two (or more) people at the same time . . . you just love them differently and you conduct yourself appropriately so that neither is hurt or damaged in any way. I don't think that I am schizoid when I say that I live in two worlds and that they don't collide. The Borderland world has made me better in the "real world" than I probably would have ever been if I had not had the experiences I had.
>
> [Emphasis in original.]

Kalsched describes how trauma fragments the drive towards cohesiveness in the impacted child and "fixes" (i.e. sets in place) these split parts of the psyche developmentally. He cites Ferenczi, who observed that "one part of the ego *regresses* to the infantile period, and another part *progresses*, i.e. grows up too fast and becomes precociously adapted to the outer world, often [but not always] as what D. W. Winnicott calls the 'false self.' "[26] Kalsched then suggests, "the *progressed part* of the personality then caretakes the *regressed part*." He points out how both regressed and progressed aspects seem to be involved in the dissociation or "out of body" experience that preserves life for the incarnate person suffering unbearable experience (trauma). He says, "If we think of the 'personal spirit' as that part of the 'great spirit' that 'wants' to incarnate in *this* body as the *soul of a unique particular person*, then trauma constitutes those times when the soul can no longer remain in the body and must 'return' to the spirit realm for sanctuary – such as the woman who wrote about her out of body experience (see above). It then returns, but your Borderland personalities never forget their 'true home.' Trauma often gives people life-sustaining access to this area."[27]

In this context, Kalsched begins his approach to this archetypal domain through the dynamics of trauma, i.e. the approach is through the pathology of traumatic assault on the child. My approach and emphasis begins with the Borderland (archetypal) domain and acknowledges traumatic wounding as the portal that *may* have provided initial access to the Borderland. The emphasis makes a difference. Neither is right or wrong – both are descriptive of real intrapsychic process. *The issue is the experience and perception of the individual.* How well that experience appears to work for the individual – how syntonic it is with their life needs and experience – determines authenticity more than how the individual got there, i.e. trauma. For some of the Border-land individuals I have cited here, although they acknowledge the trauma portal as their initial access to the Borderland, they are adamant in their insistence that their Borderland existence not be seen as an extension of, or attached to, their traumatic experience – i.e. pathologized. Many have said that when therapists and friends insist on this connection, they experience that insistence as re-traumatizing. Typically, in reaction, they will then shut down and hide their Borderland existence. *They do not want it pathologized.* When it is pathologized, it feels like a profanation of something sacred.

In a number of ways this description *partially* sums up the dynamic of the genesis of a Borderland personality on the part of *some* individuals as a result of trauma. The regressed part of the psyche fixes at a level of development *prior to* that threshold point, the theoretical threshold between Parts 2 and 3 in Figure 7.1 (see also Part 2a) and the more developed parts caretake the latter. But here, is the Borderland the *progressed* or *regressed* part of the psyche in this context?[28]

Some individuals, adults as well as children, have had a sustained ego-syntonic (ego-comfortable) connection to the Borderland prior to the onset of the trauma. In some of these cases, the reverse seemed to be the case, i.e. the Borderland connection within the person's psyche seemed to caretake and sustain the traumatized parts of the psyche. One woman reported:

> I believe that I was born with the ability to enter liminal space. I also believe that the death of my beloved grandmother and the subsequent beatings by my father [trauma] brought that ability to the fore. I believe that it came as a gift to show me that this is not the only world.

In other words, this woman's Borderland connections sustained and nurtured her through her traumatic experiences.

A typical clinical interpretation of this circumstance would deny the reality of the "other world" this woman was able to enter. It would suggest that this woman's psyche "split" into a regressed state – the Borderland – in order to not feel the pain of her trauma. Clinically, the goal would be to help her feel the feelings (grief) associated with these traumas so that she wouldn't need the "other world". Clinical psychology is suspicious of that other world and can only see it as an artifact of experience in "this" world. But this respondent said that she "was born with the ability to enter liminal space," i.e. that that was a *natural* part of her *healthy* orientation to life. In a sense, she had an ability to go from one (psychic) room to another by choice, prior to the later trauma that she describes in her life. So did her psyche "split" – an *unconscious* defense mechanism – after her grandmother's death and the onset of her father's beatings, or did she simply use the *conscious* tools at her disposal – the reality of the Borderland – to protect herself from harm?

One of the questions contained in the questionnaire (see Appendix) I sent to individuals who contacted me was the following: "Looking back . . . what would you have changed in terms of your actions?" Significantly, this woman's response was, "Nothing." Another question in the questionnaire was: "If you could have realized significantly better intimacy with others in the first half of your life, would you choose to do so if it meant sacrificing some of the Borderland connection/experience that you had? Would you choose to do so now if that choice were available to you?" Her answer: "No, I would choose to be the way I am all over again and I continue to do so today."

The crucial point here is that this woman's experience of her Borderland personality was positive and life saving. It supported "the other side" of her personality, including the traumatic phases of her life (after her grandmother died). She said, in response to item #14 in the questionnaire: "I did not discover my Borderland connection in [10 years of] therapy. Rather I came to love myself and my "Borderland ways." She reported that with one minor, short-lived exception, her experiences with two therapists were very positive. She noted in particular that these two therapists were positively receptive to her "Borderland ways." She credits one in particular with helping her to identify some heretofore unrecognized trauma in her life. There is little doubt that had her "Borderland ways" been received with skepticism or clinically labeled (pathologized) – a possible traumatic experience in itself – her life circumstance would likely have been qualitatively different as a woman, a wife and as a mother.

A woman in her mid-60s wrote:

> My parents . . . told me I was a witch and crazy and contributed to making my existence a hell. There was also much emotional and physical abuse, and a big part of my childhood was spent being a hypochondriac and wanting to end my life.
>
> I have had . . . five successful careers, and the various directions which

my adventurous, risk-taking nature has led me. With the trauma I endured in my earlier years and periodically throughout my life, by all accounts, I should have ended up in an institution. Yet, with what can only be Grace, and with much gratitude, I recognize that I have been given an amazing gift and the privilege of an incredible growth experience; as well as the ability to participate and experience fully in what has turned out to be an eventful, creative and wonderfully enlightening journey.

It seems that the Borderland is both a dimension that can be opened by the experience of trauma and one which can preexist experiences of trauma. In either case it can be a powerful support for both the regressed and "progressed part of the personality," in Kalsched's terms, and assist it in sustaining the individual through the experience of trauma.

In some cases, the Borderland connection provides the *primary* sustenance for an ego in the throes of trauma. This distinction is critical. If the Borderland as a dimension of psychic experience is viewed only as a by-product of trauma then it is likely to be viewed, clinically, as being exclusively a *symptom* of trauma, i.e. aberrant. And this one dimensional view of Borderland experience can itself be experienced as the greater trauma for some individuals.

One person who was forced to view satanic rituals as a child stated:

> The trauma began when I was a toddler, possibly at birth . . . I know these experiences [which included being forced to witness the torture of animals] contributed to my learning compassion and empathy. To this day, I often suffer deeply emotionally if it occurs to me that I have hurt someone or if I witness someone else's pain. I thought for years that this was merely "codependence," which I know is part of it, but it is also about a greater level of empathy and compassion . . . I know that these experiences in my early life planted seeds which in the last few years have developed into the Borderland experiences. Again, I used to think that my reactions to animals in the present was all about my processing the pain I witnessed and felt many years ago, and that is part of it, but there is also the Borderland, which for me manifests as a mystical empathy.

When asked if she would be willing to sacrifice some of the Borderland connection/experience that she had in the name of less life struggle she replied:

> The answer is an unqualified no. Painful as these Borderland experiences are, they feel very important, they feel sacred, they feel like something I even long for. They were and are so very much more than simply an antidote to despair.

As was the case with Hannah, painful though her experiences were vis-à-vis "the cows," the greater pain – and she would say, "trauma," – came from having her *experience* denied and labeled as a symptom, as something less than real. For her, and for other Borderland personalities with whom I have had contact, the denial of her subjective reality – particularly in the face of her feeling of not having had her experience *even considered* as being real – left her feeling crazy and pathologized by the therapy itself. Every single Borderland individual with whom I have dealt, either in my clinical practice, or via correspondence, has expressed the same subjective experience.

However, this does bring us to a conundrum: Some individuals suffering from trauma do carry defenses to their traumatic experience that do impinge on the quality of their lives and that, in a clinical model, could rightfully be viewed as "pathological." Trauma theory would hold that these individuals live on the "other side of the window" from life's reality, in a "transitional zone," as Kalsched would put it, seeking a safe haven from perceived threats from the outer world and from "traumatic anxiety." In his model, Kalsched states that:

> Repeated exposure to traumatic anxiety *forecloses transitional space*, kills the symbolic activity of creative imagination, and replaces it with what Winnicott calls "fantasying." Fantasying is a dissociated state, which is neither imagination nor living in external reality, but a kind of melancholic self-soothing compromise which goes on forever – a defensive use of the imagination in the service of anxiety avoidance . . .
>
> Psychotherapists must be very careful . . . to distinguish between genuine imagination and fantasy, which is the self-soothing activity of the daimon. This self-soothing really amounts to a self-hypnotic spell – an unconscious undertow into non-differentiation to escape conscious feeling. Here a retreat into "oneness" replaces the hard work of separation necessary for "wholeness." This is not regression, as we like to think of it in the service of the ego, but "malignant regression" – regression which suspends a part [of the patient] in an auto-hypnotic twilight state in order . . . to assure the survival of [the patient] as a human person.[29]
>
> [Emphasis in original.]

In some cases, I think the above description of fantasy as regression would be quite accurate. Here the individual would be using "fantazying" as a defense against anxiety associated with trauma. Some individuals who described their experiences as "Borderland experiences" might be viewed as confusing my description of Borderland dynamics with what Kalsched (and Winnicott) describe as fantazying.

However, Borderland experience does not represent either "fantazying" or "genuine imagination." It is not an *intrapsychic* relationship between ego and self. It is *experience*. It is a vis-à-vis *relationship* between the individual and the transrational dimension of reality. Historically, this relationship has been attributed as "magical," i.e. *not real*. But for the Borderland personality it is experience of transrational *reality*. Hannah didn't fantasize or imagine or project the pain of the cows. She *felt* it. Young children feel these things too – as did the woman above who in first grade experienced insects dying in the sleeping jar.

The very question of what did they "really" feel,[30] *in and of itself*, has the effect of drawing one into a bifurcated left-brain realm hostile to the right-brain realm that can/does experience transrational reality. One has to "re-ask" the question out of a linked right/left brain context. Yet our very *logos*-dependent language does not provide the words that permit a question that reflects at least the *possibility* of an experience of transrational reality. As Borderland consciousness evolves in the context of the western psyche, presumably new language constructs will come with it. Daniel Siegel, addressing the neurobiological substrates of this point says: "*The left hemisphere's drive to understand cause–effect relationships is a primary motivation of the narrative process. Coherent narratives, however, require participation of <u>both</u>* the inter-preting left hemisphere and the mentalizing right hemisphere. Coherent narratives are created through interhemispheric integration."[31] [Emphasis in original. Underlining added.]

One can see how easily Borderland experience could be confused with "fantazying." This can be all the more disconcerting when both dynamics are present in the same individual. This confusion can take place on the part of the individual in therapy and on the part of the therapist as well. Therapists who are unfamiliar with Borderland phenomena and its prevalence in particular personality types are particularly prone in this regard. This will be discussed in greater depth in the next chapter. One can also readily see how patients are wounded, even traumatized, by their therapy when their experience of "wholeness" and the "sacred" – which often includes the Borderland dimension – is branded, directly or indirectly, as "malignant regression." The challenge for clinicians, particularly those working in the trauma field, is to learn to differentiate between an "unhealthy response to trauma," a "healthy response to trauma," and a Borderland connection, which is neither.

The problem is further confounded by the fact that these boundaries – between (nonpathological) Borderland experience and (pathological) "fantazying" or malignant regression – are seldom clear cut. At the same time, a therapy which pathologizes nonpathological experience of the patient in itself can be traumatizing. As clinicians, it is indeed a fine line that we must walk with such individuals. And if the prevalence of Borderland personality types is in the process of increasing exponentially, then these problems will become increasingly prevalent in our clinical practices.

Notes

1 Kalsched, 1996: 142.
2 The three portals are not totally boundaried, i.e. they sometimes overlap and interact psychodynamically.
3 Jung, in one context refers to nature as "simply that which is, and always was, given" (Jung, 1972: 210, fn.121).
4 Jung referred to this source as the "psychoidal dimension" (Jung, 1972: 176f).
5 George Lakoff, Professor of Linguistics, University of California at Berkeley, in a 2003 Santa Fe Institute lecture asserted: "The only mathematical ideas we can have are ideas the brain allows ... Like other abstract ideas, mathematical ideas arise via conceptual metaphor – a mechanism for adapting the brain's sensory-motor system to constitute abstract thought ... the conceptual metaphors built into mathematical ideas, and the cognitive theory of mathematical ideas" (Lakoff, 2003).
6 In personal communication with David Abram, author of *The Spell of the Sensuous*, he informed me that scores, if not hundreds of individuals who have read his book, and who fit the description of the Borderland personality, have identified themselves to him. My experience has been similar to his – being contacted by individuals who are desperate to have their experience of reality witnessed and validated by people whom they think can and will hear them. Without this validation, they feel branded by the culture as "looney."
7 The fact that *all* children before age 7 *naturally* experience life in its totality, i.e. without a split between nature and the mundane world, speaks to an inherent psychic yearning for a return/reconnection to what was naturally wondrous in the early years of life as the ego emerged out of immersion in the self. (See Figure 7.1, Parts 1 and 2 in Chapter 7.)
8 We all know examples of this apparent genetic link where one of several children is psychic "just like father or grandmother or Aunt Sadie" while their siblings are not.
9 See Part 2a in Figure 7.1.
10 Unfortunately, the Salt Institute ceased to exist as of the fall of 2001.
11 Bernstein, 2000.
12 Part 2 (Figure 7.1) is the "place before" time and story. It is personal and impersonal. Because it is "before" it is unknowable by the ego. For the Navajo, unlike westerners, it is "knowable" and experiencable both through their cosmology story *and* its enactment through the healing ceremony. It is the possibility of connecting with the "place before," i.e. Part 1, that heals. The Navajo, because of their psychic structure that is never not connected to the transpersonal and conceptualizes the infinity of time through their emergence myth, can *do* through experience (e.g. the healing ceremony) what we, with our western ego can do only through inference.
13 I say night, because, psychodynamically speaking, this is when the ego sleeps and the unconscious is most active. The ego is the organ which mediates between the conscious and unconscious realms. This fact is supported both in contemporary brain and dream research.
14 Between then and when a sufficiently strong ego structure has developed to contain these "terrors," the child is comforted and made to feel safe through healthy-enough attachment to its parents and/or other caretakers.
15 I wish to thank Peter Talley of Ignacio, Colorado, for stimulating me to deepen my thinking in this regard.
16 The American Academy of Pediatrics (AAP) reports the following data collected by "Real Vision": The *average* number of hours per week that American 1-year-old children watch television is six hours. The number of hours of TV-watching

time recommended by the AAP for children in this age group is 0. Seventy per cent of *day care centers* use TV during a typical day. The *average* time per week that the American child ages 2–7 spends watching TV is 19 hours and 40 minutes. (Data were not available specifically on the 1–6 age group. Eighty-one per cent of television viewing time of children between the ages of 2–7 is alone and unsupervised.) (Data obtained from the AAP on July 15, 2002.)

One could argue that programs such as "Sesame Street" are constructive for children. I have my doubts about the concrete aspects of programs like "Sesame Street" for the under 5-year-old viewers, i.e. teaching the letters of the alphabet, reading numbers, and the like. These children will get plenty of such training once they enter formal education. The imaginal aspects – storytelling, the play between the various puppet characters – certainly is stimulating and fun. Weighing the value of even these components against the conditioning of children to get their fun passively "out of the tube" is questionable, particularly in the pre-school years.

17 I think Disney has moved a bit more towards center in its movies in the past few years.

18 This fact is amply attested to by their personal dreams and night terrors and the symbolic structure of myths and fairy tales, as for example "talking trees" in *The Wizard of Oz*.

19 I must claim one blow for the imaginal integrity of children. In the mid-1980s, I was interviewed by ZDF, the German equivalent of American public television. The interview focused on the "meaning" – essentially the archetypal interpretation – of one of the *Star Wars* films. To my surprise when I arrived at the studio for a viewing of the film the interviewer first wanted me to watch, "The Making of Star Wars." I refused. The astonished interviewer, however, agreed to make my refusal and the reasons for my refusal part of the hour-long interview for the program which was to air "The Making of Star Wars" portion. I spoke directly to the viewing parents of children in Germany and advised them to not permit their children to view "The Making of Star Wars," or for that matter, "the making of" anything else lest their children's rich *and essential* connection to the magical (and Borderland) realm of consciousness and their own inner imaginal space be significantly intruded on.

20 Kalsched, 1996: 1.

21 Kalsched, 1996: 34

22 In fact, I have heard a number of similar stories from other individuals. A stunningly similar testimony by another person states: "The most startling experience came one day when I was standing in a supermarket among the produce. I began to hear cries of the vegetables from when they were sprayed . . . I stood there stunned." Schmall, 1997: 5–6.

23 For a neurobiological exploration of the potential impact of left-brain bias in education and its deleterious impact on children, see the work of Daniel Siegel (Siegel, 1999: 330–337).

24 This integration would carry forward the archetypal ebb and flow eluded to above but would not, in the majority of cases, carry forward an ego still floating in an archetypal "soup."

25 Distinct from "psychic personalities." See above.

26 Winnicott, D. W. "Ego Distortion in Terms of True and False Self," as cited in Kalsched, *Ibid.*: 3.

27 Personal correspondence with the author in 2003. All emphasis is that of Dr. Kalsched.

28 In his book Kalsched speaks about how when the personal spirit falls through the

"basic fault" opened by trauma, it falls into an archetypal world already there to catch it. See Balint, 1969. The Borderland realm can be viewed as a kind of archetypal realm in this regard.

29 Kalsched, 1996: 35.
30 See the Introduction to Part I regarding what Hannah (and other Borderlanders) "really" feel.
31 Siegel, 1999: 331.

Chapter 11

Borderland/Borderline

> The doctor especially should never lose sight of the fact that diseases
> are disturbed normal processes and not *entia per se* with a psychology
> exclusively their own.[1]

A colleague, in reading some of the material on the Border*land* personality[2] that I published prior to publication of this book, asked if, by using the term *"Borderland"* and its seeming allusion to "Border*line*," I intended to push the clinical limits of the Borderline personality syndrome.[3,4] My answer was, "Yes." However, the distinction between the two is not easily made.

The word "Border*land*" came directly out of my work with Hannah. She introduced the word to me. She had just begun to read the book, *Borderlands: La Frontera*, by Gloria Anzaldúa.[5] It traces the migrations of pre-Aztec Indians from what is now the US Southwest to central Mexico and then, centuries later, back again as mestizos, individuals with mixed Indian and Spanish Conquistador blood. Hannah had spent several years of her childhood living in South America. The title had caught her eye. As the dynamics described in Chapter 2 unfolded in our work together, I resonated to the word "Border*land*" as one that best describes the phenomena that are the subject of this book.

In my review of the literature on the Borderline personality, I discovered that indeed the word Border*land* was first used clinically by C. Hughes in 1884 to describe individuals who were on "the Border*land* of insanity . . . who pass their whole life near that line, sometimes on one side, sometimes on the other."[6,7] From then it was employed by a handful of others in various contexts, sometimes along with the word, *Borderline*. Eventually, the word *Borderline* personality disorder or *Borderline* personality organization stuck, largely through the work of Otto Kernberg, and the word *Borderland* dropped from use in the clinical literature after 1919.[8]

I do not intend here to discuss the personality structure of the Borderline personality or treatment modalities per se. However, I do wish to introduce the idea that some of the dynamics that I have labeled Border*land* are of a transrational nature. They are sometimes mistaken for symptoms of underlying pathology and are used as a basis for diagnosing Borderline pathology – and worse.

Harold F. Searles, psychiatrist and psychoanalyst, in a 1960 monograph entitled, *The Nonhuman in Normal Development and in Schizophrenia*, describes human maturation as "involving the individual's struggling to achieve and maintain a sense of identity as being human and as being differentiated . . . from the nonhuman realm of his environment."[9] Certainly such differentiation on the part of the individual is fundamental and essential for healthy psychological development.

However, it is important to realize that this axiom applies to the post-Genesis ego construct – particularly what I have labeled here as the western ego construct. Prior to that time, it is likely that the ego was significantly enmeshed/identified/fused with the collective unconscious and with nature. Individuals functioned as much, if not more, in the context of a group self than in an individual self. But for the most part, the compelling psychological dynamic was the group self, most particularly as expressed through ritual cycles of their tribal cultures. These tribal groups and the individuals within them were the guardians of nature's secrets and cycles, charged with the responsibility from their center of reality for assuring that the earth would rotate on its axis, that the sun would rise in the east and set in the west, for giving thanks for food obtained, and for the rain that fed the earth so that she in turn would be generous to the people and yield them food.[10]

From the standpoint of the post-Genesis 20th-century ego (Figure 7.2, Part 5), it is easy to relegate all of this to "superstition" or "animism." And yet . . . and yet, when those of us who do attend the dances at the pueblos and at Hopi, or the healing ceremonies at Navajo, many of us can *feel* that something palpably different is taking place. We can *feel* spirit's presence. We *know* that these ancient "archaic" rites have potency even when we can't make rational sense of that *knowing*.[11]

It is important to remember too that we, who constitute [western man and] western culture, descend from tribal cultures – the Hebrews, the Gauls, the Norse, the Celts, etc. The roots and arcane vestiges of the group self to which our ancient ancestors once paid homage through the enactment of the rituals and rites demanded by them still reside in the collective unconscious, which continues to impinge on our psyches throughout our lives, however subtle and unseen. Indeed, this concept is no different from the notion that the collective unconscious contains the cumulative learning of the cultures that are the psychic font from which we all draw our capacity to learn. Reading does not have to be re-invented anew as a technology with the coming into this world of each new individual. Neither does language, for that matter. The *technology* along with the cumulative learning of the culture resides in the collective unconscious available to all who draw on it.

So what does all of this have to do with the Borderline and *Borderland* personality? Prior to the Genesis call for the development of what ultimately was to become the western ego construct, the psyche – everyone's psyche – was partially identified with what Searles refers to as the "nonhuman environment." That was the normal state of psychic existence. As I have endeavored to demonstrate in Chapter 3, the evolution of what has become our highly rational, technology-oriented, non-magical, western ego construct, was dependent on what was ultimately to become an *absolute split* of the ego from its nonrational roots in the collective unconscious. Searles seems to be making this point clinically when he says:

> I describe the major roots of the patient's transference-reactions as traceable to a stage in ego development prior to any clear differentiation between inner and outer world . . . Hence the therapist finds that these transference-reactions and attitudes of the adult borderline patient cast him, the therapist, in roles strangely different from those he commonly encounters in working with the neurotic patient, whose transference casts him, say, as a domineering father or a sexually seductive, masochistic mother. Instead, the therapist finds the patient reacting to him in limitlessly extraordinary ways, most of which have a nonhuman, or less-than-fully-human, feel to them. The patient reacts unconsciously to him for example, as being nonexistent, or a corpse, or a pervasive and sinister supernatural force, or as God, or as being the patient's mind.[12]

Another way of saying this is that the ego structure of the Borderline personality is insufficiently separated/split from its roots in nature, thus giving rise to a Borderline personality structure.

Searles asserts that this is clearly a determining, etiological factor in Borderline personality structure. In the next paragraph he attributes this lack of differentiation of the Borderline personality "from his nonhuman environment" to "parent-figures [who] were not predominantly whole, well-integrated individuals . . . but [who were] a collection of poorly integrated, and sometimes seemingly innumerable introjects, only precariously managed by the parent-figure's relatively weak own self." So, from Searles' point of view, this differentiation deficiency of the individual ego from its "nonhuman environment" largely, if not predominantly, derives from insufficient parental imagos of one sort or another.[13]

I fully subscribe to what Searles says above about deficient early interpersonal dynamics as the etiology of the problem of the Borderline personality. This is indeed the case as far as it goes. However, I propose that in some, if not many, individuals diagnosed as having Borderline personality disorder, what appears to be a lack of differentiation of the individual "from his nonhuman environment" is in fact the presence of Border*land* features, which in their essence are not pathological.

In another forward-looking (1972) paper entitled, "Unconscious Processes in Relation to the Environmental Crisis," Searles addresses another, *impersonal*, etiological source of Borderline personality structure:

> [O]ver recent decades we have come from dwelling in an outer world in which the living works of nature either predominated or were near at hand, to dwelling in an environment dominated by a technology which is wondrously powerful and yet nonetheless dead, inanimate. I suggested that in the process we have come from being subjectively differentiated from, and in meaningful kinship with, the outer world, to finding this technology-dominated world so alien, so complex, so awesome and over- whelming that we have been able to cope with it *only* by *regressing*, in our unconscious experience of it, largely to a *degraded* state of nondif- ferentiation from it. I suggested . . . that this "outer" reality is psycho- logically as much a part of us as its poisonous waste products are part of our physical selves.[14,15]
>
> [Emphasis added.]

He seems to be saying that environmental degradation and the encroach- ment of "dead" – I would say, soulless – technology can result in a regressed state similar to that of the child with poor parental imagoes, both giving rise to a Borderline personality structure. And certainly the combination of the two would argue for a high risk of Borderline personality structure. Both can produce the kinds of splitting, distortion, paranoia, and defense mechan- isms in one's personality structure that contribute to what is referred to as Borderline personality structure.

Searles talks implicitly about nature as if she were not only dominated by, but – psychologically at least for the individual – displaced by, technology. He suggests that these Borderline patients can have difficulty differentiating themselves from that overwhelmingly "wondrously powerful and yet none- theless dead, inanimate" outer world of technology and its poisonous waste products. For Searles such a state is pathological in its essence. It is an infec- tion of the outer world resulting in regression; it blocks differentiation of the ego-self from the nonhuman dimension. Nondifferentiation results in pathology.[16]

However, might it be possible that some of the patients whom Searles diagnoses as Borderline could be having equal, if not more, difficulty dif- ferentiating their human self from *actual* experiences – *nonpathological* experiences – of nature? Might it be that the "problem" here is not a regres- sion, but a lack of differentiation, or perhaps erroneous interpretation by both patient and therapist?

In other words, what if some of those individuals are perceiving what I have called objective nonpersonal, nonrational phenomena occurring in the natural universe that are barely liminal (i.e. phenomena that are at the threshold of conscious awareness)? Namely, what if they are perceiving

Border*land* phenomena? And what if at least some of these experiences are not distortions so much as they are new psychic quanta entering into the cultural collective? One Border*land* woman reported: "My sensitivities to all things animate and inanimate were with me from my earliest memories. I would touch my bedroom door and it would 'tell' me about the forest it came from." These were warm and positive feelings for her. She said that by age 4 or 5 she had learned never to speak of them although they were, and continue to be, central in her relationship to the outer world. And if, as I assert, there has been an unfolding evolutionary shift since the mid-20th century reconnecting the western ego with its split-off roots in nature, there has been and continues to be an ever-increasing number of people who have nonpathological Border*land* experiences in a culture that is unaccepting and/ or hostile to their experience. While Searles emphasizes the *outer* circumstance – poor parental imagos and an increasingly degraded technology-dominated environment – I am emphasizing *internal* dynamics, namely a growing number of individuals with heightened sensitivity to and apperception of nonrational reality. The latter is occurring due to an apparent evolutionary structural shift in the nature of the western ego. (See Figure 7.3, Part 6.) Jungian analyst David Sedgwick in his book, *Jung and Searles*, says:

> Jung's hypothesis of an impersonal "collective unconscious" lends itself to this distinction between the defensively avoided and the not yet understood. The irrupting contents from the unconscious may be "archetypes," whose strangeness, power and impersonality make them initially incomprehensible. These "internal selves" [Searles' term] do not have a personal reference point or history against which the client might be defending. The heavy emotional overtone of this type of complex is not a function of defensive operations in Searles' sense; it is inherent in the archetypal experience itself. . . . If defenses do arise, according to Jung they will most likely be reactions to the "objective", inner activity of the psyche.[17]

I would add that defenses might arise due to the therapist treating an objective experience as if it needed to be defended against as regressive and unreal.

This is my thesis and my emphasis here with regard to the Border*land*/ Borderline realms: The clinical interpretations of what these individuals are experiencing may well be distorted because of a built-in cultural, and thus a clinical, bias against nonrational experience, i.e. "archetypal dynamics," in Jung's terms. Here is the nexus where Border*land* phenomena can be unconsciously turned into pathology by the treating therapist.

In reviewing the literature on the Borderline personality I have been struck by the degree to which therapist-writers seem to have no questions regarding the actual threshold of conscious and unconscious contents as reported by the patient. What appears to be a distortion to the therapist is taken as such.

(Interestingly, Searles in the above quote comes to the threshold of such a consideration of variable liminality in the normal spectrum, but doesn't cross the line.) The literature is replete with statements about the patient's "flawed sense of reality" and the patient's "distortions." It seems to me that a question that needs to be much in our minds here is: To what extent is there distortion on the part of the patient, and to what extent is the perception of distortion in fact a result of a perceptual limitation on the part of the therapist?

It is precisely here that Jung's theories of the Self, the archetypes, the collective unconscious, and the psychoidal dimension make a profound difference.[18] Without them, one is left at the object level with nowhere to go. To put it more accurately, one is stuck within the limits and grandiose inflations of the western ego. Without Jung's theoretical constructs, psychological and emotional experience are considered either normal, namely rational, or they are abnormal, namely irrational. Psychologically speaking, no room is made for a link to a transpersonal realm outside of religion and personal *belief*. Thus the kinds of experiences reported by Hannah and others could only be seen as irrational and pathological in a non-Jungian context. And this was the problem for Hannah: She could not heal, could not get well, from the Borderline features that she did manifest and the deeper wound of having her Border*land* experiences denied – until her experiences of reality were acknowledged as such and not pathologized.

In a March 1990 presentation by Charles McCormack, at the Washington School of Psychiatry, the Borderline personality was described as follows:

> The core of the borderline difficulty is a fundamental incapacity to self-soothe. This results from a lack of assimilation in early childhood of a relationship capable of helping the child to manage its anxiety. This developmental shortfall results in the borderline adult remaining dependent on others to mitigate his experiences. In other words, he seeks out others to contain his anxiety.[19]

For many individuals, of course, this analysis/diagnosis is accurate. Note, however, that this view is limited to an *object-centered* psychology which does not recognize the validity of nonhuman, archetypal, and spiritually based connections as a *primary* self-care system and a source of anxiety alleviation and self-ordering of the personality.[20]

In numerous communications with individuals, some of whom have been diagnosed as having Borderline personality disorders, many have described to me the preciousness of their connection to these nonhuman dimensions, their reality, and their genuine healing power. Some have described these experiences as sacred. Others contend that there is no question that they could not function in the world without them. And virtually all have expressed their need to be secretive regarding this dimension of their life experience. Many have described the wounding experience of having these connections pathologized in therapy. Some individuals were driven out of therapy never to return.

Clinically, it is important to look at the data: Hannah remained chronically depressed and largely unrelated to the outer world, except to the world of nature. She had particular difficulty relating to people – and when she tried, it usually turned out disastrously for her. She was isolated in her connection to nature because she herself believed that her experiences were "crazy" (her word). *She* believed they were pathological. She did not *want* to give them up because they were and had been her primary source of anxiety alleviation and self-ordering. *As long as others did not know* that she lived in a parallel world alongside her relationships with others, and as long as she could keep secret her deep connection to nature and animals, she could function – even be happy at times. At the same time, she felt that her parallel life had to be kept from others lest they ridicule her and brand her as "crazy." Western culture does not admit nonrational experience as legitimate, neither did the psychology she encountered through the various therapies in which she had engaged. Her experiences fed a chronically paranoid and schizoid pattern. Most therapists on initially encountering Hannah would likely have given her a diagnosis of "Borderline personality disorder." But this diagnosis was not the whole story, or necessarily the primary diagnosis.

Critically in my work with Hannah, it was when I began to acknowledge that I thought what she was reporting was coming from a parallel reality and was not pathological, that the work began to change. The more I listened to, witnessed, and took seriously her transratonal reality, the more her Borderline features seemed to melt away. I mean just that – they seemed to melt away. Whereas prior to our encounter around her distress over the cows, focusing directly on her actual pathological content and behavior invariably would set off her angry defenses and splitting. By the same token, the more we focused on her Border*land* reality – not only in the manifest content of the material that she brought, but also in her dreams and art – the more her Borderline features would seem to dissolve.

So, in answer to the question posed at the beginning of this chapter, yes, I am trying to push the boundaries of what we consider to be reality in the context of the Borderline personality. It is my conviction that some patients are diagnosed as Borderline personalities in part, and sometimes substantially, because they have experiences of the Border*land* realm that are pathologized by the therapist. And for even those individuals for whom a diagnosis of Borderline personality is appropriate, some have Border*land* experiences similar to those I have been describing. It is important that their Border*land* experiences not be pathologized – that they be differentiated from their pathological parts. To the extent this differentiation is not made, the picture is confounded and healing is obstructed. Indeed, it can and does make the individual more sick.

Specifically, the personalistic bias in object-relations ego-based therapies that insists that all (other than chemically induced) neurosis results from faulty object relations, itself is a source of the difficulty in the treatment of Borderline personality disorders. In some cases, such as Hannah's, this is not enough. Validation of the patient's experience of transrational reality is an essential part of the equation. The insistence that healing, "self-soothing," can be attained *only* through a healing relationship with another individual, *and that that relationship alone is sufficient for healing*, can derail and totally shut down the therapeutic process for the Borderline personality with Border*land* features.

Individuals who experience Border*land* phenomena know something of the sacred that oftentimes we, as therapists, do not. They can try to tell us. But what are we open to listening to and letting in? To the extent that we are closed, both therapist and patient may lose.

While acknowledging the central importance of the transpersonal dimension in human experience, Donald Kalsched warns us that: "In trauma . . . all investment of libido in 'this life' is resisted by the self-care system in order to avoid further devastation. Energies of the numinous world then became substitutes for the self-esteem that should come from embodied gratifications in the human world. *The transpersonal is placed in the service of defense.*"[21] [Emphasis added.] Although his statement is undoubtedly true in many traumatized individuals, it is not necessarily true in the case of others. In Hannah's case it was both true and not true.

Hannah would qualify clinically as a traumatized individual. She had been sexually molested at age 9, and had palpable somatic memories of being sexually molested at very early ages, perhaps by members of her own family. When we began our work together, my initial experience of her in the transference was similar to Searles' description when he speaks of the patient reacting unconsciously to the therapist as a "pervasive and sinister supernatural force," or as "nonexistent."[22] This kind of transference was reflected also in her dreams. In this sense, Hannah's experience of the transpersonal dimension was "placed in the service of defense," as Kalsched suggests. But – and this is important – a major reason for this defensive stance was that no one, including her previous therapists and me, took as valid her experience of transrational reality. Ultimately, when I did, her capacity for "embodied gratification in the human world" broadened and deepened.

Did she feel the cows or not? Certainly my object relations stance early in the work was that she did not, that hers was an "as if" experience, not a "real one." It was her anger at me in the session described in Chapter 2 that moved me as her therapist from a defensive stance wherein *I* discounted her insistence that she had a genuine experience of the transrational. To let that notion in was too disquieting *for me*. Subsequently only when I did witness and acknowledge *her* reality, did the nature of the transference change and with it her relationship to me and others including her family, and to the transpersonal dimension.[23]

So for some individuals, as Kalsched suggests, the experience of trauma puts their relationship to the transpersonal (spirit) dimension in the service of defense,[24] with serious personal and interpersonal consequences including the risk of somatic complications. For some, like Hannah, her trauma *may* have put her experience of the transpersonal in service of defense. But an equally, *if not more causal factor* in this regard was the absence of any available witness, particularly her therapists, to her genuine experience of transrational reality. And in some cases, it is the therapy itself that inadvertently serves to undermine the patient's experience of the transpersonal and spiritual dimension in the service of defense. Sedgwick says of Searles' attitude towards these transpersonal contents: "Searles' generally negative opinions about mysticism suggest that the theory of the collective unconscious might itself be an immature defense against painful 'Good Mother/Bad Mother' emotional experiences on the personal level." He goes on to say that Searles attributes "infantile omnipotence" to such transpersonal experiences.[25]

Pathologizing Border*land* dynamics can have the effect of "teaching" the individual with a Borderline personality disorder to behave in a more Borderline-like manner than would otherwise be the case. For example, when I suggested to Hannah, albeit quite subtly, that some of her experiences of and with animals were not real and had nothing to do with the animals themselves, i.e. that she was only projecting her own trauma and depressed feelings onto the animals, I was in effect encouraging her to deny and split off parts of her experience of reality while substituting mine. This produced rage (slamming the floor with her shoe) so typical of Borderline personalities.

We can see this dynamic as it is portrayed quite dramatically in Hans Christian Andersen's tale of "The Emperor's New Clothes," a fairytale one theme of which is the differentiation of what is "real" from what one perceives to be real or unreal – and one's capacity to deal with it. At the end of the tale, after the little boy pointed out that the Emperor had no clothes, the Emperor and his court behaved as if he did, *even when they knew better*:

> The Emperor took off all his clothes, and the impostors pretended to hand him one article of clothing after the other. They pretended to fasten something around his waist and to tie on something at his neck. This was the train, they said, and the Emperor turned round and round in front of the mirror. "How well His Majesty looks in the new clothes! How becoming they are!" cried all his followers. "What a design, and what colors! They are most gorgeous robes."
>
> "The canopy which is to be carried over Your Majesty in the procession is waiting outside," said the master of the ceremonies.
>
> "Well, I am quite ready," said the Emperor. "Don't the clothes fit well?" Then he turned around again in front of the mirror, so that he should appear to be examining his handsome new suit.
>
> The chamberlains who were to carry the train stopped, felt about on

the ground and pretended to lift it with both hands. They walked along behind with their hands in the air, for they dared not let it seem that they did not see anything . . .

"But he hasn't got anything on," said a little child.

"Oh, listen to the innocent," said his father. And what the child had said was whispered from one person to the other. "He has nothing on – a child says he has nothing on!"

"But he has nothing on!" cried all the people at last.

The Emperor writhed, *for he knew that it was true*. But he thought, "The procession must go on now." So he held himself stiffer than ever, and the chamberlains fussed and straightened the invisible train. And the procession goes on still![26]

[Emphasis added.]

In my work with Hannah, I was like the emperor, the imposition onto her of my object-relations training was like the "imposters" and the child was like the child in Hannah that kept protesting the false reality "we" kept presenting to her. Finally, unlike the emperor, I had to admit the previously disconcerting (to me) truth of her perceptions and desist from pressuring her to believe otherwise. On a more subtle level, this fairytale suggests how, as clinicians, even the best of us can be seduced by the patient's (unconscious) personality dynamics and our own countertransference reactions. Damage is done if the therapist (as does the emperor in the tale in the name of the "procession going on") presumes, *a priori* that his/her reality is more "real" than that of the patient, even in the face of feelings/thoughts/doubts/intimations on the part of the therapist that perhaps there could be some validity to the patient's representations. Even the best of us can, at the expense of our patients, succumb to a denial of our own countertransference anxiety or even our pathology.

The sometimes intractable and frustrating dynamics that those of us, as clinicians, have all encountered in our work with Borderline patients can harden not only our own defenses as therapists, but sometimes our minds and hearts as well. That is one reason why I was so moved and deeply touched by Searles' book, *My Work with Borderline Patients*. He has worked consistently for decades with some of the most difficult cases. Notwithstanding, it is my conviction that the Borderline personality is often unconsciously and palpably scapegoated.[27]

There can be a lowered expectation of healing and greater countertransference resistance to some of the patient's subjective reality. We may not be inclined to "listen" to what our patients bring, let alone to what the patient considers sacred. And I do not mean that everything the patient considers sacred is free of pathological elements. I do mean that "listening" needs to include the possibility that the patient has a connection to a "reality" that goes beyond that of the therapist. The therapist needs, for the sake of the patient, to be open to the possibility that all that does not appear rational is not necessarily pathological – that the patient may have a relationship to the transpersonal, to the transrational, that is both sustaining *and healthy*. The *Psychiatric Dictionary* defines countertransference as:

> The total reaction of the therapist, both the transference reaction and the realistic reaction, to all aspects of the patient's transference and general personality; the effect on the analyst's understanding or technique of the therapist's own unconscious needs and conflicts. Countertransference reactions, sometimes called analytic stumbling, are manifestations of the therapist's reluctance to know or learn something about himself. They may impair the analyst's interpretive capacity and his ability to deal with resistances *by distorting the therapist's perception of the patient's unconscious processes.*[28,29]

[Emphasis added.]

It is my view that the point of breakdown between what is authentic from the patient's perspective and the therapist's *interpretation* of what is authentic comes when the therapist *leaves his or her feeling body and prematurely* **thinks** about what he/she is experiencing/perceiving from the patient. This is what happened initially in my work with Hannah. Psychoanalyst Nathan Schwartz-Salant, in his book on the Borderline personality says that "The process requires that the therapist allow himself or herself to be affected by the patient's material without having to resort to interpretation, which would at best prove to be a defensive maneuver."[30] If the patient's authentic reality is different from any known reference point of the therapist, then the therapist lacks a frame for grasping what is being communicated consciously and unconsciously, and all the more so for transrational contents. On a subtle level, the therapist may be thrown back onto his/her fragmentation complex (see Chapter 4). At this point the therapist's own anxiety may create a need to pathologize the patient's authentic reality in an attempt to protect his sense of psychic and emotional cohesion.

I can't offer a simple formula for differentiating Borderline and Border*land* dynamics in session. I can share some of my own experiences: With Borderline patients I often feel a pervasive anger present in the room. There is a hardness, an anger – sometimes rage – not too far below the surface if it is not overt, and a demandingness that is present to greater or lesser degree. And, of course, splitting is usually evident both in the manifest content offered by the patient and in the emotional content. In terms of the countertransference, I sometimes find myself wrestling with my own resentment of the Borderline patient, as well as a certain guarded feeling, particularly in my upper body. And I, too, feel split – sometimes disembodied and fragmented. For me, I experience my own splitting more on a body level than on a mind level.

With individuals whom I have come to refer to as Border*land*, more than anything else I feel their sadness and a pervasive mournfulness, sometimes a Great Grief. So many appear to be in a state of chronic mourning – seemingly, at least initially, unconnected to anything. Oftentimes the patient seems to disappear in the session – without warning or any manifest reason. Ultimately what emerges is a secret life that is quite conscious to the patient and closely guarded. A mother wrote me that after reading an article of mine on the Border*land* personality, she "came out" (her term) to her 20-year-old son about what he must have perceived as her weird behavior when he was young. She reported that her son seemed to understand both her process and her dilemma and had empathy for her struggles. For him, it was a kind of "Ah ha!" recognition regarding his childhood experiences with her. In terms of the countertransference, it is much as I described my reactions with Hannah – a feeling of something missing, something not happening in the sessions, some part of the patient missing. Sometimes it feels as if some part of *me* is missing in the room, a kind of two-dimensional experience of my feeling self. Sometimes I have the sense of being in the presence of the sacred, that the sacred has entered in, even when there is no such indication in the manifest dynamic of the session. And, notably, I don't feel many of the dynamics – particularly rage – I described above with regard to *Borderline* patients.

With regard to other characteristics common to the Borderline personality disorder such as a chronic feeling of emptiness, emotional volatility, poor impulse control (e.g. gambling, indiscriminate sex, binge eating), and self-destructive behaviors (e.g. self-mutilation, overdosing prescription medications and illegal drugs), some or all of these can be experienced in conjunction with Border*land* dynamics. As pointed out previously, the interactions between these different types of dynamics (Border*land* and Borderline) in the same individual often confuse the individual with regard to what is "abnormal" and what is "ordinary" transrational experience as reflected in their own patterns of behavior and personality structure. Because the individual does not know how to interpret his/her own behavior, these interacting patterns of behavior are often self-reinforcing. The result is often that Border*land* dynamics inadvertently reinforce Borderline patterns of behavior and there is an overall exacerbation of symptoms and personality dynamics. (Early in our work this was the case with Hannah.) At the same time, it is my experience that Border*land* personalities welcome a process of differentiation of their Border*land* and Borderline parts. Nearly all are fully aware that they have pathological parts. Many would acknowledge having some Borderline features. The identification and authentication of Border*land* dynamics can significantly improve difficult behavior patterns and the self-image of individuals diagnosed with Borderline personality disorder.

Well-trained therapists, particularly psychoanalysts, constantly use the countertransference in their work with Borderline (and other) patients. But the countertransference can be used either to heal or to hurt. And for the same reason, when the therapist cannot remain open to the possibility of a transrational reality outside of his/her own experience, the countertransference can be a powerful implement for wounding – the therapist as well as the patient.

In the last 50 years there has been a proliferation of new schools and theories in psychology and psychiatry. The object-relations school of psychology, particularly, has become prominent, if not dominant, in psychotherapeutic practice in the United States. It opened up and broadened the understanding of the underlying dynamics of psychopathology and put forth whole new approaches to treatment – particularly with regard to narcissistic disorders and the Borderline personality. I personally found this training indispensable and, when integrated with Jungian theory, it helped my own understanding of psychodynamics and my personal approach to treatment.

However, with the evolution of these new schools and theoretical orientations comes a heavy emphasis on etiology and psychopathology. The very term – "*object* relations" – depersonalizes the individual, and because it is so one-sidedly ego based, it leaves out the transpersonal dimension. For me, it blurs the boundaries between psyche and soul. The nature and language of the theory is a detraction in this regard, and there seems to be an inexorable drift toward looking at the individual pathologically to the exclusion of the soul. "Normality" too often has become merely the absence of pathology. Most important, the locus, the frame of reference, for addressing psychic contents seems to have become more and more centered in the theory and less centered in the frame of reference of the patient and the patient's own experience of his/her inner processes and life connections.

Freudian and neo-Freudian schools of psychoanalysis contributed more than their share to what sometimes seems to me to be name calling. Stephen M. Johnson, Professor of Psychology at the University of Oregon observes:

> [T]he psychoanalytic and particularly characterological labels for characteristic adaptations are singularly negative and pathological; there is relatively little emphasis on where the absence of pathology will lead. There is little attention paid to what we really could be, and none to what this melodrama of life is all about. In traditional characterological terms, one has the choice of being one of the following or something equally horrible: Oral, schizoid, masochistic, psychopathic, narcissistic, rigid, hysterical, obsessive-compulsive, etc. While . . . we need to label psychopathology to communicate and think about it in a systematic way, these labels are, unfortunately, often powerful negative suggestions that convey judgmental attitudes and further separation between those whom one considers healthy and those whom one considers sick.[31]

More recently, the "intersubjective" school of thought takes a significant step closer to what is needed to address this problem. The intersubjective perspective differs from other psychoanalytic theories in that it does not posit particular psychological contents (the Oedipus complex, the paranoid and depressive positions, separation–individuation conflicts, and so on) that are presumed to be universally salient in personality development and in pathogenesis. It holds that the child's, and subsequently, the adult's derivative experiences are the product(s) of mutual *interaction* between the individual and the primary care givers as well as other significant individuals in the person's life. Robert D. Stolorow, faculty member of the Institute of Contemporary Psychoanalysis and clinical professor of psychiatry at the UCLA School of Medicine, asserts:

> [A]ny pathological constellation can be understood only in terms of the unique intersubjective contexts in which it originated and is continuing to be maintained . . .
>
> Psychoanalytic theories that postulate universal psychodynamic contents also tend to prescribe rigid rules of therapeutic technique or style that follow from the theoretical presuppositions . . .
>
> The doctrine of intrapsychic determinism and corresponding focus on the isolated mind in psychoanalysis has historically been associated with an objectivist epistemology. Such a position envisions the mind in isolation, radically estranged from an external reality that it either accurately apprehends or distorts. Analysts embracing an objectivist epistemology *presume to have privileged access to the essence of the patient's psychic reality* and to the objective truths that the patient's psychic reality obscures . . . the intersubjective viewpoint . . . is best characterized as "perspectivalist." Such a stance does not presume either that the analyst's subjective reality is more true than the patient's, or that the analyst can directly know the subjective reality of the patient.[32]
>
> [Emphasis added.]

Although this theoretical viewpoint significantly addresses the limitations of many other theoretical approaches, it is still limited to an object-relations context. It does not make adequate space for the role of nature even as a significant other, let alone as a "primary caregiver," as is the case with some individuals.

Developmentally, for the insecurely attached individuals, trauma often provokes an attachment crisis – both interpersonally with others and between the individual and his/her own body experience. We have seen earlier how for Border*landers*, nature can become the positive, if not life-saving, "primary caregiver," when the interpersonal dimension of treatment and healing have been spoiled. Here Mother Nature, herself, becomes the safe parent – *in lieu of an individual's* (i.e. object attachment) – as the primary caregiver. I am proposing that when the interpersonal/intersubjective level of relating is so damaged and compromised as to be functionally unavailable to the individual as a primary part of the individual's developmental attachment system, *the* *individual seeks out a "safe enough" impersonal primary caregiver and partner in the attachment drama.* Oftentimes this primary caregiver/attachment partner is nature. This instinctual gravitation toward nature as the *impersonal* safe enough primary caregiver is given further impetus by what I have described in earlier chapters as evolutionary process taking place vis-à-vis the western psyche. To insist, in the therapeutic context, that the individual repair what, from his/her soul's standpoint, seems unrepairable (object constancy as their primary attachment), can lead to further stress, re-traumatization, and despair. Indeed, resistance by the therapist to the transrational dimension of the patient's reality experience, may be a significant dynamic in reinforcing Border*line* features in the therapeutic process itself.

If we are open, we can find Border*land* dynamics in virtually any diagnostic category. However, I wish to be clear that although I believe that the Borderline personality is particularly accessible to experiencing Border*land* phenomena, not all people who experience Border*land* phenomena are Borderline personalities. Indeed, as I have put forth in previous chapters, I believe that the experience of Border*land* phenomena is not in itself a neurotic experience. Rather it is a natural evolutionary occurrence, and that the prevalence of such experiences has been rapidly developing in a substantial proportion of people in the United States.[33] There are many individuals whose lives are quite functional and who do not seek psychological help – people whom I perceive as "Border*land* personalities." I have reserved the term "Border*land* personality" to refer to individuals for whom this realm is consciously lived and is an enriching part of their reality. Many of them are quite aware that they fit the profile of Border*land* personality. Since I have begun to publish material on the subject, scores of these individuals have identified themselves to me. All that I have heard from are immensely relieved to have words put to their experience – and, for many, to their secret. Without exception, they have expressed a longing for recognition and connection with others like themselves – a longing for community.

Notes

1 Jung, 1935: para. 5.
2 For purposes of clarity in this chapter I use the italicized form "Border*land*" to distinguish it from the word "Borderline."
3 The *Quick Reference to Diagnostic and Statistical Manual of Mental Disorders IV*, defines Borderline personality disorder: It is "a pervasive pattern of instability of interpersonal relationships, self-image, and affects, and marked impulsivity beginning by early adulthood and present in a variety of contexts as indicated by five (or more) of the following: (1) frantic efforts to avoid real or imagined abandonment (2) a pattern of unstable and intense interpersonal relationships characterized by alternating between extremes of idealization and devaluation (3) identity disturbance: markedly and persistently unstable self-image or sense of self (4) impulsivity in at least two areas that are potentially self-damaging (e.g., spending, sex, substance abuse, reckless driving, binge eating) (5) recurrent suicidal behavior,

gestures, or threats, or self-mutilating behavior (6) affective instability due to a marked reactivity of mood (7) chronic feelings of emptiness (8) inappropriate intense anger or difficulty controlling anger (9) transient, stress-related paranoid ideation or severe dissociative symptoms."

4 Association, 1994: 280–281.

5 Anzaldúa, 1987.

6 I came across the use of the term "*Borderland*" in the psychological literature at least three years after I began to employ the term to describe the transrational phenomena and personality dynamics I have described in my work with Hannah.

7 As reported in Grinker and Werble, 1977: 12.

8 *Ibid.*: 12–13.

9 Searles, 1986: 60.

10 See pp. 12–14; 17; 71–73.

11 It is pertinent here to recall that only 20 years ago the medical/pharmaceutical world generally pooh-poohed the claims of tribal and other "alternative" healers regarding herbal remedies for the treatment of disease. Estimated expenditures for alternative medicine professional services increased 45.2% between 1990 and 1997 and were conservatively estimated at $21.2 billion in 1997, with at least $12.2 billion paid out of pocket. This exceeds the 1997 out-of-pocket expenditures of all US hospitalizations. Total out-of-pocket expenditures relating to alternative therapies were conservatively estimated at $27.0 billion for 1997, which is comparable with the projected 1997 out-of-pocket expenditures for all US physician (allopathic) services. The research indicates that the increase is attributable primarily to an increase in the proportion of the population seeking alternative therapies, rather than increased visits per patient (Eisenberg, Appel, Wilkey, van Rompay, & Kessler, 1998).

Shamans and other native healers come to their knowledge of medicine through their *intuitive experience* and by observing animals and plants – another source of wisdom in nature – which was/is the core of their science and religious practice.

12 Searles, 1986: 28–29.

13 Searles, 1986: 29. Sedgwick, 1993: 29–31, 36, 47.

14 If this was his assessment of the environment and our resultant relationship to it in 1972, one can only imagine what might be his assessment in 2005 of the degraded state of our environment and its impact on human personality!

15 Searles, 1986: 60–61.

16 Sedgwick, 1993: 62.

17 Searles, 1986: 50.

18 Although the term, the "self", is utilized in ego psychology and self-psychology, it is not utilized in those disciplines in the manner in which Jung used the term. Jung's concept of the Self connects the personal realm with the transpersonal dimension, what Edward Edinger refers to as "subjective identity" and "objective identity," respectively.

19 McCormack, 1990.

20 Kalsched, 1996: 4, 12, 142.

21 Kalsched, 1996: 143. John Welwood calls this a "spiritual bypass." See Welwood, 2002: 12–13.

22 Searles, 1986: 29.

23 See Chapter 2 for description of the session. Also see the Introduction to Part I and Chapter 10 for a discussion of whether she "really" did hear the cows.

24 See Chapter 15.

25 Sedgwick, 1993: 51.

26 Andersen, 1871, 1872: 86–87.

27 A great deal of controversy surrounding the validity and legitimacy of "Borderline personality disorder" has arisen since the 1990s. On the one extreme, some clinicians hold that the diagnostic category is not legitimate in its own right and that virtually all individuals perceived as Borderline personality disorder represent a particular symptom complex resulting from early (usually pre-Oedipal) childhood trauma, particularly sexual abuse. On the other extreme, others have asserted that there is a biological basis for the Borderline personality syndrome. Both of these positions offer *some* compelling data in support, but in my view there is not enough data to conclusively support either position.

In my own experience, although certainly I have encountered individuals who would fit the Borderline personality disorder, I have also worked with individuals who fit the diagnostic pattern of Borderline personality whose history(ies) presented no dramatic pattern of abuse. Although I would acknowledge that many individuals with the diagnosis have experienced abuse, I also hold that a Borderline personality structure, including and independent of abuse/trauma issues, does exist. I also believe that we are not close to a definitive answer regarding the role of the biological make-up of this disorder. See the work of Judith Lewis Herman (Herman, 1992), the *Journal of the California Alliance for the Mentally Ill* (1997), and the work of TARA Association for Personality Disorder (Goodwin & Porr, 1999). More recent research by Allan Schore and others suggests that Borderline personality disorder takes its etiological roots in severe attachment disorder as well as in early trauma, Schore, 2004: 335.

28 Campbell, 1996: 162.

29 This is less than a full definition of countertransference but sufficient for purposes of the points illustrated below.

30 Schwartz-Salant, 1989: 177.

31 Johnson, 1985: 5–6. Also see Carl G. Jung's essay, "Medicine and Psychotherapy" (Jung, 1945: para. 195, 197).

32 Stolorow, Atwood, and Brandschaft, 1994: x–xii.

33 I have asserted that the Border*land* phenomenon results from an evolutionary process and is aimed at adapting and transforming an overspecialized western ego that threatens the survival of species *Homo sapiens*. It would follow that the phenomena that I have described above in the United States would be following a similar pattern in other cultures where the western ego construct is dominant, i.e. western Europe, Australia, New Zealand, etc. However, since I have had no *direct* clinical experience in any of these cultures, I cannot assert that the same phenomenon is taking place in those cultures.

Part III

Chapter 12

Introduction to Part III: A new emerging consciousness: Building a clinical bridge between the mind–body split

Indians experience and relate to a living universe, whereas western people – especially scientists – reduce all things, living or not, to objects. The implications of this are immense. If you see the world around you as a collection of objects for you to manipulate and exploit, you will inevitably destroy the world while attempting to control it. Not only that, but by perceiving the world as lifeless, you rob yourself of the richness, beauty, and wisdom to be found by participating in its larger design.

In order to maintain the fiction that the world is dead – and that those who believe it to be alive have succumbed to primitive superstition – science must reject any interpretation of the natural world that implies sentience or an ability to communicate on the part of nonhumans . . .

If you objectify other living things, then you are committing yourself to a totally materialistic universe – which is not even consistent with the findings of modern physics.[1]

In Part I, we explored the threat to the survival of species *Homo sapiens* by an overspecialized western ego too inflated with its own power complex to contain its grandiosity and competition with God. It is important to note before moving on that although I have placed necessary emphasis on this threat to our survival, *all* dimensions of experience have both a negative and a positive pole. Thus, that western ego that I have described as so menacing to our survival, is also an indispensable instrument for our potential salvation. What the *final cause*, in the Aristotelian sense, might be remains yet a mystery. And, by definition, mysteries are never fully known. The ultimate challenge is whether we can take advantage of our new consciousness so as to be able to participate as an aware coevolutionary partner in reining in our own self-destructive nature. Doing so holds the prospect for crossing a threshold into a broader and deeper relationship with all of life, and for embracing the intriguing mystery of the greater fullness of who we are and who we are intended to become – not merely who we choose to be.

I have asserted that, since the 1960s, there has been a compensatory evolutionary shift in the collective unconscious in an attempt to rein in this runaway western ego. A hallmark of that evolutionary shift is a reconnecting of the western ego with nature. Through that process the western psyche is being forced to integrate the transpersonal and transrational dimensions of life from which I propose it began to split some 3,000 years ago. However, this reconnection with nature is not a regression to previous psychic states, such as animism or a Rousseau-like idealized romanticization of nature. The integration of these dimensions – the transpersonal and the transrational – holds the potential to contain the western ego construct and its self-destructive intoxication with its own technological prowess.[2]

One by-product of this evolutionary process appears to be the emergence of a new kind of consciousness, which I have called the Borderland. Some of the characteristics of what I have defined as the Borderland personality have been evident in *individuals* past and present. However, historically, its prevalence has been far from the mainstream consciousness of western culture. To review, I will remind the reader of the particular characteristics of this emergent Borderland consciousness are:

- A western ego at a high level of psychological development with an elastic ego boundary capable of being in connection with nature without falling into a state of *participation mystique* with nature.[3]
- An ego capable of containing its own fragmentation complex.[4]
- A resultant greater capacity for maintaining a simultaneous connection and dialogue with, and integration of, the rational and transrational dimensions of life.[5]
- An evolutionary process that holds the prospect of a new kind of *collective* consciousness that will be familiar not only to the few, but that will be common to the many. Indeed, it may become the predominant form of consciousness emergent in the 21st century.[6]

I have come to these realizations gradually over a period of 30 years of clinical practice as an analytical psychologist and in my contact with Navajo and Hopi cultures. As I worked with some patients, increasingly I began to see that their patterns of experience and psychological reality did not fit the clinical models in which I had been trained. Broadening my clinical awareness through reading and further training helped, but did not quite answer the questions: "What's this all about? What are they talking about?" For many years, largely unconsciously, I succumbed to the subtle pressure of squeezing my understanding of patient experience into the boundaries of familiar clinical models. Yet, all the while I was searching for new meaning.

For many years I followed this Ariadne thread, which suggested a consciousness different from the ones I lived and worked in, mostly through my experiences with Navajo medicine and healing ceremonials. I was able to relate western and Navajo *concepts* of healing. But I never succeeded in translating the one into the other clinically or in adapting the wisdom that I had garnered over 30 years in my contact with Navajo religion and culture in a manner that would satisfactorily inform my work. These concepts remained for me, both personally and professionally, two separate worlds, clinically, with no bridge between. Perhaps a telephone wire, but no bridge. At the same time, it became more and more obvious to me that there were dimensions of consciousness and transrational experiences in an increasing number of people that needed a new kind of clinical container, one that was more accepting and less judgmental of transrational experience.

During this process I never lost sight of the fact that I came to my training as an analytical psychologist through my encounter with Navajo healing and Hopi religion and culture, not the other way around. There was something in the deep wisdom of their "way" that inexplicably took root in my mind and soul, and that I intuitively knew was central in the journey towards my work. Ironically, I began that journey looking at western healing through the other end of the telescope – from a cultural and archetypal center that was not mine and could never be mine. That sense of dislocation and confusion led to a push/pull of what was figure and what was ground, and an endless series of questions and "yes, buts."

I began Part I of this book with the chapter on Hannah because it was in my clinical work with her that these pieces fell into place. It was when my knowledge and expertise as an analytical psychologist came to an obvious dead end with Hannah that I began to learn to listen differently. Instinctively I fell back on that clinical center that was both strange and familiar and yet not mine, and from which I had begun the journey towards my work as an analyst. The chapters in Part III will further broaden the psychological and clinical explorations undertaken in Part II of the book. In Part III I will discuss how, finally, a way to build a bridge between Navajo medicine and western approaches to healing presented itself. My intuition and my experience told me that a broader clinical model was needed to embrace what appears to be an increasing prevalence of what I have called Borderland reality. For me, that broader clinical model would emerge out of a joining of western and Navajo healing approaches.

Jungian theory is clearly the essential connecting link between these two worlds. Jung's psychology remains the only one that unqualifiedly embraces transpersonal experience and spirituality as an integral part of normal human experience and an essential consideration in clinical practice. Jung's theories of the collective unconscious, his theory of archetypes, and his concept of the Self (as differentiated from the *self* in object relations theory and other Freudian and neo-Freudian modalities), are the indispensable building blocks of the clinical bridge that follows in the rest of this book.

Notes

1   Deloria, 2000: 6. Vine Deloria is a Native American writer, Yankton/Dakota Sioux, retired Professor of History, Law, Religious Studies, and Political Science at the University of Colorado in Boulder.
2   The prefix *trans* is from the Latin, meaning "across, beyond, or to the other side of."

The *Chambers English Dictionary* defines "transpersonal" as, "going beyond, transcending, the individual personality: Denoting a form of psychology or psychotherapy that utilizes mystical, psychical or spiritual experience as a means of increasing human potential" (1988: 1560). In the context that I am using the term, it alludes (but is not limited) to Jung's concepts of the "collective unconscious" and the "transcendent function," both concepts previously discussed. It also alludes to the relig*ious function* (as opposed to relig*ion*), in essence to life's transpersonal mysteries. Thus such definitions as "transpersonal" can never be precise and therefore it is suggested that the reader focus on what is alluded to, rather than precise concepts and definitions.

I use the term "transrational" to refer to phenomena that are not provable in the rational, statistically provable, sense of the word – simply stated, observable phenomena and connections that do not "make sense" by generally accepted scientific and rational criteria.
3   See Part 2 in Figure 7.2.
4   See Part 2 in Figure 7.2.
5   See Figures 7.1–7.3 in Chapter 7.
6   Ray, 2000.

Chapter 13

A cookout: Fundamental differences and points of linkage between Navajo and western healing systems

Of their religion, little or nothing is known, as, indeed, all inquiries tend to show that they have none. The lack of tradition is a source of surprise. They have no knowledge of their origin or of the history of the tribe. Their singing is but a succession of grunts and is anything but agreeable.

Jonathan Letherman, MD of the US Army, 1855[1]

Balancing the individual balances the world.

Johnson Dennison, Navajo medicine man, 2000

A while ago a group of 12 or so medicine men and medicine women came to Santa Fe to research old and extinct healing ceremonials and chants preserved in the archives of the Wheelwright Museum. One evening after a day of research, my wife and I hosted a cookout at our home for them and their family and friends. After half the group had gone home, someone commented that since there were three "Biligana" (white/western) practitioners and half a dozen Navajo medicine people present, it was a unique opportunity to compare and explore differences and similarities in the Navajo and western approaches to healing. There was particular curiosity about what therapists (as opposed to counselors) and most particularly, psychoanalysts, *do*.

One of the medicine men present gave a "case presentation": A family brought their child of 7 to the medicine man because the child had been having chronic and severe digestive problems. The medicine man sent the family to a diagnostician who gave them the following diagnosis: When the mother was pregnant with the child, the father killed a dog. This was the source of the child's ailment. A "reconfiguration of dog ceremony" needed to be held to restore order and harmony in the child's life.[2] The ceremony was held and the child's symptoms cleared up within a week of the ceremony and did not return. The medicine man then turned to us, the western practitioners, and asked, "How would that diagnosis be translated in western medicine?"[3] That was a showstopper of a question if ever I heard one!

But there is an answer of sorts to his question. It is that the view of illness and its related diagnostic system is as much determined by the culture and its underlying cosmogony as by "objective" data. And, of course, within each system the data available *are* by definition the "objective" data. Navajo and western systems of healing are parallel systems, complete unto themselves from diagnosis through treatment, and it is not essential for either to be translated into the cultural context of the other for its efficacy to be valid. It is true that microbes are microbes and they remain what they are across cultures. But when one adds in the fact of the immune system – the primary place of meeting and "dialogue" between psyche and soma – and the influence of psyche on the immune system, the gulf between these two views of the same problem seems not so huge after all.[4]

Another case example presented that night by a medicine man was more relatable in the western context: A young pre-school age child was chronically agitated and difficult to manage. It was known by the child's maternal grandmother that the mother had intended to abort the pregnancy. Intervention at the last minute by the maternal grandmother prevented the abortion. The child's mother was not in the picture as the primary caretaker. A diagnostician was consulted, and a "returning back the consciousness through the corn pollen path ceremony" was prescribed for the child. The ceremony would address the intrauterine wound to the child's psyche by virtue of the mother's initial decision to abort the pregnancy, and would restore psychological balance and harmony for the child and in the universe. In Navajo thinking, an "unnatural act" – and abortion would constitute an unnatural act, albeit perhaps at times medically necessary – is a wound to the cosmos or the universal psyche as well as to the individuals involved. To heal the one – the individual psyche – is to heal the other – the universal psyche. They are not separable from the standpoint of Navajo cosmology and medicine.

In western terms we can more readily relate to the wound carried in the psyche of the child in this example, leaving the wound to the universal psyche by the mother unaddressed. In this case, there was a wound to both the child and the universe. The healing of the one without addressing the healing of the other would make no sense in Navajo medicine. The ceremony was performed over the child and simultaneously addressed the wound to the universal psyche. As this case was described, the child's behavior and overall well-being improved after the ceremony. Research in developmental psychology in recent years has begun to address intrauterine consciousness and trauma to the fetus.[5] It is noteworthy that with the exception of some psychoanalytic writings, the notion of intrauterine consciousness and psychic wounding has gained broader acceptance in the psychiatric community only in the last decade. In Navajo medicine it has been a "truth" within their cosmological and medical system for centuries.

Navajo religion and healing

In the Navajo system most "illness" results from some kind of disturbance of the natural balance in the cosmos. Much of Navajo etiology is based on a wound to/from nature. An individual can cause that imbalance, consciously as well as unconsciously. In addition to the examples described above, such disturbances might be bad dreams, being witched by another individual, being physically present in an area recently struck by lightning, entering an area that has not been ritually cleansed too soon after a death, transgressions against animals, among others. Navajos also certainly would attribute illness to eating spoiled food, dehydration, and other similar types of harmful behaviors and treat them with "medicine."

In the case presented earlier where the father killed a dog in the proximity of the pregnant mother – an act that disturbed the psychic balance of the world surrounding the developing new life form, i.e. the child – the wound to be healed was the transgression against the dog. By restoring psychic and spiritual balance with the spirit of the dog, the latter would be inclined to "release" the child from the negative karma resulting from the father's act. Thus the "reconfiguration of dog ceremony" to address the etiology of the child's illness.

For the Navajo there is no split between mind and body. Although some Navajo medicine practitioners will talk about "mental illness," this is a new term intruded into the Navajo system by western medicine.[6] While tradition-ally the Navajo acknowledge that certain functions reside in certain parts of the body, i.e. thoughts originate in the mind and the "mind" (i.e. the place of thoughts) is located in the head, psyche and soma are still one system for the Navajo.

Similarly, Navajo religion and healing are one and the same system. Navajo religion is expressed in detail through their cosmology, which includes all their myths regarding the origins of the Navajo people – the Diné. Within those myths are the stories of the various mythological figures, including the "Holy People," particular groups of beings who are called forth in the various Navajo healing ceremonies. The Holy People do not heal per se, but they are the agents for constellating the powerful energies that do heal the patient, repair the cosmos (in this context what Jung calls the "objective psyche"), and restore order and harmony.

Because Navajo religion and healing are inseparable, the Navajo are always connected to the transpersonal dimension of life and existence. There is no dichotomy between religious life and secular life. Religion resides in and is reflected by every aspect of their environment and being. What for us, through the eyes of western culture, are inanimate lifeless/spiritless objects, are, for the Navajo, forms of existence, each with its own indwelling spirit and place and function in the order of the cosmos. In one sense, one might say that all Navajos are Borderland personalities – with the significant exception that they do not have the left-brain-dominating ego construct of western culture that splits western man from nature.[7]

Navajo healing ceremonials are divided into "chantways," all of which trace their roots to some portion of a very elaborate cosmological story.[8] Donald Sandner reported that as of 1938, there were approximately 26 different chantways, some with many variations and branches. Besides these there were various shorter blessingways, hunting and war rites, short prayer ceremonies, and minor rites.[9] Some of these have since died out and others may soon follow. At the same time, Navajo interest in healing is currently at an all-time high, and medicine men report increasing numbers of younger Navajos who wish to apprentice with them to become medicine men in their own right.

Perhaps Navajo religion and healing can be best described in the words of Carl N. Gorman. As I mentioned earlier, Gorman was a Navajo artist, code talker, teacher of Navajo culture and religion, and the first director of the Office of Native Healing Sciences within the Navajo Nation governmental system:

> For the Navajo, religion is a very personal relationship with that which we call nature – nature with a capital "N". Our religion is a way of life, a path which we follow, called the Corn Pollen Path of Beauty.
>
> We have a complex ceremonial system with a mythology that tells of the creation of the earth, sky and man; and man's relation to that creation. Symbols from our religious stories and ceremonies are used in our everyday life reminding us of their meaning. One of these is the manner in which traditionally our hair is tied. It is tied in a knot [siyelth] shaped similar to a figure eight [or hour glass] and tied with white wool . . . It has a very sacred meaning. It is the bringing together of the head, or reason, and the heart or love, in a creative way. When these two are in balance, there is harmony . . . [See Plate I.]
>
> Everyday activities and religion are woven together in our lives the way our women weave strands of wool into rugs of the most beautiful designs. Our thoughts weave all things together into the fabric of life, making it a path of harmony and beauty.
>
> Thought is probably the one most important concept in our religious philosophy. We believe that everything originates in thought, that the power of thought is real, for good or evil . . . thought is energy, the energy that produces dreams . . . and it is the energy that molds our environment. Thought is perhaps the root substance of creation from the mind of the great unknown power. . . .
>
> We believe that men, animals, plants, mother earth, the sun, the moon, all physical bodies, have some of this great power or spirit within them which is indwelling intelligent life, each one having its own special form and work to do . . . each thought-form from the mind of the creator has its own song, or vibration . . .

Plate 1 Carl Gorman with *siyelth*.

We believe in the duality of all things. Everything has its opposite, or its positive and negative side.[10]

It is important in reading the above quote not to equate "thought" with "thinking." "Thought," really, "thought-form," for the Navajo is more than mental construct as it is in the context of the western ego. Their use of the word in this context is closer to Jung's (not Freud's) concept of libido, or psychic energy. Thought for the Navajo embodies such additional concepts as attitude, symbolization, intention, focused feeling, intuitive knowing, and above all else, mythological truth. It includes magic and the magical dimension, but is not synonymous with it. It is a constant, aware meditative state of being and inextricably includes the spirit dimension. The western concept and usage of the word "thought" for the most part is as mental construct separate from spirit and soul.[11]

Beauty

Beauty, *hozho*, is a word of power and healing. It contains the Navajo feeling about the fullness and sacredness of life. There is a numinous and transpersonal connotation as well as a personal and temporal meaning. It represents a *power*[12] that comes from the cosmos, reflected in the soul and spirit, and one that is interactively communicated between the perceived and the perceiver – including inanimate objects in nature. *Hozho* holds the knowing of the wonder of life and the great spirit that gave rise to it and that sustains it.

This is why a Navajo seldom uses words like "belief," or has a need for a traditional *logos*-based religion. He needs no explanation for what is given and what he knows experientially. The "proof" is in the knowing, not in any explanation. It is all given in their cosmology. Thus Navajo ceremonials focus much energy on re-establishing harmony and awareness of the beauty of life and ultimately the beauty of the individual life of the one who is sick.

Western approaches to healing

Western medicine traditionally has split psyche and soma – mind and body.[13] This has been particularly true since the middle of the 19th century with the rise of scientific medicine and the work of Agostino Bassi, Louis Pasteur, Joseph Lister, Robert Koch, and others. In 1900 Freud published his landmark work, *The Interpretation of Dreams*. We talk about mental health and physical health, and the patient enters one system or the other in western medicine.[14] However, in the last ten years, there has been a growing interest in, and systematic bridging of, the split between mind and body within western medicine. There has been increasing focus on psychosomatic medicine, and the relationship between mental states and disorders such as asthma, various skin disorders, and a host of autoimmune disorders – multiple sclerosis, cancer, and others.

At the same time, the decade of the 1990s was known in psychiatric, psychoanalytic, and other clinical research circles, as the "decade of the brain" because of the heavy focus on brain research and the links between the various psychotherapies and their impact on the brain. Comparative double-blind brain studies using the technology of positron emission tomography (PET), brain single photon emission computed tomography (SPECT), computed electorencephalographic topography (CET), and functional magnetic resonance imaging (FMRI) scans now demonstrate that "talk therapy", as well as the use of psychotropic drugs, produces alterations in the brain – something that psychoanalysts and psychotherapists have known and asserted for years, but without the "hard" data to support their clinical observations and intuitive awareness.[15,16] By confirming many psychoanalytic observations and theories held over the years, brain research has also led to major advances in developmental psychological theory, in psychoanalytic theory involving early childhood and infants, and in the treatment of trauma.[17]

In addition, major bridging is taking place between mind–body interaction, making possible the treatment of some psychological disorders such as early childhood trauma and environmental illness by accessing the one dimension (psychological) through the other (physical). This ultimately utilizes a synergy of both dimensions, where heretofore such access seemed impossible – an approach that has been characteristic of Navajo medicine for centuries.[18]

With regard to a comparison of Navajo and western healing approaches then, we may make the following observations:

1. Western medicine splits mind and body.
2. Navajo medicine treats mind and body as one inseparable integrated whole. Therefore, no treatment distinction is made between physical disorders and mental disorders.
3. Dominant western approaches to the treatment of psychiatric/ psychological disorders discount the spiritual and transpersonal dimensions as legitimate considerations in both diagnosis and treatment.
4. Navajo medicine integrates spiritual and transpersonal dimensions in the core of its approach to diagnosis and treatment.
5. Navajo medicine most suffers from the absence of western medicine's comprehensive system of pathogenesis, antibiotics, and its surgical technology.

Huston Smith, internationally renowned teacher of world religions, suggests the following situation:

> Imagine a missionary to Africa. Conversion is slow going until a child comes down with an infectious disease. The tribal doctors are summoned, but to no avail; life is draining from the hapless infant. At that point the missionary remembers that at the last minute she slipped some penicillin into her travel bags. She administers it and the child recovers. With that single act . . . it is all over for the tribal culture.[19]

One can imagine the same events taking place in Native American tribes with the same outcome. I have witnessed this dynamic myself. However, what might be said in regard to tribes other than the Navajo, to a significant degree has not been the case for Navajo culture, religion, and healing.[20] The fact is that within most extant Native American tribes, little, if anything, of their rich native medical practices (oral traditions) survive. The Navajo, contrariwise, are another story.

The Navajo Tribe, comprising over 255,000 registered members,[21] constitutes one-third of *all* tribal Indians extant in the United States. Its survival in terms of numbers and the preservation of its culture are due to three primary factors:

- They reside on the largest reservation in the USA with a land base comparable to that of the entire state of west Virginia. This gives them access to western culture in surrounding towns, as well as some degree of protection of their own culture.
- Their roots are those of a nomadic hunter/gatherer tribe with the related aggression inherent in such a lifestyle, enabling them to survive in the midst of an alien and sometimes hostile culture.

- The Navajo are extremely adaptive, taking on *the functional* characteristics of their host culture (whatever they might be), while retaining the
  core of their own.[22]

This last characteristic – learning to functionally adapt and embrace particular aspects of their host and other cultures – is something that other tribal
cultures have tried to resist. For these other tribes, maintaining cultural integrity meant dealing with another culture only as necessary for survival, while
eschewing its social systems. But the hallmark of the Navajo is adaptation,
and this has enabled them to proliferate as a people.

Navajos have been relatively successful in adapting to western medical
technology and wisdom. There is an extensive system of health clinics and
hospitals, most developed and operated through the US Indian Health Service (IHS), on the reservation. Navajo medicine men, for the most part, have
accepted the benefits of western medicine and do not resist their patients,
family and friends, obtaining allopathic medical treatment. Indeed, a number
of medicine men and women come into those allopathic clinics and perform
blessingway and other ceremonies on in-patients. Recently the Tribe received
a substantial grant from the IHS to employ Navajo medicine men to help
translate the nature, treatment, and prevention of diabetes – a disease endemic
on the Navajo as well as most other reservations – into terms understandable
within Navajo culture. The grant includes cross-cultural training of allopathic physicians and nurses and Navajo medicine men. Although this cross-
cultural training appears to be more focused on transposing western medical
concepts into the Navajo context than the other way around, it represents a
dramatic and essential step in beginning to bridge and integrate Navajo and
allopathic medicine.

However, like most native tribes subjected to genocide, defeat, and
imprisonment by western culture, the Navajo have a lingering sense of
assumed or supposed superiority – in terms of raw power, if nothing else – of
the dominant culture. Furthermore, what western medical practitioners *do* is
still more of a mystery than not. Thus, although Navajo medicine men believe
that their traditional medicine is superior in some ways to the western, they
do not *know* it. In part, their culture and social norms – their natural humility
– would not let them make such a claim. They carry a deep psychic wound of
inferiority from the ignorant disrespect they feel from western culture as a
whole, and the condescension of western medicine towards their culture and
their healing practices. Tragically – for us as well as for them – the quote of
Jonathan Letherman at the beginning of this chapter carries more currency
than any of us would like to acknowledge.

In my opinion, there is no question that Navajo medicine has much to
offer western medicine, particularly in the fields of psychiatry and psychology
and in the growing field of what I think of as "Borderland syndromes," e.g.
environmental illness, chronic fatigue syndrome, some autoimmune disorders,

and the broad area of psychosomatic disorders. There are aspects of Navajo medicine that are clearly superior to western forms of treatment. Because of the non-splitting of mind and body, one obvious example is the use of the body to gain access to what we, in western psychology, would call highly defended or split off areas of wounding and trauma. These areas of Navajo medicine will be the focus of much of the rest of Part III.

Notes

1 King, 1943: 3.
2 This is the literal name of the ceremony given to me by the medicine man presenting the case. The actual ceremony was performed by his wife's grandfather who was a medicine man.
3 In the Navajo medicine system there are three types of "medicine men/women:" 1. Diagnosticians whose role solely is to do diagnosis – in this case diagnosis includes a statement of the source (etiology) of the problem and identification of the remedy, usually a particular healing ceremony; 2. herbalists whose sole function is to prescribe herbs; and, 3. the chanter or *hatathli* who presides over particular healing ceremonials. The boundaries between these three types of practitioner often overlap to some degree. The role of the *hatathli*, however, can never be taken over by one of the other two categories of practitioners since one has to be "certified" to perform given ceremonials after years of apprenticeship to an older medicine man/woman who is a practitioner of the given ceremonial. Typically, a given medicine man/woman performs only two or three "minor" ceremonies and/or one major ceremonial. I will not endeavor to present here a comprehensive overview of the complex structure and details of Navajo healing. To do so would be like trying to give a detailed overview of psychiatry, endocrinology, or orthopedic surgery. For a more detailed discussion of Navajo healing, see Sandner, 1979.
4 The medicine man often has a number of others skills at his disposal such as the use of sweats, osteopathic/chiropractic-like manipulation, visualization, ethnobotany, and psychoanalytic-psychotherapeutic skills, among others. However, this would require more complex discussion than can be engaged here.
5 Erskine, 1994: 7, 20–21; Piontelli, 1987; Piontelli, 1992; Tustin, 1992: 130–133; Winnicott, 1975: 182–189, 248. Also see the work of Daniel J. Siegel on attachment, which points to intrauterine trauma as a possible source of manifest dysfunction in later life (Siegel, 1999: 67–120).
6 One medicine man who works in a community mental health clinic by day and practices as a traditional Navajo medicine man at night and on weekends, asked me how one can fit these kinds of Navajo condition/illness to the DSM-IV. I responded that if I tried to do that it would probably make me crazy.
7 In my experience this statement is true even of those Navajos who are western trained and educated. There are some exceptions that I have encountered, but very few.
8 The healing ceremonials are called "chantways" because the core unifying theme of each is the chanting and invocation of the prayers, blessing and mythological themes and figures (the Holy People), by the medicine man who is known in Navajo, as an *hatathli*, the Navajo word for "chanter." The length and complexity of the many ceremonials vary. A few can be done in 40 minutes to an hour. Some may last nine days and nine nights.
9 Sandner, 1979: Chapter 3, 41–78.

10 Gorman, 1971.

11 It is important too to remember here that not only are we translating from one language to another (Navajo to English), but we are also bridging oral tradition and the written form of language which are structurally and psychically different. Navajo language is metaphorical in structure. There are layers within layers of meaning in the language.

12 Actually, if we are true to Navajo psychic and language structure here, we would say, "female (not feminine) power" – just as they acknowledge male and female rain, for example.

13 The splitting of mind and body in western medicine was also, of course, a positive development in the evolution of modern allopathic medicine. Among many benefits deriving from this split are the medical specialty of modern psychiatry as well as the numerous specialty fields within physical medicine. The question always remains one of tradeoffs and ultimate losses due to overspecialization. The challenge today is how to retain the major gains in psychiatry while compensating for narrowness due to overspecialization. (See footnote #12.)

14 With regard to the use of the term "mental health" in the context of western medicine, I include all those disciplines, including non-medical disciplines, that focus on mental health treatment or more broadly speaking psychotherapy in the broad sense of the word. This would include clinical psychology, psychoanalysis, clinical social work, clinical mental health counseling, pastoral counseling, marriage and family counseling, etc., as well as psychiatry.

15 While most of the data involving "talk therapy" have come from the specific field of cognitive therapy, there is a growing body of research involving other psychodynamic modalities such as psychoanalytic-psychotherapy, self psychology, object relations therapy, and the like.

16 Friedman, 2002: D5.

17 Unfortunately, during this same period, psychiatry itself – that branch of allopathic medicine that focuses on mental health – has steadily diminished its focus and training in "psychodynamics," i.e. the art of psychotherapy of one sort or another. Its near-exclusive focus on the development and use of psychotropic drugs to alleviate *symptoms* has had the intended and unintended impact of de facto equation of symptom alleviation with healing of the psyche. Although there is an obvious connection between the two, they are far from synonymous. There seems to have been a blurring of the lines between etiology and symptomatology. As is well known in western medicine, particularly in the field of psychiatry, even more so than in physical medicine, individuals experiencing emotional and psychological discomfort tend to resist seeking treatment until the discomfort associated with their symptoms forces the issue. The Ariadne thread leading to the nature of the healing that the psyche seeks lies in the symptoms that indicate underlying psychological needs and wounds. Symptoms need to be listened to and monitored throughout treatment to assess whether treatment is headed in the direction that the psyche of the individual prescribes. Thus the premature alleviation of all symptoms within the patient can have the unintended effect of blocking or derailing treatment of underlying wounds and trauma. And of course, when symptoms are so intense (e.g. obsessive thinking, panic attacks) that their intrusion blocks psychotherapy, the use of psychotropic medication to contain overly intrusive symptoms may be essential in order to make psychotherapy possible. While psychopharmacology has produced revolutionary advances, and in some cases – it would not be an exaggeration to use the word "miraculous" – it has also had the effect of squelching the highly developed art of psychodynamic psychotherapy.

18 See the works of Damasio, 1999, Levine, 1997, Schore, 1994, Siegel, 1999, Stern, 1985, and Whitmont, 1993, among others.
19 Smith, 2001: 61. I wish to thank Donald Kalsched for acquainting me with this aphorism by Huston Smith.
20 From my point of view, the greater and more imminent threat to Navajo healing was evident when I first visited the reservation in 1971 because *the language* was dying. The US government through the agency of the dreaded Bureau of Indian Affairs (BIA) forbade the speaking and the teaching of Navajo language as well as its religion and culture – oral, not written systems. It is when the language dies that there is no hope for survival of the integrity of the culture. Beginning in the late 1980s, the teaching of Navajo religion, language, history, and culture has been mandatory in all schools on the reservation. Because of the Navajo culture's unique ability to adapt to alien cultures, the use of penicillin or any aspect of western medicine would not necessarily threaten their traditional medicine.
21 The Washington D.C. Office of the Navajo Nation, Vital Records Office.
22 This trait has been no minor sore point with other native tribes such as the Hopi. Navajo crafts people have become quite adept at carving *kachina* dolls, archetypal sacred figures of the Hopi people. Navajo carvers became a real economic threat to Hopi doll carvers. A few years ago, the Navajo Nation agreed, after much pressure, to identify Navajo carved dolls as such.

Chapter 14

Clinical adaptations between Navajo and western healing approaches: Bridging the mind–body split

> The intuitive mind is a sacred gift and the rational mind is a faithful servant. We have created a society that honors the servant and has forgotten the gift.
>
> Albert Einstein

> Imagination is an act born of the body. It arises out of a matrix of confusion and disorder. Faith, rather than mastery of understanding, is its midwife.[1]

> Trauma is not, will not, and can never be fully healed until we also address the essential role played by the body.[2]

> The point is that, for every scientific "discovery," there may exist one or more alternative ways of understanding natural processes. But we can't know what these alternatives are until we absolutely reject the idea of forcing nature to reveal its secrets and instead begin to observe nature and listen to its rhythms.[3]

In approaching this chapter, the reader should bear in mind that Borderland features in individuals are virtually always mixed with/accompanied by pathological features. I have emphasized that differentiating Borderland features from pathological features is essential[4] to avoid pathologizing non-pathological contents in the therapy, which inevitably wounds the patient. By differentiating the two, it brings pathological elements into a clearer perspective for both the patient and the therapist, enabling more direct and less defended focus on those dimensions of the therapy.

It is always more comfortable to have clear categories when reading clinical material. In the material that follows, however, I will sometimes be talking about Borderland contents and pathological contents *as if* they were separate and distinct. The reader should bear in mind that this is seldom the case. We will always be discussing them in the context of endeavoring to differentiate the one from the other.

Clinical links: The transference dynamic

There is much that is different between Navajo healing and western-based clinical psychology. One significant difference is the nature of the "transference" dynamic in the clinical relationship. In western psychology, the transference and countertransference are seen as interpersonal. They are the result of a dynamic tension between two people – the patient and the therapist.

In Navajo medicine, however, the medicine man is not the therapist per se. Rather he is the facilitator and mediator of the transference. Here the transference is between the patient and what Jung called the Self, externally represented and portrayed in the drama of the healing ceremony itself, a drama that is wholly based in the symbolic and archetypal representation of unconscious contents of the patient's psyche. The medicine man mediates and directs that transference relationship but, unlike the western therapist, he is simultaneously outside it.[5] In western culture, there is nothing comparable with this transference dynamic as it takes place in Navajo medicine.

However, when considering *Jungian*-based clinical approaches there are critical points of convergence – the three most prominent are:

1. The archetypal/symbolic approach to healing.
2. A dynamic metaphor of transformation such as alchemy, which was Jung's primary metaphor in the healing process.[6]
3. The primacy of archetypal dynamics in the transference.

In *Jung and Searles: A Comparative Study*, David Sedgwick highlights the differences in theoretical stance between Jung and Harold F. Searles, Searles representing a more classical psychoanalytic standpoint. Sedgwick observes:

> [The] Jungian notion of a union via symbols . . . places the dynamic emphasis somewhat beyond the actual transference relationship, which now seems to be the support or ground rather than the direct focus of treatment. In [other psychoanalytic] theory, the relationship between client and therapist is always the center of the transformation . . .
>
> Whereas for Searles [and more traditional psychoanalytic schools] the synthesis of the client's fragmented personality first occurs in another person (the analyst), for Jung it is mediated by symbols. Because it happens in the therapist, [therapists] must postulate a re-introjection or identification by the client with the wholeness seen in the therapist. *Jung's theory does not need this step: the remediation theoretically is happening already via the symbol. Furthermore, this is the only way it can occur in Jung's system, because the unified "third" thing is by nature transcendent.[7] It can only be suggested by an image approximating the unknown reality.[8]*
>
> [Emphasis added.]

And:

> [T]he "impersonal" nature of Jungian introjects means that they are only
> to a minimal extent composed of personal, repressed elements (images,
> feelings).[9]

And finally:

> Jung's focus is also on what is happening in the unconscious, as mediated
> by these symbols . . .[10]
>   Jung's alchemical reference point is still farther away [from more trad-
> itional psychoanalytic theoretical stances]. His presentation is not
> grounded in a human relationship at all, but in a ritualistic, archaic
> science.[11] Still, all this is in accord with Jung's view of the unconscious
> as a non-personal acquisition.[12]

Transculturally and psychodynamically speaking, these aspects of Jung's
conception of the transference leaves us at the threshold of the "transference"
dynamic as it manifests in the context of Navajo medicine.

Navajo clinical context

In an earlier discussion (Chapter 13, footnote #3) I have referenced three
categories of "medicine men": The diagnostician, the herbalist, and the
hatathli. From this point forward when I use the term medicine man it will
always reference the *hatathli*, the chanter. For purposes of the clinical discussion to follow, I will be using the context of what is sometimes referred to as
the "major" Navajo healing ceremonials. These are the longer, more complex
ceremonies, which employ the full panoply of Navajo clinical tools and
skills. Since the ceremony with which I am personally most familiar is the
"Yei-Bi-Chai" ceremony – one that lasts nine days and nine nights – it will
represent the clinical context and framework through which the following
material is presented. It is not necessary for the reader to be familiar with this
ceremonial in order to understand the clinical material that follows.[13]
   The Yei-Bi-Chai ceremony takes place within, and in the area immediately
surrounding, a medicine *hogan* specifically constructed for the occasion. The
hatathli presides over and personally directs every aspect of the entire nine
days and nine nights of the ceremony. Although there are many components
of the ceremony, such as various purification rites, sweats, emetics, medicinal
herbs, etc., the centerpiece of the ceremony is the very elaborate and highly
detailed recounting and enactment of a central myth from Navajo cosmology.
This is done in chant by the *hatathli* over a period of several days, and is
enacted by variously masked and costumed figures representing the mythological figures in the story. To say that these individuals are (merely) masked

and dressed to represent these mythological figures in the drama is mislead-
ing. *Every* detail, *every* participant, and every part of their dress is ritually
sacralized so as to carry the numinous qualities of the archetypal figures *and
context* that they incarnate.

During the sixth, seventh, and eighth days of the Yei-Bi-Chai ceremonial
there are sand painting rituals, which will be discussed later in this chapter.
On the seventh and eighth days there are masked dancers and singers performing the various chants and holy songs associated with the mythic core of
the ceremonial. The drama and intensity (and sleeplessness) build over the
nine days and nights, culminating in the last night when the rituals, chants,
singing, and dances take place without cessation until dawn.[14]

It is of note, and will be discussed further in this chapter, that this event is
attended by as many as 200 or more people. The patient's immediate and
extended family are almost always present as well as clan relatives. Any member of the community who wishes to attend may do so on the last two nights
of the ceremony. Many bring food and other tokens of support for the patient
and for the event. On the last evening of the ceremony, the entire assemblage
is fed by the family of the patient.

The Self and the *hatathli*

I will be using primarily Jungian clinical concepts to build a bridge from
Navajo clinical practice to western clinical practice. Jung's concept of the Self
is the primary psychic construct from which all other personality structures
(ego, shadow, anima, animus, persona) emanate. It contains all the unconscious identity of the individual and, in conjunction with secondary processes
(i.e. outer influences), shapes the emerging ego identity of the individual. The
Self is a "conscious unconscious," aware of itself, and one that knows more
about the individual than he/she knows about it. Within it lies the blueprint
of the character and personality make-up – the psychic genes – of the individual. It is also the agent for psyche/soma connection in the individual.
Unlike the concept of the self in other psychological modalities, Jung defines
the Self as the organ through which the individual maintains connection to
the transpersonal dimension and the collective unconscious, however
unconscious or conscious that connection may be.

Thus it is through the Self that the individual connects to the archetypal
realm, and it is through the Self that this realm influences the individual.
From the standpoint of analytical psychology, the "prescription" of what
constitutes health for the individual comes from the Self; it is not prescribed
by the therapist.[15] The therapist acts more in the role of a kind of midwife,[16]
guided by the patient's manifest content that he/she brings to the sessions, as
well as his/her unconscious content through dreams, fantasies, somatic realizations and symptoms, and by the transference–countertransference process
in the therapeutic work.

What we are describing here is a therapeutic process that relies as much, if not more, on intuition and feeling as it does on thinking and analysis. It recognizes synchronicity as a valid parameter of experience as well as trans-rational dimensions of psychic experience such as dreams, intuitions, and waking fantasies.

From the standpoint of Navajo medicine, the *hatathli* can be viewed as an embodied linking/guiding function of the Self of the patient. In addition, as the Navajo medicine man, Johnson Dennison, points out, "balancing the individual, heals the world." From this standpoint, the *hatathli* is also the intermediary for healing the collective or objective psyche through the agent of the patient.

Typically, a diagnostician makes the formal diagnosis of the etiology of the patient's illness. Based on the determination of the etiology of that illness, the appropriate healing ceremony can be prescribed. The *hatathli* determines the specific ceremony (treatment) called for, sets the parameters for the cere-mony, presides over all rituals and "treatments," calls forth the Holy People associated with the particular ceremony, selects and presides over the making of the necessary sand paintings, and is the singer of the chants, songs, and invocations.[17] He is in every sense the link between the archetypal realm – the mythological drama that is invoked on behalf of the patient's healing – and the patient. He presides over the enactment of that drama, which calls forth those archetypal figures and the powers they represent in incarnated form. Thus the entire healing ceremony is a direct link to the cosmological roots of the Navajo people and invokes their collective spirit and libido on behalf of the patient.[18,19] (See Plates 2, 3, and 4.)

Clinical implications

In classical psychoanalytic and psychoanalytic-psychotherapy models clini-cians are taught to respect and gradually work through the defenses of the patient. This is necessary so as not to trigger massive resistance, even unconsciously, to the work by the patient and to not inadvertently open up areas of pathology not previously evident to the therapist or for which the patient's ego is not adequately prepared to address. Psychological defenses develop as an essential protection of the individual's psyche.[20] This is one of the reasons why psychotherapy can take such a long time (and psychoanalysis even longer). And indeed it *is* important with many patients to do just that – respect their defenses.[21]

In the case of the *hatathli* and his patient, consideration of defenses is left outside the healing context. They are neither dealt with nor rejected. Once the diagnosis is made and the ceremony prescribed, *everything* that occurs from beginning to end is contained within the mythological content (the story) of the ceremonial itself. The ego–self axis is enacted in the externalized *temenos*[22] of the healing ceremony itself. The patient is thus simultaneously

Plate 2 Traditional Navajo *hogan*.

Plate 3 Navajo medicine man, Ronald Brown, and apprentices.

Plate 4 Navajo medicine man, Johnson Dennison, gathering plant medicine.

both witness to, and beneficiary of, the transformative process of the ceremonial.[23]

The great need of Borderland personalities is to have their connection to nature and transrational reality validated, not analyzed, not interpreted – simply witnessed. Since these dimensions of their reality result from a connection to the self that is less filtered through their (western) ego, that link tends to sit outside their ego defenses. In the clinical context, it is not the therapist's acknowledgment of the Borderland connection that is threatening, it is the patient's anticipation of the therapist's rejection of it and worse, pathologizing it, that is defended against. Paradoxically in respecting those defenses, it is the therapist's caution that sometimes heightens them – particularly if this caution is accompanied by analysis and interpretation. In my experience, therapeutic interventions that go directly to Borderland traits without interpretation and without addressing a patient's defenses do not tend to set off resistance, neither do they inadvertently set off areas of pathology disruptive to the therapeutic process. Indeed, addressing Borderland traits directly helps differentiate pathological and nonpathological components of the individual's personality. This differentiation process often is diagnostic: *Those contents that tend to be consistently and highly defended are likely to be pathological contents; whereas those transrational contents that consistently tend to be not defended are likely to be Borderland components.* Differentiating out Borderland traits renders pathological elements more discernible and therefore more accessible to treatment. Typically, once the Borderland dimension of the patient's personality has been witnessed, it heightens trust in the transference and, in my experience, the patient tends to be less defended around his/her pathological features. In my work with Hannah, once we had established a pattern where she consistently felt witnessed around her *Borderland* reality, many of her Border*line* features seemed to melt. This was her subjective experience as well as my observation.

With regard to individuals who have been the victims of trauma, the classical analytical model of working through the defensive structure of the patient "on the way to" addressing the core trauma itself usually is counterproductive and is contraindicated. Too often this approach will re-activate the trauma, derailing the therapy and in extreme cases, seriously damaging the therapeutic relationship, as well as re-traumatizing the patient. When the therapist is perceived as trying to access the core trauma wound, patients sometimes tend to naively drop their defenses – as they did as a child – thus opening themselves to re-traumatization. And, too often, an unaware therapist inadvertently walks into that space of naive trust, mistaking it for grounded trust in the transference, triggering the core trauma and re-traumatizing the patient. In my experience, the trauma core should virtually never be directly accessed in the therapy. The therapy should focus on *the field* attendant to the trauma core.[24] In this manner the therapist can witness *the fact* of the trauma incident(s) and the attendant emotional trauma while not treading on the wound itself. Abreaction, which is used to bring unconscious material into direct consciousness of, and expression by, the patient, in almost all instances is contraindicated.

It is very difficult for the therapist to monitor the trauma field as described above. I have found that the process is best achieved through the monitoring of bodily reactions – the body of the patient and/or the body of the therapist – through the psychodynamic of projective identification.[25] In this process the therapist relates to the patient through the agency of the Self, from deep within his own psychic core, opening himself up to the unconscious processes of the patient. It permits an experience as if the therapist and the patient were merging across the boundary that typically separates the therapist and the patient, while at the same time permitting the therapist to maintain a separate stance outside the merged field as observer and monitor. It is akin to reading the body via telepathy. Focusing on communications emanating from the patient's body through picking up micro-subtle body movements in conjunction with the use of projective identification, can be quite effective in monitoring patient anxiety and defenses. In this manner the therapist can know when the process is too intrusive, too rapid, or getting too close to the trauma core. Peter Levine, leading trauma researcher and the developer of a technique called "somatic experiencing," observes:

Trauma is traditionally regarded as a psychological and medical disorder of the mind ... for thousands of years, oriental and shamanic healers have recognized not only that the mind affects the body, as in psycho-somatic medicine, but how every organ system of the body equally has a psychic representation in the fabric of the mind. Recent revolutionary developments in neuroscience and psycho-neuro-immunology have established solid evidence of the intricate two-way communication between mind and body. In identifying complex "neuro-peptide messengers," researchers like Candice Pert have discovered many pathways by which mind and body mutually communicate. This leading-edge research echoes what ancient wisdom has always known: that each organ of the body, including the brain, speaks its own "thoughts," "feelings," and "promptings," and listens to those of all the others.[26]

Levine says that trauma can never be adequately healed without considering the central role of the body. The above quote gives a western conceptual overlay to what Navajo medicine has known and practiced over the course of centuries.

Taking another step closer to the Navajo model, Donald Kalsched points out that in the case of trauma, the wound implicates the Self more than it does the ego, leaving the ego to defend not only against perceived external threat but against the Self which has become an agent of survival, i.e. an archaic defense instead of a guide. Thus, trauma disrupts the Self's healthy function of being the most informed and sagacious ally on behalf of the total being of the individual. He sums up this point well when he says:

[T]he ... optimistic understanding of the Self must be modified by an understanding of what happens in the inner world when trauma interrupts normal "incarnational" processes. With trauma, the Self has no chance for transmuting humanization and thus remains archaic. The Self then appears in the form of radical opposites which are at war with one another; good vs. bad, love vs. hate, healing vs. destruction. This way of understanding brings Jungian theory into line with object-relations, with the important addition of Jung's awareness of the numinous dimension of the Self's archaic dynamisms on the one hand, and their mythological equivalents on the other.[27]

Speaking of myth, Kalsched goes on to say that: "These great archetypal stories give us rich imagery about the process through which the Self unifies and becomes incarnate in history ... That is to say, it is only in the life of the individual that these great archetypal dynamisms can integrate."[28] That is precisely the role played by the *hatathli* in Navajo healing ceremonials. Because the Self's "normal incarnational processes" have broken down in the patient, a return to his/her mythological origins through a *participation mystique* within the safety of the healing ceremony is necessary, to reconnect with the archetypal dynamics of his/her developmental origins. The *hatathli* serves as ally and guide in a process of re-ordering and re-balancing the individual through a re-ordering of the mythological world, and a re-ordering of the world, through a re-balancing of the patient. In Jungian terms the ceremony invokes the transcendent function. The *hatathli*, in this context, is its agent.

Story as clinical tool

The chanting of myth in ceremonial context is one of the oldest forms of medicine known. In the context of Navajo medicine, the healing ceremonials invoke the origins of life *in the now* and with it the archetypal figures and all of the power and mana associated with them – all of it constellated on behalf of the patient.[29]

In the western clinical context, of course, we do not have ceremonial *hogans*, *hatathlis*, and the like. We *do* have the weekly ritual of coming to the therapist, rites of entry into the clinical space, and other subtle rituals attendant to the clinical process. Neither do we have origins myths per se.[30] However, from an existential standpoint, all individuals are born in the context of unique patterns of archetypal influence and characterological definition. The notion that one is born with an identity and character already in tact at the moment of birth is consistent with Jung's concept of the Self.[31] As we emerge into our being, into our unique personality, we become revealed to ourselves. That "revelation," in its fundamentals, emerges from that origin story with which we are born.

I do not mean here that each individual is handed a kind of archetypal script at birth. I do mean that some individuals appear to be influenced by particular archetypal energies seemingly independent, and even in spite of, environmental and genetic inheritance. All of us are familiar with the family member whose nature appears to come from "beyond," whose personality and behavior in no way resembles anyone familiar, present or past, in the family constellation. Likewise there are individuals who seem "driven" by forces beyond themselves to become someone, e.g. priest, healer, leader, without seeming support either from social environmental or genetic factors. Jung alludes to this when he observes:

> [T]ranspersonal contents are not just inert or dead matter that can be annexed at will. Rather they are living entities which exert an attractive force upon the conscious mind . . .[32]
>
> We shall probably get nearest to the truth if we think of the conscious and personal psyche as resting upon the broad basis of an inherited and universal psychic disposition which is, as such, unconscious . . .[33]
>
> One of the essential features of the child motif is its futurity. The child is potential future . . . In the individuation process, it anticipates the

future that comes from the synthesis of conscious and unconscious elements in the personality . . .[34]

Myth . . . emphasizes . . . that the "child" is endowed with superior powers . . . The "child" is born out of the womb of the unconscious, begotten out of the depths of human nature, or rather out of living nature herself. It is a personification of vital forces quite outside the limited range of our conscious mind . . . a wholeness which embraces the very depths of nature. It represents the strongest, the most ineluctable urge in every being, namely the urge to realize itself.[35]

In the case of Borderland personalities who have arrived at that dimension through the personality structure and evolution portals, the personal story that they bring with them into this life is one of living in a Borderland realm. That is their original story, their personal "Genesis," with which they entered this world. Their "wound" is that the culture at large and the people most important to them do not accept the reality of their story and they feel compelled to hide their "origins story" and to go along with the collective story of the culture *as if* it were their personal story. The collective story *is* the story of the world in which they live. However that story is secondary to their personal Borderland reality, which they are forced to hide.

Clinically, this picture becomes complicated when the therapist cannot recognize Borderland reality and the therapist and the therapy devolve into the kind of resistance that the individuals experience in their outer life.[36] On the other hand, when the therapist does recognize and witness the Borderland reality of the patient, the recognition has a powerful healing effect similar to the numinous experience of the Navajo patient, whose personal mythological origin is portrayed right in front of his eyes in ceremonials.[37] The western patient then "comes out of hiding" in the therapy, and his Borderland reality becomes a matter of course in the treatment, as opposed to an issue. This reality takes its central and routine place along with the rest of the patient's life, as an integral part of his story. Clinically, it is as if a field of obstructing overgrowth has been cleared away so that the patient's pathological features and content can come into view and can be more readily focused on by both therapist and patient.

In the case of individuals who encounter the Borderland realm through the trauma portal, the clinical picture is more complicated. They too have come into the world with their "origins story" in place at birth. However, the impact of their traumatic experience(s) overlays a new and powerfully charged story – a trauma story – which, because of its impact on the self, takes on numinosity *as if* it were their "origins story." The fact that, as Kalsched points out, this shifts the self's energies from individuation to archaic defense, tends to leave the individual cut off from his pre-trauma "origins story" with which he came into the world *as if it never had existed*. Indeed, most trauma victims have no sense that they carry an encapsulated pre-trauma origins myth as a personal archetypal existential story.

One man in his late 40s, with whom I worked for nine years and who suffered from severe posttraumatic stress syndrome (PTSD), about three years into the work one day walked into my office and began the session by saying, "I think I need a new story for my life." When I asked him what he meant, he said that he had no idea where that statement came from or why he said it. When I asked him to imagine what a new life story might be, he could not. He could only offer that the one he was living was pretty "fucked up," and it made his life a nightmarish misery. We did not return to the theme of his story until six years later in his analysis.

Then, in the ninth year of our work, after we had incrementally reduced the frequency of our sessions from four a week to two and were about to reduce to one session per week, he had the following dream:

> I awoke in the morning to the sound of the doorbell. I was naked. I went to the door anyway. It was the postman. He had a special delivery letter for which I had to sign. He made me produce my driver's license as I.D. saying that he could deliver the letter only to . . . [name] who lives at . . . [address]. I signed for the letter.
>
> When I opened it, the letterhead was a symbol of my astrological sign. The letter said: "Your work has entitled you to know: For the first ten years of your life your primary parents were animals in the forest. The human parents you had were your secondary parents. Your animal parents protected you from your human parents. You are strong enough. It is time for you to be weaned."

This dream came to this man, the first of three children, after his obsessive thought patterns and compulsive behaviors were controlled sufficiently through a combination of medication and cognitive behavioral and psychoanalytic psychotherapy, to enable him to relate to his trauma story as a real but inauthentic statement about the reality of his life. Or to put it another way, the therapeutic work had been successful in enabling him to see that the trauma story that he had been living was in fact an overlay burying a more personal and authentic story *and that the trauma story came externally from sources outside of himself* and therefore was inauthentic as his personal origins myth. It was his *experience* of the trauma – his interpretation of his own suffering – but it was not his existential "origins story," the source of which is transpersonal.

This man's trauma resulted from very hostile and life-threatening emotional abandonment beginning at birth by a probably psychotic mother. The severity of his trauma was such that he could not trust his very clear images of a nurturing mother in his later life. Thus the dream reveals his psyche had reached into the Borderland realm for nonhuman parents – animals.[38] These encapsulated archetypal nurturers, unbeknownst to him, had carried him into his full adulthood and protected his sanity, thus enabling him to survive and function. It was only then, towards the end of our work, when his psyche determined he was ready, that it revealed a piece of his pre-trauma origins myth. The dream was explicit: A threshold had been crossed and he was on the way towards more fully realizing this other "origins story" that he had not known existed. His newly discovered "origins story" now was carrying more valence psychologically than the trauma story. But, and crucially, it was now necessary for him to embrace his "origins story" by *choosing* to be weaned. His ego must consciously embrace, choose to live by his "origins story" and reject the trauma story which had been overlain on it.

The dream also prescribed an essential part of the next phase of the clinical work: He had to give up the comfort of being suckled, of being dependent, and wanting to be taken care of. This latter included the comforting role that supportive psychotherapy had played in his life over the past several years. Apparently, the dream was stimulated, in part, by the movement towards fewer sessions and the imminent change from two to one session per week. His psyche was telling him that it was time to take care of himself.

Kalsched cautions that trauma victims "will [often] present themselves as innocent victims seeking support, but they are really unconsciously engineering self-damaging situations that they inwardly enjoy. Until they realize this and break the self-destructive pattern, supportive psychotherapy will not help them."[39] It is precisely at this point – when a threshold has been crossed and the therapist has the relief of knowing that now *the patient himself* knows that the trauma story is inauthentic as his "origins story" – that both therapist and patient are at risk. The therapist cannot afford to let down his vigilance about the vestigial parts of the trauma defense as a kind of trickster energy that waits patiently in the background until defenses are down and then pounces to reinvigorate the trauma story.[40] This in fact did happen with this patient several times in our work, including after the patient had this dream.

In my experience, one way of guarding against a resurgence of this dynamic, once the threshold has been crossed from the archaic inner world of the trauma to the patient's living out his more authentic "origins story", is to reduce the frequency of the therapy to the minimal number of sessions necessary to address the specific work at hand. In the case of this patient, it was the number of sessions needed to focus on learning to wean himself, i.e. to take care of himself as a self-reliant adult – how to live in the world operating out of his "origins story" rather than his trauma story – and learning new behaviors. In addition, I would caution sparsity with regard to empathy – particularly when the patient comes into the session reciting his miseries because of his internal conflicts. Trauma victims can become quite adept at manipulating empathy, which is counterproductive in this context. The therapist can be supportive without being overly empathic. Sometimes empathy is perverted into an incentive for the patient to remain in therapy beyond what is indicated and necessary. In this context it can become an incentive to regress before the patient gets well enough to "have to" leave the therapy and the therapist (and the therapist's empathy).

In the case of trauma victims in particular, once this threshold has been crossed and sufficiently integrated by the patient, I think the model of periodic ceremonies employed in Navajo medicine would work well with trauma victims in the western clinical context. In the context of the Navajo medical model this would be a ceremonial every few months or years, as needed. The nature of the specific ceremony would go from the more "major" and elaborate ceremonial to the less complex and shorter ceremonials. In the western clinical model, viewing the therapy session as a form of ceremonial, this would mean periodic sessions anywhere from several times a year to, ultimately, a handful (five or fewer). This approach would tend to reduce the risk that the ritual of the therapy would regress into a repetition compulsion more characteristic of earlier stages of the therapeutic work. The focus of these sessions would be for the patient to have a *temenos* (not unlike the specially constructed medicine *hogan* of the Navajos) to which he could return to recite parts of his "origins story" as it continues to reveal itself to him, i.e. to discuss and witness the non-traumatic/healing/healed aspects of his life. The role of the therapist would be a combination of ceremonial witness/authenticator and mythological technician assisting the individual to differentiate those parts of his "origins story" that are still contaminated by his archaic trauma story.

The body

As previously noted, the work of Peter Levine stresses the need for tracking the body in the treatment of trauma patients, focusing on the neurological imprinting and body memory of the trauma. Because the study of the neuropsychological aspects of trauma is a relatively new field, the treatment of trauma *can* remain split between psyche and soma, i.e. when psychological treatment and neurophysiological work are not done by the same practitioner. The nature of the transference is crucial here. By definition, depth (psychoanalytic) work, of the nature described in Kalsched's book, takes the transference process to the deepest and most primitive levels of the psyche. At the same time, when the transference relationship is secure, it is often possible for the patient to obtain needed body work from a separate practitioner specialist as an extension of the transference relationship with the analyst.[41] This would not necessarily constitute a split. In all cases, there is some risk of "splitting" when more than one practitioner is involved. I have found the risk of splitting significantly lower in cases involving trauma once a secure transference attachment is in place.

As Levine stresses, no treatment of trauma can be sufficient without focus on the body. The figurative "threshold" described above could be an efficacious point for initiating body work as an adjunct therapy along with the psychotherapy. Obviously "efficacious" timing in this regard is variable and depends on each patient and each treatment. Since most trauma victims begin their treatment with a psychotherapist, initiation of body work should take place when the patient is ready to work with another practitioner while continuing his psychotherapy.[42] "Readiness" in this context would be when the patient is secure in his relationship with the psychotherapist and sufficiently trusting to engage in adjunct therapy with a second therapist.

There is one further consideration with trauma victims and their "story." Many trauma victims experience their trauma in childhood prior to ages 6 to 7, when living in a Borderland-like dimension is a normal developmental state. When trauma takes place before their natural developmental process takes them beyond the Borderland realm (see Part 2a in Figure 7.1) at ages 6 to 7, these children tend to remain with the Borderland dimension as a fixed part of their personality and psychic experience. This tends to be true even if treatment of their childhood trauma is highly successful. The question poses itself then as to how "authentic" their Borderland existence is.

Witnessing as clinical tool

One of the key differences between the western and Navajo medical models is that the Navajo incorporates witnessing as a clinical dynamic. *All* aspects of the healing ceremonial are attended by witnesses. Some elements of the ceremonial are carried out in relative privacy inside the medicine hogan. Some, as described above, are performed in the immediate vicinity outside of the medicine *hogan* and, as in the case of the last night of the Yei-Bi-Chai ceremony, this portion of the rite is attended by as many as 200 or more people. Usually all or parts of the ceremony are attended by witnesses – from the two or three family and or clan relatives who attend the more "private" parts of the ceremonial inside the *hogan* to those standing outside the *hogan* after the sand painting rite on the eighth day, when the medicine man and the patient go into the *hogan* for a "private" rite, to the scores of people who attend the dances and songs on the last night of the ceremony. All are witnesses – for the rite and for the patient. In Navajo way the mana that is constellated by the presence of these witnesses is part of the energy that heals the patient along with the various rites and medicines of the ceremonial itself. And since the ceremony calls forth the Holy People of Navajo cosmology and incarnates that part of their origins myth in the ceremonial, all present benefit from the healing energies that these archetypal figures and enactments constellate, witnesses as well as patient.

Since Navajos are never not connected to the transpersonal dimension of existence and their cosmological roots, these witnesses, members of the community in which the patient lives, carry with them those connections that have been reinvigorated by the ceremonial. Thus the power does not end with the final rites of the ceremonial. These psychic links are present in direct and subtle ways when the patient returns to his community and is surrounded by individuals who were witnesses at his healing ceremony. They serve as symbolic reminders, and continue to reflect the power and mana of the ceremony for weeks and months after the event itself. Ann Belford Ulanov, a Jungian analyst in practice in New York City and author of numerous books and articles on the link between spirituality and psychology, says, "All of us depend on someone to mediate the world to us. And, then, we each need to develop our own personal relationship to what is mediated . . . We need to be witnessed to feel real."[43]

John Welwood, a clinical psychologist and psychotherapist and a leading figure in bringing eastern and western psychology together, says that, "The core wound we all suffer from is the disconnection from our own being."[44] In the case of Borderland personalities, however, often it is the opposite. The core wound for them is not having their Borderland reality witnessed and valued by others. As I discussed in previous chapters, many experience that wound as devastating – so much so that they have chosen to live parallel lives within the culture and with their loved ones. They are emotionally forced to live as if they lived a reality other than the one they know and value most profoundly. That is why the mother in her 40s who, after reading my Borderland piece in *The Salt Journal*, used the phrase, "I decided to *come out* to my son" in deciding to share with her 20-year-old son some of her deepest experiences as a Borderland personality during his developmental years.

This wound is not just the personal loneliness of not being witnessed by the important people in our lives. For some, it is also the loneliness of being given one of God's splendid secrets – and feeling forbidden to speak of it with another. Sometimes it is the awesomeness of beauty that is the more difficult to hold in silence.[45] For others, holding God's secret in silence *is* the awesome beauty. For them, that silence, the secret, is their contentment. For some, the Borderland represents a terrible secret. Their experience is inexplicably frightening, seemingly without point. Theirs is a loneliness of a different kind.

"Witnessing" is one of those "obvious" psychodynamics that most of us nod our heads to and don't think much about. In developmental psychology we talk about how the mother mirrors the child (I would say that she is witnessing the Self in the child, in the Jungian sense, as well as mirroring the child's behavior and being) and how central and indispensable this mirroring relationship is to healthy ego development and overall psychological well-being.

I was Hannah's essential witness in authenticating her Borderland reality. She knew that reality, lived it, and even fought for it. But she did not have emotional and psychological title to it. That required an authenticating witness. There had been no one there for her to witness that reality; she could not witness for herself. The need to be witnessed is true of every Borderland person whom I have encountered. For most, it is their core need.

From a clinical perspective, it is helpful to differentiate witnessing for those whose access to Borderland reality was other than the trauma portal from those who entered through the trauma portal.

Other than trauma portals – evolution and personality

Synchronistically, while I was in the process of drafting this section on witnessing, I received an unsolicited email from someone I had never heard of. I shall call her Kristin and with her permission, present below her email in its entirety:

Dear Mr. Bernstein,
Recently I was reading a book by the name of *The Tao of Equus*. As I'm sure you know, the author discusses your discovery of people you call "Borderland Personalities". When I read this, I was brought to tears. I felt that there was someone out there who could actually understand my thoughts and feelings related to the natural world and its spirit within. I immediately researched your name on the web. Again I was very moved when I read your article "On the Borderland". I found mention of the fact that you have a book coming out by the name of *Listening to the Borderland: Differentiating the Pathological from the Sacred*. Has this book been published yet? I have looked everywhere I can think of and can't find it. If it has been published, do you know where I can get a copy? I believe your book would be such a comfort to me. I have always been intrigued by Jungian Psychology as well as Native American spiritual views because of their respect for nature.

"Hannah" is a very fortunate person to have found someone like you with your compassion, insight and wisdom. As you mentioned, people who feel this connection with nature are usually seen by our society as crazy. I have never understood this overwhelming sadness I feel over our society's mistreatment of animals and the natural world. It eats at my soul. My only explanation was the theory you mentioned called "projection". My mother called it "My cross to bear." It makes it very difficult to lead a normal life. Like many of your patients, I have never found my niche in life. I have gone from job to job and abused alcohol and drugs to numb the sadness. My passion is animals but I can not go into an animal related career because I cannot handle the emotional end of it which makes me feel like such a coward.

Anyway, I don't mean to get off on a tangent. I just wanted to write you and see if your book was available yet and to tell you thank you for doing such heartfelt work.

Sincerely,
[Kristin]

Kristin felt witnessed by the Hannah piece, which she read in the *IONS Review*.[46] It is not possible to know what impact, if any, feeling witnessed after so many years of depression and feeling misunderstood in her therapy might have on a new approach to therapy were she to take one. The essential clinical point here is that for those individuals who live in the Borderland and who were not victims of trauma, witnessing as a psychodynamic can occur readily in the transference as part of the transference–countertransference relationship, in a manner similar to the way it occurs in Navajo medicine.

Witnessing for trauma victims

Psychodynamically speaking, witnessing of trauma victims must take place on a somatic level as well as on a psychological level. For them, the impact of the trauma has the effect of blocking the "object level" of transformation – the interpersonal underpinnings of the transference–countertransference relationship – in the clinical context. In this context, witnessing is pre-transference – or at least, extra-transference. For witnessing to take place, the therapist must stand outside the transference, even while being in the midst of the transference. As I see witnessing, it is the essential first step towards the establishment of trust on the level of the Self. Trust can be readily established on an ego level – actually, more often than not, on the level of the "false self" in D. W. Winnicott's terms.[47] We "work it out" together as patient and therapist. We "know" how it works – or at least how it is *supposed to work*, in terms of the false self. Thus, for trauma victims, authentic trust seldom gets beyond the level of the false self.[48] However, if healing is to take place, trust must reach to the deeper realms of spirit and soul. When we speak of spirit and soul, we must take into account the somatic level of being, since spirit and soul do not operate with a split loyalty to either psyche or soma. Trauma victims hold in encapsulation those dimensions of their story – their trauma experience and the attendant Borderland realities associated with them – waiting to be witnessed so that trust can enter in, and with it, healing at the deepest levels.[49] They relate to their therapists *about* the trauma experience, holding the three-dimensionality of their experience in their encapsulated safe place, watching, waiting, for the authenticating witness who would make it sufficiently safe to reveal their deepest wounds to soul, spirit, and body. Often, because the wounds to their bodies were so profound, in some cases at a pre-verbal stage of development, their memory is held more on a somatic level than on a psychic level. Or more accurately stated, psychological apprehension of the wound must be accessed through somatic memory.

Ironically, in the circumstances described above, oftentimes empathy prevents authenticating witnessing. It tends to keep the therapy fixed at the level of the false self while the soul's yearnings of the authentic Self remain hidden away. The problem with empathy in this context is that empathy depends on understanding and comprehension.[50] Being "understood" is an abstraction for the trauma victim, and at least one step removed from a *knowing* of what soul and spirit have suffered and still suffer. Understanding can satisfy the false self; it cannot satisfy body and soul. Trauma victims *know* that the therapist cannot know the patient's reality, which in almost all instances, *stands outside normative experience* and therefore cannot be "comprehended" by even the most well-trained therapist. Theirs is a unique isolation, and even the suggestion that it can be understood is felt as a violation. Indeed, it is the very concept of "understanding" that is proof to the patient that the therapist cannot know the mystery of his or her profound suffering. For the trauma victim, the therapist's "understanding" is two dimensional and leaves a feeling of being objectified, analyzed, classified, and abandoned.[51] And, in reality, the patient is usually correct. Too often the therapist mistakes understanding for witnessing. In the initial stages of the work with trauma victims, before deeper trust can be established, the patient's trauma can only be witnessed, acknowledged – nothing more. For the therapist to witness the patient's trauma, in my experience the therapist must shut down empathy – even the desire to be empathic. And above all else, he must learn to shut down his mind.[52]

Since, as Kalsched points out, all trauma experience contains an archetypal core, there is always an archetypal and therefore transpersonal dimension to the patient's experience and reality.[53] On the archetypal level, the therapist is a stand-in for an absent God, since the trauma victim (and many Borderland personalities who have not been victims of trauma) feels unwitnessed, if not forsaken, by God.

Notwithstanding the profoundly personal and unique reality of the trauma, there is an *impersonal* dimension to the victims' reality. Although the experience is personal in the extreme, it is outside the realm of any graspable sense of what is human or even real. Their experiences fall into the liminal space between what they know and have experienced and what is unknowable and beyond that which can be experienced. Because of this, their experience is deeply personal and yet is almost always connected to and mediated through the transrational and the transpersonal. Thus authentic witnessing must take place apart from the personality of the therapist because it would otherwise bring a personal dimension into a space where it doesn't belong and where it can only be intrusive.[54] Here the psychoanalytically and psychodynamically oriented therapist cannot be a partner in this process – only an accepted presence. It is a space where, for the trauma victim, feeling is dead (split off).[55] For them there are always the questions – "Did what I experience *really* happen? Was it *really* that bad? Was it my fault?" Too often trauma occurs in the absence of a third party who is not a perpetrator. And even when others may have been present, for a host of reasons they are not available as reliable witnesses, psychologically and emotionally.

As evolutionary process expands the boundaries of the Borderland within the western psyche, more and more people – trauma victims and people who have not been victims of trauma – will experience the Borderland dimension of reality. As clinicians, it would behoove us to think as much in terms of authenticating witnessing as we do in terms of analytic interpretation. Indeed, if we want to engage in the latter effectively, we will have to become more sensitive and more adept at witnessing our patients. That means learning to be more in *our* bodies when we are with our patients and learning to listen through our bodies as much, and sometimes more, than we do with our minds.

Sand painting, dream work, and the mind–body connection

The mythologist, Joseph Campbell, remarked that "a myth is a conscious dream, and an [archetypal] dream is an unconscious myth." The fact that myths deal with eternal (sacred) time and origins – the first stories about the genesis of life and the life of the gods – gives them a timelessness and numinosity in the now that invokes transpersonal healing powers.[56] For the Navajo, this takes place in the form of the telling of the mythic stories and through sand painting rites connected to their cosmology (see Plate 5).[57]

Plate 5 Navajo sand painting.

The Navajo word for sand painting – *iikaah* – means "the place where the gods come and go." And so it is also with archetypal dreams: they are also the place where the gods come and go.

For the Navajo the *temenos* where the sand painting rites occur is in the medicine *hogan*. The sand paintings are made by the medicine man and as many as six to eight helpers near the center of the *hogan*, in front of the altar constructed by the medicine man at the beginning of the healing ceremony. When a given rite calls for a sand painting, it is constructed in this space, whether it be a "major" ceremony like the nine-night ceremony, or whether it be one of much shorter duration (an hour or more). Not all healing ceremonies entail sand paintings. Most of the "major" ceremonials do.

Typically, the process begins by grinding stones of various colors to make the sand. (No artificially colored sand is used.) The paintings can be as large as 10′ by 12′ or larger. Smaller sand paintings are sometimes made for child patients. Often the sand painting is a reproduction of a painting that a hero figure in the chant has obtained from the Holy People on one of his mythic journeys. Sand paintings are identical in nature – from one medicine man to the next – down to the last detail and color. They often take from six to eight hours to construct by several sand painters, so exacting is the care to detail in their construction. The patient does not see the sand painting being made; he is not in the medicine *hogan*. When it is complete and consecrated by the medicine man, the phase of the ceremony begins in which the patient is brought in and sees the sand painting as a whole. Sand paintings remain intact only during this particular part of the ceremony, usually less than an hour; sometimes for as little as 15 minutes. Most are made in the afternoon and destroyed by sunset. Great care is taken in dispersing the sand from the sand painting outside the *hogan* because of the numinous power sand paintings are believed to contain.[58]

A central part of the rite is when the patient is seated in the sand painting itself. Various incantations, prayers, and infusions of herbs and medicines brought by masked figures, as well as other rites are performed while the patient is seated in the painting. The crucial part of the rite that I wish to focus on here takes place at the end of the sand painting ceremony when the sand of the hero figures in the painting is applied onto the body of the patient – sand from the foot of the hero figure(s) to the foot of the patient, torso to torso, arm to arm, head to head. This rite constitutes a direct application of the mana of the mythic hero figures to the body–psyche of the patient – bearing in mind that for the Navajo there is no mind–body split. It is an extraordinary rite to behold. The intensity, solemnity, and obvious respect for the numinous power contained in these sand paintings infuses everyone in the *hogan* with awe. Indeed, very often when the above rite is completed, and a moment before the sand from the painting is removed from the medicine *hogan* and scattered to the winds, it is common practice for others present to scramble forward and apply the sand from the remnants of the sand painting to their own bodies.

One analog for these sand painting rites in the western clinical context is dream analysis. When the therapist enters into the rite of dream analysis with the patient, particularly when the dream symbolism contains archetypal symbols and "story" dynamics, he is engaged in a process similar to the sand painting rite. Dream analysis places great emphasis on meaning; sand painting rites do not emphasize meaning other than the telling/chanting of the mythic story that identifies the patient with the archetypal figures and the drama of the origins myth. The transference of archetypal mana to the patient in the sand painting rite is direct; it is indirect and symbolic in the context of western dream analysis. The sand painting rite is externalized and concrete in process. Dream analysis, although it is not concretized in a similar manner, however, aims at the same goal: the release of archetypal energy within the patient to invoke transpersonal healing dynamics along with object level healing dynamics in the transference.[59] Since there is no mind–body split in Navajo medicine, the sand painting rite impacts the patient on the mind/body level.

And that is the point. In my view, western healing modalities are too accepting of the mind–body split. As Peter Levine puts it:

> The practice of modern medicine and psychology, [gives] lip service to a connection between mind and body . . . The welded unity of body and mind that, throughout time, has formed the philosophical and practical underpinnings of most of the world's traditional healing systems is sadly lacking in our modern understanding and treatment.[60]

Although Levine's focus is specifically on the treatment of trauma, I think his point is well taken for most, if not all, western therapeutic treatment. Analytical psychology as well as other schools of psychology are too comfortable with the symbol and the symbolic as abstraction. Even the focus on meaning as a mental process is overemphasized at the expense of body integration of symbolic content as well as psychic integration. And sometimes, when the body does speak through dream symbols – as in the form of dreams that *directly* address pathology in the body[61] – the therapist may miss the concrete level of the dream (e.g. the presence of undiagnosed cancer) in a process that abstracts the concrete to the detriment of the patient.[62]

It would behoove western practitioners to learn to apply dream content directly to the body of the patient in the therapeutic process. Such an approach would not necessarily entail physical touching of the patient by the therapist. The therapist could employ such techniques as those developed within gestalt psychology to have the patient embody dream content. Techniques such as having the patient role play a dream figure, or to engage in outloud dialogue with a dream figure have been described in the literature of gestalt psychology. On a more subtle level, the therapist can ask the patient to find and point to the place(s) in his body where he feels a given emotion portrayed in a dream. The patient can then be asked to inquire of that part of his body what it has to say. In most instances, the patient will hear/feel the body's answer. Active imagination with *physical* dynamics in a dream (e.g. a dream figure stroking an animal, or the emotion perceived in the eyes of a dream figure) can release powerful archetypal energies within the patient's body/psyche. Suggesting to a patient that something said by an archetypal figure in a dream can be used as a mantra chanted silently and/or out loud, can put the patient in touch with the transpersonal energy associated with the dream symbol outside of the *temenos* of the office. He can bring it to life through the medium of chant. It can, as in the case of most chant, through its resonance at deep levels within the body, put the individual in touch with transcendental transformative processes.

Images of the patient himself in a dream can put the patient in touch with emotion from which heretofore he has been cut off. For example, a dream image might portray unfamiliar great grief and sadness in the patient or perhaps an unknown anger. By using some of the above techniques to identify where that emotion resides in the patient's body, the patient can learn to access that particular emotion outside the *temenos* of the therapeutic setting by touching (patting, stroking) that part of the body (e.g. the heart, the diaphragm, eyes, feet.) And the therapist must be open to the same process in the countertransference. This is what happened to me with Hannah when she was insistent that it was the cows – not her projection onto the cows – that she was feeling. Although *I* did not feel the cows, eventually I came to the place of feeling Hannah's feeling for the cows. This was sufficient for me to witness her reality, which was the turning point in our work. In my experience, the use of projective identification by the therapist through the countertransference can be one of the most powerful tools for monitoring powerful subliminal emotional reactions in the patient.[63]

Certainly I am not suggesting that the symbolic be given up for the concrete. On the contrary, I am suggesting that the power of the symbolic approach can be greatly enhanced by integrating more of the psychotherapeutic process at a body level as well as on a symbolic mental level. This point is dramatically illustrated by an experience that one patient, a man in his early 50s, suffering from posttraumatic stress syndrome, brought to a session. I asked him to write down what he shared with me in the session. What he wrote seems to address what Peter Levine is referring to when he says that: "Each organ of the body, including the brain, speaks its own 'thoughts,' 'feelings,' and 'promptings,' and listens to those of all the others."[64] The patient wrote:

> For the past few weeks I have been having spontaneous . . . I don't know what to call them, perhaps hypnotic images. They just occur – no rhyme or reason, they just occur.

At first I was really frightened of them. They could just happen while I was walking down the street, sometimes at night, but just when they wanted to. They were weird. At first it looked like little worms that were wriggling and kind of reaching for one another. Then, after I got used to them, I realized that they were nerve endings in my brain and sometimes elsewhere in my body. I came to know that because I could *feel* them wriggling in my body. I thought I was going crazy.

But then I realized that the body sensations were comforting, notwithstanding the weirdness of the images. And after a while I kind of learned to watch and feel the feelings in my body. It was healing. I realized that it was healing. My body was healing. That child in me was healing.

After a while, as I realized more and more of the body feelings, some of them felt funny, like a kind of itch like when the skin is healing. When I realized that it made me laugh. It kind of tickled. What a wondrous thing the body is. My mind is mind-blowing!

Here, we have an example of body (literally the patient's brain and neurological system) intervening on behalf of healing where the object level has been so damaged that its capacity to offer hope and direction had been severely curtailed. With this "mind-blowing" realization of the healing power of his psyche/body in the midst of acute suffering and terror, the patient's body gave him a vision of healing that he himself could not imagine on a psychological level. It offered transrational data for a rational healing process, data that his mind could not generate. This vision was offered up by his body and at one and the same time it embraced and transcended our connection in the transference. In a subsequent session some months later, this patient referred to the above experience of somato-psychic healing as a "miracle." Einstein once said, "There are only two ways to live your life: One is as though nothing is a miracle. The other is as if everything is. I believe in the latter."

Synchronicity

Carl Jung developed his theory of synchronicity during the 1950s – as quantum physics was taking a front seat in explaining certain phenomena that did not fit the statistically based model of cause and effect. Jung credited Albert Einstein for sparking the notion of synchronicity that he applied to psychic phenomena.[65] He observed that under certain circumstances the connection of events is of a nature different from causal, and thereby demands a different principle of explanation. He defines synchronicity as "the timely coincidence of two or several events that cannot be causally related to each other, but express an identical or similar meaning." Jung also observed that in the macro-physical world it was difficult to find non-causal events simply because we could not even imagine occurrences that were not causally related.[66,67]

Since Jung developed his theory, the word "synchronicity" has taken its place in the lexicon of psychological literature and in the day-to-day language of individuals attuned to psychological processes.[68] In the world of the Navajo, particularly in the context of Navajo healing and religion, psychic life operates more in the realm of synchronicity than it does in the context of causal relationship. I once asked a Navajo acquaintance what time a ceremony was going to begin. He responded, "When the people arrive." I then asked what time the people would arrive. He responded, "When it's time to start."[69] What in the western context would be a non sequitur, such as the above responses, for the Navajo are honest responses in the context of a psychic world that operates more in circular, synchronistic time, than in linear *kronos* time–space.

I would like to share an experience I had while attending a Yei-Bi-Chai ceremony in the late fall of 2000. On the eighth day of the ceremony a large sand painting was completed. It was about 6′ long by 5′ wide and took between five and six hours to complete by up to eight individuals working on it at various intervals during the day. It was completed between 2–3 pm on a bright, cloudless sunny day.

This sand painting depicts a mythic place to the north where the Holy People obtained many rites of the night chant. The myth holds that rainbows illuminated the holy dwellings. One could see the rainbow along both sides of the sand painting. At the bottom the rainbow passes through a cave and emerges at the other end, to the left. The hands of the rainbow are open to receive bowls of medicine from the Holy People.

After completion of the sand painting the patient was brought in as described above and the sand painting rite performed where sand from the painting was applied to the body of the patient. Unlike other sand painting rites, this one on the eighth day is followed immediately by additional rites that take place outside, directly in front of the medicine *hogan*. At this particular place on the Navajo reservation, the vista is flat for nearly as far as the eye can see, with mountains to the west and east in the far distance. It was a bright sunny day – no clouds, not even a wisp of a cloud. When we emerged from the *hogan*, to the left – to the north – was a rainbow arcing across the sky. It remained there for nearly ten minutes (see Plate 6).

One might say this was a synchronous event – the presence of a rainbow to the north at the moment of completion of the sand painting rite depicting a mythic place to the north from which these particular healing rites were obtained. Not a single Navajo attendant at this ceremony commented on the rainbow, although all saw it. When I asked one or two about it, they said that of course a rainbow was present. It meant that the Holy People had come and the ceremony had been right.[70]

Significantly and without exception, the handful of individuals with whom I have shared this experience *instantly* began to search for causal explanations (e.g. there was humidity in the air) of "why" the rainbow appeared at that

Plate 6 View from a medicine *hogan*.

instant in a cloudless sky on a sunny afternoon. It seemed that my recounting of this incident had sparked their fragmentation complex on a deep uncon-scious level and the event could not be permitted to take its place as one of the kinds of miracles to which Einstein was alluding. In this context, the "miracle" is the experience of awe, not the apprehension of meaning. For the Navajo, this is their world. It needs no explanation. For me, who came to that place from the other side of time, it was an experience of the Borderland – the place where the gods come and go.

Notes

1 Schwartz-Salant, 1989: 176.
2 Levine, 1997: 3.
3 Deloria, 2000: 10.
4 In any professional therapy, the therapist is always endeavoring to differentiate "normal" from pathological contents presented by the patient. In the case of Borderland dynamics, this process becomes highly complicated because of the transrational nature of Borderland dynamics.
5 A common misunderstanding about Navajo medicine and the role of the medicine man/woman is the belief that the latter function out of a shamanic tradition. Medicine men are not shamans who, at a basic level, according to Michael Harner, "journey to nonordinary reality in the shamanic state of consciousness" (p.7.). He goes on to say that, "*most* medicine men and women are not shamans . . . An important difference . . . is that a shaman journeys and otherwise works in another reality while in a substantially altered state of consciousness, whereas priests work basically in ordinary reality" (Harner, 1998: 9).
6 I am aware that alchemy, as we know it, is of western origin and based in Christian mysticism, symbolism, and texts. (Indeed, the roots of alchemy go to Arab origins

as well.) In this context I am using alchemy as a generic concept to reference a dynamic metaphor for transformation, i.e. transforming base metals into "gold," or in Jung's psychic alchemical metaphor, transforming pathological elements through what he defined as the "transcendent function." In this context "alchemy" refers to any dynamic system that is based on transmutation of substance and/or (psychic) form where the end "product" is a "third" that transcends the initial input. Jung's concept of the "transcendent function" is a psychic analogue for alchemical transformation. At the same time both western alchemy and Navajo symbology are based on primary elements, i.e. earth, fire, wind, and water. (Jung, 1948: paras 89–91, 1959.)

7 However, the therapist is a symbolic figure (i.e. a symbol) as well as being the "other" in an interpersonal relationship between client and therapist as referenced in Searles' model.

8 Sedgwick, 1993: 81.

9 Sedgwick, 1993: 81.

10 Sedgwick, 1993: 112.

11 Here Sedgwick is referring specifically to the European-based practice of alchemy prevalent largely in the Middle Ages as represented in the extensive research of Carl Jung.

12 Sedgwick, 1993: 113.

13 However, for those who wish to read some material on that ceremony, it can be found in Donald Sandner's "Symbols of Navaho Healing," and in "The Night Chant: A Navaho Ceremony," recorded by Washington Matthews. (Matthews, 1902; Sandner, 1979.)

14 There are varying intervals during the day and in the night when the patient is absent and can sleep – as for example during the several hours it may take to make a sand painting (see below). Similarly there are periods during which the medicine man may sleep. (Oftentimes while the medicine man sleeps, his apprentices are preparing paraphernalia and the setting for a next stage of the ceremonial. However, after the fifth day, periods and length of sleep diminish as the ceremonial approaches its dramatic climax.)

15 There are some exceptions to this axiom, notably in the case of trauma when, as Kalsched puts it, trauma interrupts normal "incarnational" processes and they remain in an archaic state (Kalsched, 1996: 189).

16 In the best sense, because Jungian analysts/therapists work on the transpersonal level through the recognition of archetypal dynamics in the work, it would be more accurate to say that they act as a kind of *hatathli*, as well as midwife.

17 As indicated earlier, the patient sometimes first goes to a diagnostician and the diagnosis is presented to the *hatathli*. But it is the *hatathli*, whether he makes the diagnosis himself or is given one through a diagnostician, who determines the specific ceremonial and other healing measures that will be employed on behalf of a given patient.

18 In going back and forth between the oral tradition of the Navajo and the written more abstract context of western language and concept formulation, I will sometimes be using terms referencing comparable clinical contexts common to both, but different in structure. The term "archetypal realm" is used in the context of western healing where archetypes are understood to be symbolic, i.e. not embodied or enacted as is the case with the Navajo. That "realm" for the Navajo is not so much an imaged symbol as it is an *embodied experience* of the symbol – it is absent the "as if" context of symbols as in the western psyche. In the healing ceremonies themselves, they are embodied physical representations (e.g. masked figures and dancers and ceremonial paraphernalia) enacting mythological truth.

Thus, for the Navajo these "symbols" are not "as if." They simply *are* what they represent.

19 Jungian work on the archetypal level often bypasses the patient's ego defenses, as does Jungian dream work. However, Jungian therapists are trained to differentiate when by-passing the patient's ego defenses may be appropriate and when it is not.

20 However, as the individual matures developmentally, oftentimes these "defenses" do not mature and become archaic. Thus what may have been a protective defense often devolves into an obstructive block to healthy psychological development.

21 Some individuals have encapsulated or split off psychotic parts that if activated could be deleterious to the patient's well-being.

22 Sacred space.

23 For a discussion of ego–Self axis see Chapter 7 and Part 4 in Figure 7.1.

24 By "the field attendant to the trauma core" I mean the more ethereal body sensations/memories, feelings *about* the incident(s), fantasies associated with the experience, and attitudes towards the event. It is also suggested here that the therapist's experience of "the field" can be used to maneuver the work in a way that circumambulates around the trauma core while at the same time avoiding being pulled into the gravitational field of the trauma core itself.

25 Projective identification is by definition an unconscious dynamic that occurs between therapist and patient wherein the patient projects personal contents (rage, sadness, anxiety/panic, fantasies, sexual feelings, disgust, confusion) into the other. In this instance I am proposing that the therapist, when aware of the contents being "put into him" by the patient, can use the dynamic as a conscious clinical tool in monitoring the trauma field of the patient.

26 Levine, 1997: 2–3.

27 Kalsched, 1996: 189.

28 Kalsched, 1996: 189.

29 The *New Shorter Oxford English Dictionary* (1996) defines "mana" as: "an impersonal supernatural power which can be associated with people or with objects and which can be transmitted or inherited." C. G. Jung's definition is "Mana: Melanesian word for extraordinarily effective power emanating from a human being, object, action or event, or from supernatural beings and spirits. Also health, prestige, power to work magic and to heal. A primitive concept of psychic energy." Jung, 1963: para. 396.

30 Of course, in the context of western culture we do have the Hebrew scripture and its creation myth common to both the Jewish and Christian religions. But in our secularized society we cannot assume that creation myth is an integrated and embraced component of an individual's psychological reality, notwithstanding the fact that it is the archetypal roots of western culture.

31 This idea takes its roots in the Jewish mystical tradition of Kabbalah as well as a number of other mystical traditions of other religions.

32 Jung, 1938: para. 230.

33 Jung, 1938: para. 234.

34 Jung, 1951: para. 278.

35 Jung, 1951: para. 289.

36 See the story of Kristin below.

37 Although, in the case of Navajo medicine, the mythological stories are fixed, i.e. they relate to specific aspects (chapters) of Navajo cosmology and do not change, the story telling of the ceremonial is personalized for the patient in that it is the specific component of the total myth that is related at that moment in time to this specific patient's story in the earthly realm. Because the diagnostician has related the etiology of the patient's illness to some component of the Navajo

cosmological story that reflects the dynamics of the source of the patient's illness, it is the story of his illness and how he became ill. It is the enactment of that story at that particular point in mundane and mythological time on behalf of this specific patient which personalizes it.

38 One is reminded here of the myth of Romulus and Remus, mythological founders of Rome, who were abandoned to die by their great uncle and were found and suckled by a she-wolf. There is a myth in Hopi tradition where an abandoned boy was suckled and raised by deer. Similar myths exist in several cultures.

39 Kalsched, 1996: 116.

40 Another metaphor for this dynamic derived from myth would be the figure of Set, the dark dismembering force, in the "Osiris/Isis" myth of Egyptian mythology. Kalsched refers to this dynamic as an internal "protector/persecutor."

41 I am distinguishing between a male *analyst* and male *psychotherapist* where the unconscious transference dynamics are charged as opposed to male "body workers," where the transference relationship is more limited because their specific role – body worker – is delimited.

42 The treatment of trauma is rapidly becoming a discipline in its own right. Many psychotherapists who treat trauma victims are training and becoming certified in disciplines that focus on neuropsychological patterns imprinted in the body as a result of trauma, e.g. eye movement desensitization reprocessing (EMDR), developmental needs meeting strategy (DNMS), the technique of shifting consciousness through dimensions (SctD), and somatic experiencing (SE), among others. Thus the trend is toward practitioners who will be proficient in both psychotherapeutic techniques and neuropsychological tracking in the treatment of trauma.

43 Ulanov, 2001: 16, 153.

44 Welwood, 2002: 15.

45 Indeed, in Navajo healing ceremonials, the word for what the medicine man invokes on behalf of healing and health is *hozho*. *Hozho* means beauty and harmony.

46 Bernstein, 2000.

47 Winnicott, 1960.

48 By "authentic trust" is meant trust at the level of the Self in the Jungian sense of the word.

49 See Chapter 10, particularly the section on the "trauma portal."

50 Campbell, 1996: 241–242.

51 Susan Griffin observes: "Even with the most sensitive practitioners, you will seldom be asked to give full witness to the life of your body. And because on an unspoken level of mind, you learn how to treat yourself from the way that you are treated by others, especially authority figures, the effect of this narrow focus can be to limit the range of your own attention. Many times after visiting a doctor who did not listen well, I have found myself turning away from the habit of awareness, trying to ignore what I feel myself" (p. 282).

"A week or two after I returned from Germany I began to make small entries in my journal, trying to trace the arc of events in my body. Years before, I had been asked by a doctor to keep a record of symptoms. The request seemed bothersome, and I failed the task. But this was different. As if my gaze were softened somehow and by seeing I could make an alliance with my body" (Griffin, 1999: 294).

52 It was only when I stopped talking/interpreting in my sessions with Hannah and realized that I understood *nothing* of what she was trying to convey, that I shut down my mind and listened through my body. She began to feel witnessed and her world began to open to me. See Chapter 2.

53 Kalsched, 1996: 4.

54 Susan Griffin: "Heisenberg's [uncertainty] principle applies in this dimension too. To see the life of the body is to affect it" (Griffin, 1999: 293).

55 For the child in second grade who experienced the horrors of the "sleeping jar" when she was crouching in the corner in the bathroom to hide from the cries of the insects, it could have been empathic for the teacher to ask what was upsetting her. But once the child experienced the teacher's judgment – "She must have thought that I was mentally ill" – her feeling was split off and that part of her became dead to herself. It was not the *event* that needed witnessing at that point, it was the dead space/place that needed authenticating witnessing for her. Only then would she be able to experience empathy, to come back into her feeling and her soul. This particular child chose, somewhat later, *consciously*, to shut down her Borderland reality, i.e. to encapsulate it. The experience of the "sleeping jar" and the teacher's judgment were traumatic for her. It was only well into her adulthood that that place was witnessed for her so that she felt secure enough to reclaim it.

56 Part 1 in Figure 7.1 can be viewed in this light. In this figure the ego of the child/infant is represented as a nascent germ, totally immersed in the timelessness of the (archetypal) mother. Mythologically, it is the "place before" time and story. It is simultaneously personal and impersonal. Because it – the "place before" is *before*, i.e. in mythological time, it is unknowable by the ego. One is reminded here of the Borderlander who wrote me that she "was born with the ability to enter liminal psychological space," and the woman who had the out of body experience and went to her "real home," "*the place I lived before I came into this body*." For the Navajo, unlike westerners, it is "knowable" and experienceable both through their cosmology story *and* its enactment through the ceremony. This holds significant clinical implications for doing healing work with non-Native individuals at the deepest layers of the psyche and with individuals who have experienced trauma in the pre-verbal stages of psychological development. (See Chapter 10, footnote #9.)

57 Navajo sand paintings are mandalas. Of the mandala, Mircea Eliade says: "The mandala is primarily an *imago mundi*; it represents the cosmos in miniature and, at the same time, the pantheon. Its construction is equivalent to a magical re-creation of the world . . . The operation certainly has a therapeutic purpose. Made symbolically contemporary with the Creation of the World, the patient is immersed in the primordial fullness of life; he is penetrated by the gigantic forces that, *in illo tempore*, made the Creation possible" (Sandner, 1979: 195).

Also see Carl G. Jung's essay, "Concerning Mandala Symbolism," in Volume 9i, of the *Collected Works*.

The Navajos primarily relate to dreams as diagnostic of illness and as a tool for determining the kind of ceremonial a given individual may need. For the most part they do not practice on-going dream work as is done in the context of western psychology.

58 The Catholic priest always finishes the remaining consecrated wine and wafer in similar fashion.

59 When I use the term "object level," I am referring to the healing process that does or does not take place in the *interpersonal* transference–countertransference dynamic between patient and therapist. The phrase is derived from the "object-relations" school of psychology.

60 Levine, 1997: 2.

61 See Chapter 16.

62 See Chapter 16 for clinical examples of this point.

63 It is my intention here to stimulate thought about the use of the body in "standard" psychotherapeutic process. It is not my intention to have anything approaching

an in-depth discussion of the use of "body techniques" in therapeutic work. That is much too complex a subject for discussion here. The reader who wishes to explore this dimension might pursue the literature regarding EMDR (eye movement desensitization reprocessing) particularly when it is coupled with the technique of active imagination, developmental needs meeting strategy (DNMS) techniques, Peter Levine's "somatic experiencing" (SE) technique, the technique of "shifting consciousness through dimensions (SctD)" pioneered by Lee Cartwright, Ron Kurtz's "body-centered psychotherapy", and the work of Robert C. Scaer, Daniel Siegel, D. Stern, and Allan Schore, among others.

64 Levine, 1997: 2–3.
65 Mindell, 2000: 352.
66 Gebser, 1949, 1953: 399–402; Whitmont, 1980: 70. Also see Jung's essay, "Synchronicity: An Acausal Connecting Principle" in Jung, 1972.
67 We notice what we are open to noticing.
68 Indeed, it is often over-used by individuals seeking psychic connection where there are little grounds for making that claim.
69 This remark was simultaneously tongue-in-cheek since he knew how a biligana would take the comment, as well as a genuine response.
70 Obviously, a rainbow is not visibly apparent every time this sand painting rite is performed. I am not sure what the Navajo would say about that if asked. Typically, I would expect them to say nothing at all. The question is a white man's question. It is a question of cause and effect and simply would not "fit" – would not be meaningful – in Navajo cosmogony and in the world of synchronous time.

Chapter 15

Spiritual redemption or spiritual bypass

Psychology is the only science that has to take the factor of value (feeling) into account, since it forms the link between psychic events on the one hand, and meaning and life on the other.[1]

There are men too gentle to live amongst wolves.[2]

Clinical psychologist John Welwood, in his book, *Toward a Psychology of Awakening*, discusses "spiritual bypassing" as a major obstacle to self-realization, individuation, and healing. He defines spiritual bypassing, a term which he coined in 1984, as "a common tendency . . . among western spiritual seekers to use spiritual ideas and practices to avoid dealing with their emotional unfinished business."[3,4]

Welwood also recognizes the illegitimate use of therapy as a kind of pseudo-spiritual practice constituting a spiritual bypass by people caught up in the fascination of delving "into their feelings, archetypes, dreams, and relationships [so] that they become endlessly absorbed in working on all their psychological material." He says that this kind of unfocused self-examination "as the ultimate journey" often turns into an "egocentric dead end."[5] In nearly 30 years of clinical practice, I have seen several instances of the kind of illegitimate use of spirituality that Welwood talks about. The ego's hold on it and its hold on the ego can be so powerful that if a therapist addresses this dynamic directly, the patient – feeling threatened and/or angry at having his defense brought into the light of day – may make a swift departure from the therapy itself.

In discussing his concept of spiritual bypass, Welwood speaks of the "tendency to avoid or prematurely transcend basic human needs, feelings, and developmental tasks." He goes on to state:

Spiritual bypassing is particularly tempting for people who are having difficulty navigating life's developmental challenges . . . involvement in spiritual teachings and practices can become a way to rationalize and reinforce old defenses ... [and can] result from trying to use spirituality to shore up developmental deficiencies ... [it can be used] to transcend your personal feelings altogether ... Spirituality becomes just another way of rejecting one's own experience ... as a compensation for low self-esteem.[6]

Borderland personalities present their own unique qualities which require particular focus. Typically, individuals living in the Borderland are spiritually very aware and very alive. Unlike individuals who have a western ego split off from connection to nature, Borderland personalities have an ongoing connection to the transpersonal dimension of life, in a manner analogous to that of the Navajo – yet, not a *participation mystique*. Therefore for many, living in the Borderland more than not constitutes a spiritual practice, in that "practice" refers to a way of life that incorporates conscious spiritual connection and relationship.[7] We can see this in the various personal statements of Borderland individuals quoted in previous chapters. It is not clear if Welwood had the Borderland personality type in mind when he addressed the problem of spiritual bypass. However, this personality type is particularly vulnerable to appearing to be invested in spiritual bypass. Their connection to the transrational is both incomprehensible and threatening in the culture at large and dismissal of these individuals as spiritual bypassers is a convenient defense.[8]

No doubt there are Borderland people who do engage in the kind of "spiritual bypass" of which Welwood speaks – to their detriment. I say to their detriment because to the extent the Borderland is used to bypass essential and life enhancing dimensions of their lives *that are available to them*, then by definition they suffer a qualitative deficit in terms of their life potential and their life needs. The reader will note that I have used the phrase, "dimensions *that are available to them*." The question in this regard is not just what one *does* or does not *do*, but what is essential for the fulfillment of that individual and what is *possible*, internally and externally.

One example might be a Borderland person who substitutes intense involvement with nature and wildlife for desired and *available* relatedness with another human being. For many years Hannah fit this description. Although she had significant friendships with women, given her childhood history of abuse by older men and her history in her adult years of failed relationships with men, including a marriage, she could not imagine the possibility of a wholesome reciprocal relationship. Consequently she used her relationship to nature and to her art to avoid the issue altogether. Frankly, it was easier for her to relate to dogs than to contemplate a workable relationship with a man.

In Hannah's case, her primary limitation was internal. Presumably there were men out there somewhere who were "available" for relationship with Hannah had she been available emotionally for relationship with them. Her cynicism regarding men that derived from her early experience, along with the fact that the unworked-through unconscious emotional dynamics of her early history attracted her to dysfunctional men, resulting in a dysfunctional cycle that became self-reinforcing and that dead-ended in despair. This was a natural set-up for Hannah to use her Borderland connection as a spiritual bypass regarding her unfinished work with men and with living in the outer world. In that context she increasingly related more to animals than to people, men in particular. (See Chapter 2.)

As she engaged those aspects of her emotional history in our work, she became progressively freed from that dysfunctional cycle. Key components in the work were:

1. I am a man who did take her seriously and did engage with her in our work.
2. She was able to get angry with me and to express that anger and not only have it received, but experience its impact on me.
3. The ghosts of her early childhood sexual abuse (vague as they were) reared their heads in the transference and showed up in dreams that portrayed me in compromised settings (in bed with her), and later as a menacing sexual presence.

Neither of us shrank from these daunting images in a powerful erotic transference. It was on the heels of this phase of our work that Hannah met the man who was to become her second husband. Her need to use her Borderland connection as a spiritual bypass melted as she integrated this phase of our work together. Or in Welwood's words, Hannah had dealt with enough of her "emotional unfinished business." The work had disentangled and somewhat decontaminated her relationship to the outer world and her connection to the Borderland. As of the time of writing Hannah has been happily married for nearly twelve years.

For some, the Borderland is their primary legitimate and life fulfilling spiritual experience. These individuals are sometimes seen by clinicians as well as by the community at large as engaging in a spiritual bypass. In my experience, clinically and in the world, it can be difficult to differentiate those individuals who live positively in the Borderland from those who use their Borderland connection primarily as a spiritual bypass. Those living positively in the Borderland have a deep inner life and an outer as well as inner connection with nature that is rich and fulfilling. A number of them do have stimulating, intimate and fulfilling relationships, including families. Many do not. Their inner turmoil and consternation has to do with feeling that they have to live a life parallel to most of the people around them, including their family members and in some cases, their intimate friends. They believe that these "main streamers" presumably would not/could not understand their Borderland reality – however true that assumption might or might not be. Notwithstanding the loneliness of this position and life stance, they manage their parallel lifestyle in a more or less ego syntonic way and are more than not content with it. Their pain is in not being witnessed. They are quiet about life in the Borderland – not so much hiding, but acceptingly quiet. They have no need to proselytize or proclaim their Borderland connection. Their deepest needs emotionally are their longing to share their experience with another on a reality level – not on a descriptive, thinking level – and a deep need for community.

These individuals can be mistakenly perceived by therapists and others as engaging in a spiritual bypass. In fact, many of these Borderland individuals are leading happy, ego-syntonic lives and the spiritual bypass label is unwarranted and hurtful. Others, who might be using their Borderland connection as a spiritual bypass, need to have their Borderland connection witnessed and valued – particularly by therapists. The therapist's failure to witness a patient's Borderland existence tends to reinforce the patient's tighter hold on a spiritual bypass as a defense against external wounding.

On the other hand, the type of individuals that Welwood is describing, who are engaged in a spiritual bypass, often see synchronicity and archetypes in almost every event in their lives, as if all things in life are numinous and ordained. Unlike Borderland personalities, who do discriminate Borderland reality from a more linear cause and effect reality and who function in both, Welwood's bypassers stand ready to cast aside cause and effect relationship in their connection to life as a kind of perpetrated fraud that threatens their health and welfare. Listening to them one can often feel an undertone of desperation and anger. To see life as ordained from without takes them off the hook from having to face some of the "basic human needs, feelings, and developmental tasks" of their lives that confront them and that leave them feeling frightened, overwhelmed, and helpless to cope. Above all else, it takes them off the hook from having to accept responsibility for the dysfunctional aspects of their lives and the resulting pain.

Often such individuals invoke Jung's theories of the collective unconscious, of archetypes and of synchronicity to support their avoidance of life exigencies. They substitute a kind of pseudo-magic for relating either to individuals or to the outer world and its opportunities and demands. Jung said of these individuals that they strip archetypes of their numinosity by appropriating them illegitimately to meet their personal needs, reducing them to mere words (a kind of "Jungspeak"). He said that it is:

> [T]hen easy enough to link them together with other mythological representations, and so the process of limitless substitution begins; one glides from archetype to archetype, everything means everything, and one has reduced the whole process to absurdity.[9]

This can also be a problem in the case of those trauma victims who have a clear Borderland connection. They are perceived, by therapists as well as others, as engaging in a spiritual bypass when their behavior may be *essential for survival*. Trauma work can be humbling for therapists; it confronts therapists with the real limitations of their art. Kalsched has pointed out that therapeutically, it may be necessary for some trauma victims to go through a retraumatization in order to achieve healing. At the same time he recognizes that for some this is not a realistic option; it is more than their psyches can handle. He sensitively paints a painful picture of their dilemma:

> Unlike the usual analytic patient, we must remember that for the person carrying around a dissociated trauma experience, integration or "wholeness" is initially experienced as the worst thing imaginable. These patients do not experience an increase of power or enhanced functioning when the repressed affect or traumatogenic experience first emerges into consciousness. They go numb, or split, or act out, somatize, or abuse substances. Their very survival as cohesive "selves" has depended upon primitive dissociative operations which *resist* integration of the trauma and its associated affects – even to the point of dividing up the ego's "selves" into part-personalities. Analytic work with them, therefore, must involve "softer" techniques than the usual interpretations and reconstructions we consider mutative in analysis.[10]

I would add to Kalsched's statement that not all individuals can heal or transform their wounds – at least as defined by most clinical models. For some who have a Borderland connection, their connection with that dimension of reality *is* their spiritual and psychological grounding *of choice*. For some, it is their salvation – but not only. Most individuals whom I interviewed expressed clear preference for their Borderland connection even at the sacrifice of some healing in the traditional sense of the word. They are not willing to sacrifice their connection to the sacred for the mundane. Nor should they have to. For many, their deeper healing in the traditional sense can come *only* in the wake of a witnessing of their Borderland realm. Theirs is a clinical model of a different sort. A therapy that does not recognize the limits of its art – not just the limits of that particular form of therapy or the personal limits of a particular therapist, but a limit in the art itself – can itself become a form of abuse to patients told directly and subtly by a therapeutic process that they *should have* healed and since they haven't they are defective in some way.

These are real and sometimes quite painful countertransference issues that all practitioners must face. Being confronted by the limits of the art and science of our self-image as healers, and therein, perhaps, the limits of our own omnipotence, can be painfully humbling. There is an implicit assumption that most, if not all, wounds are and should be sufficiently healable through psychotherapy (as we practice it). This can lead a therapist to label a patient's process as a spiritual bypass when what might be called for is the acknowledgment and honoring of the patient's use of a Borderland connection to survive and thrive.[11]

Notes

1 Jung, 1961: para. 596.
2 Kavanaugh, 1991.
3 He uses the term "spiritual practice" in the formal sense, referring to a defined practice of one kind or another, such as Christianity, Zen, meditation, yoga, and so forth, although he recognizes that many people engage in a kind of informal spiritual practice, however lacking in definition and informal it might be.
4 Welwood, 2002: 5.
5 Welwood, 2002: 13.
6 Welwood, 2002: 12–13, 207.
7 *Spiritual* practice does not necessarily mean "religious" practice, in the sense of a structured religion (e.g. Catholicism or Judaism).
8 Over the years I have come to realize that as clinicians we tend to seriously under-estimate ridicule as a defense against the unfamiliar and that which threatens to unconsciously trigger the therapist's or one's fragmentation complex.
9 Jung, 1961: para. 596.
10 Kalsched, 1996: 26–27.
11 Guggenbuhl-Craig, 1971.

Chapter 16

Transrational data in a western clinical context: Synchronicity

If we can remember the past, why can't we remember the future?[1]

The intrusion of both psyche and acausality into science is ultimately paradigm-shaking and, therefore, of enormous importance.[2]

I have included this chapter on synchronicity because it is a quintessential example of the relevance of transrational reality in our lives. Because of its transrational nature, synchronicity is associated with Borderland phenomena. Since, as put forth in Part I of this book, Borderland consciousness is becoming more prevalent, personally and clinically, it is my conviction that synchronous events are becoming much more evident in our lives. Because of its transrational nature, synchronicity is easily overlooked and passed off as "just" this or that, but not something to be focused on and taken seriously. I consider transrational data in the western clinical context – dreams and what I call "synchronous interventions" – a major source of overlooked *and available* data that can be of enormous help in medical treatment, even life saving.

Synchronicity, defined by Jung, as an "acausal connecting principle," links events in terms of their subjective meaningfulness, rather than by cause and effect relationship.[3] J. Marvin Spiegelman points out that the astrophysicist and author and lecturer on synchronicity and science, Victor Mansfield, is adamant about differentiating "meaningful coincidences" (synchronicity, which Jung links to the individuation process) from parapsychological events (such as target guessing in experiments), which carry no such meaning.[4] He goes on to point out that synchronistic events are unique and nonrepeatable expressions of an experience.[5,6]

Most important, synchronistic events can be life altering. Parapsychological events, although at times intriguing, have little or no impact on human life. Moreover, the distinction between these two types of event is important since the word "synchronicity" has been confused and fused in its usage, with parapsychological phenomena. Parapsychological events can be verified statistically. Synchronous events can be verified experientially, even witnessed by a number of others, in many instances, but not statistically.[7] Marie-Louise von Franz, Jungian analyst and Jung's close colleague observed:

> Since synchronistic events seem to be irregular, they cannot be grasped statistically; nevertheless acausal orderedness can be investigated experimentally, because it is something general and regular.[8]

Asserting that synchronistic events can be life altering is not done lightly. Indeed, it is the point of this chapter. Namely, there is a large and growing body of transrational data available to individuals attentive to their own psyches and to clinical practitioners in all fields of healing, including and particularly allopathic medicine. And, if my assertions about the growing rapid prominence of Borderland consciousness holds true, then "data" emanating from some synchronous phenomena can and should become a major tool in healing and even in the prevention of premature and/or unnecessary pain, injury, and death.

But first an example of what I call "synchronous intervention." In the example to follow – apparently a failed one – the intervention took place in the collective arena as well as in an individual's personal life.

It is known from anecdotal reports and reports in the media that scores of people – probably hundreds – had premonitory dreams and waking fantasies prior to the events of 9/11. This was not only true of people who worked at the Pentagon and the World Trade Center (WTC), but people all over the country. We also know that dozens of people reported synchronous experiences that saved their lives: People who reported inexplicable dread or sudden illness that kept them away from their jobs; people who "simply" turned around and went home, inexplicably, before any of the events at the WTC or the Pentagon occurred.[9]

For a year or more following the terrorist attacks of 9/11, *The New York Times* carried, under the heading "Portraits of Grief," brief obituaries of every individual known to have been killed in those attacks. One such obituary can be found in Figure 16.1.[10]

Doe's dream and that of his wife are two poignant examples of the potency of synchronous events. It should be noted that John's dream was specific and explicit, i.e. "that the World Trade Center, where he worked, was coming down on him." Although clearly the dreams of both Doe and his wife significantly impacted them emotionally – given his wife's report of their discussion on the way to a christening only two days before his untimely death – tragically, like many people, the drama of this dream was not sufficient to impact his ego to the point of concluding that he should not go to work that day, or that he should vacate the building as quickly as possible once the attack occurred. One can only wonder whether his dreams came to mind at all as the World Trade Center literally came crashing down on him. Like most people in

---

Grim omens

Early last September, John Doe, a fire safety officer, had a dream that the World Trade Center, where he worked, was coming down on him. A few days later, his wife had a bad dream about debris, followed the next day by a nightmare about people bringing food, mountains of it. And, on their way to a christening on September 9, the couple talked about death.

"He even said to me, 'You know, if the time comes, if you need somebody to take care of you, I don't mind.' That's how giving and caring he was," she said.

"In my case, I said, 'If I die first, you are *not* getting married.' I swear to God." She laughed. "He said, 'Oh, that's not fair. How come? I'm allowing you to remarry if you need to.' I said, 'No, I don't want to share this feeling. I don't want any woman to share this relationship with you, just me. The feeling that I have, I just want to lock inside my heart.'"

On Sept. 11, John helped knock out the windows of a ground-floor child care center at the Trade Center; the grandparents of several of the children he helped rescue attended his memorial service with their pictures, said his brother.

Figure 16.1 Portraits of grief.

western culture, the Does likely were biased towards cause and effect thinking and the statistical model for scientific "proof." It would appear that their dreams did not register as literally prophetic and as an attempt by the collective unconscious at synchronous intervention.[11] As the colloquial term goes in our culture, although disturbing, these were "just" dreams.

Robert H. Hopcke, therapist and author of numerous articles on Jungian psychology, addresses this issue when he observes that:

> Jung noted that the numinous quality of synchronistic events was derived from the fact that "the emotional factor plays an important role" in these occurrences and that "meaningful coincidences – which are to be distinguished from meaningless chance groupings – therefore seem to rest on an archetypal foundation" . . . If synchronicity is above all a connecting principle, then the feeling quality produced by a synchronistic event, the numinosity and psychic energy it evokes, find their source in the deep stratum of psychic interconnections that Jung called the collective unconscious.[12]

Although the reported dreams of the Does were obviously quite meaningful to them, the "numinosity and psychic energy" that those dreams apparently were endeavoring to evoke in this couple were aborted by an educational and cultural bias that disdains transrational (i.e. non-statistical) data as valid. Had the Does been familiar with the word "numinosity," and more important, the consciousness-altering experience of the numinous, John might be alive today.[13]

Hopcke goes on to point out:

> This feeling aspect of synchronistic phenomena . . . requires . . . revision of thinking on the relationship between the physical world and the psyche. This revision would value the *quality* of an object or an event, as Chinese thought seems to do, rather than simply its *quantity*, as is emphasized by western science's single-minded attention to verifiable, quantifiable data. As von Franz . . . points out, a synchronistic event almost seems to force upon one a fine differentiation of feeling as well as the understanding that, in dealing with psychic facts as natural phenomena, the quality and intensity of feeling present are the only "measures" of quantity available.[14]

The Does discussed the *fantasies* that their dreams sparked. However, apparently, neither said to themselves or to the other, "What if this dream means what it says? What if this dream means that the World Trade Center *really* is going to come crashing down around your/my head? If it doesn't mean what it says, then what does it mean?"

Clinical examples: Dreams[15]

The example of the Does is one that was reported in the media and not one with which I have had any clinical contact, either direct or indirect. In the material that follows, I will present a number of clinical case examples to amplify the necessity of taking seriously transrational data in the clinical context. All the clinical examples that follow are direct (those of patients in my clinical practice) or secondary (patients of clinicians whose cases I have personally supervised). The reader should note that in some of the clinical examples that follow, the patient's dream was the primary source of synchronous intervention on behalf of the individual's physical health and survival. In some cases, the primary source of data supporting synchronous intervention was the patient's body intuition.

Helene Shulman points out that dreaming is an unconscious "psychic complex adaptive system" operating simultaneously with consciousness within the human.[16] In this sense dreaming is connected through the Self to the collective unconscious and to evolutionary process. As noted previously, we tend to think of evolution primarily in biological terms. But psyche evolves as much as biology. And it evolves much more rapidly. I think of the collective unconscious as the organ through which psychic evolution speaks and moves us. The collective unconscious is the repository of all human experience and learning, but, and critically, it is also the organ through which, apparently, evolution tries to guide us psychically. Jung points out that the unconscious can be a source of contents that "have never been conscious before."[17] It is also through the collective unconscious that synchronicity manifests along with and through Borderland consciousness.

Dreams seem to be the primary context through which synchronous intervention takes place on an individual level.[18] For now, we do not know *why* such intervention takes place. We only know that it does. We do not know *why* the collective unconscious intervenes on behalf of one individual and not another, but we know that such intervention does occur.[19]

Justin

The 14-year-old son of Justin was scheduled to have routine surgery for a hernia. His son was particularly anxious about the surgery, in part because he remembered being hospitalized for ten days at age 4 for a childhood illness. Justin stayed late with his son in his hospital room the night before the surgery, which was scheduled for 6.30 am the following morning. His son kept saying over and over again that his most intense fear was that, "They will put me to sleep and I won't be able to wake up." Justin took this mantra of his son as an expression of appropriate anxiety under the circumstances and repeatedly assured him that this surgery was "routine," that he was in excellent hands, and that it was natural to have such fears. All would be well. However, no amount of assurance seemed to appease his son. Around 11.30 pm the sedative that had been given to his son took effect and finally he fell asleep. His father went home to bed, setting his alarm for 5 am to be sure to be at the hospital by six for the surgery.

At 3.30 am Justin had the following dream:

> He and his son were walking into what seemed to be the Sahara Desert. It was as if they were leaving civilization and entering an ocean of sand. As they walked, Justin was suddenly hit by the worst foreboding he had ever experienced in his life. Something in him *knew* that he had to – that very instant – physically turn his son away from facing the desert. If he did not do so instantly, something profoundly dreadful would take place. He overcame the paralysis of his alarm, grabbed his son by the shoulders, and physically turned him away from the direction in which they were walking.
>
> At that instant, two atomic bombs exploded in the distance. He knew that somehow the act of turning his son away from the direction of those explosions saved his son's life. Instantaneously while still in the dream, he felt as if someone had taken a meat cleaver and split his forehead with full force. He awoke with the worst migraine headache of his life and in a panic, knowing that his son was in mortal danger.

Deeply shaken by the dream and still with his migraine headache, Justin dressed and arrived at the hospital at 5 am determined to stop the surgery. He told the nurses on duty that he wanted the surgery postponed, that he wanted to speak to the surgeon when he arrived. Then he took up a seat immediately adjacent to the door to his son's room to be sure that his son would not be taken to surgery.

When the surgeon arrived at the hospital he was informed by the staff that Justin had cancelled the surgery – giving no reason – only saying that he wanted to speak with the surgeon when he arrived. When the surgeon met with Justin, the surgeon seemed ashen and shaken. Before Justin could speak, the surgeon told Justin that when he had been informed that Justin had postponed the surgery, he went over his son's lab reports and data before meeting with Justin. And then the surgeon said: "We missed something. Your son has mononucleosis and his liver is enlarged. *If we had put him to sleep, we might not have been able to wake him*" – the precise words of Justin's son when he was so anxious the previous evening.

It seems apparent from this accounting that Justin's son had some deep unconscious body awareness of his condition which somehow had been missed by the examining physicians in the hospital and by the surgeon himself. Peter Levine, author of *Waking the Tiger*, and authority on the physiological effects and causes of trauma, makes reference to two-way communication between mind and body and "many pathways by which mind and body mutually communicate [and that] . . . each organ of the body including the brain, speaks its own 'thoughts,' 'feelings,' and 'promptings,' and listens to those of all the others."[20] It would appear as if Justin's son's liver spoke to him the night before the surgery and somehow through his son's synchronous psychic connection to Justin, communicated to Justin through the medium of Justin's dream, the mortal danger that he faced. Justin's panic on being awakened by his dream and his own physical symptom of the migraine headache forced awareness on him of the danger of the situation that provoked his extraordinary action. Justin reported that his migraine headache left him soon after his conversation with the surgeon.

It cannot be known if the surgeon might have caught the oversight of the boy's mononucleosis and his enlarged liver without Justin's intervention. Certainly the surgeon's comments to Justin suggested that the surgeon, himself, was shaken by that very possibility. And, of course, it cannot be known if Justin's son would have failed to recover from the anaesthesia, or if some other acute harm might have befallen him. What *is* known is that some kind of mind–body communication was deemed urgent enough to take place at the psychoid level of being.[21] And this intervention by Justin may well have saved his son's life.

It is important to note – as compared with the dreams of the Does above – that Justin took the gestalt of his experience profoundly seriously. At the time of this dream he had been in Jungian analysis for three and a half years and placed much stock in his dreams.[22] For him, the experience of his dream, his panic, his migraine, his body's knowing dread, was beyond question. In fact, he stated that not once did it occur to him to question the data and their import. Neither did he have the thought that "this is irrational; this doesn't make sense." Although he had had numerous dreams with images of symbolic death over the years, he said that the feeling tone in this dream made it impossible for him to take the dream imagery *and its attendant affect* only symbolically – to not take the dream as concretely predictive. As Robert Hopcke notes, it is the "feeling quality produced by a synchronistic event" that makes it such. Without that (numinous) feeling quality being registered *and accepted at some level by the individual's ego* the "event" becomes another "interesting" coincidence – something worthy of curiosity, but not to be taken seriously. And it is here – just at this point of acceptance of the feeling quality of the transrational, that we could be at the literal juncture of life or death.[23]

Margaret

I report Margaret's dream and experience as she, herself, wrote it out for me:

> *Setting*: My husband, Carlo, is in Spain for the summer researching a book on Spanish culture. I am alone in our house in La Jolla. Our children are away. A week or so before the dream I have written Carlo an extremely angry letter that I, on second thought, do not send him. I am ashamed of the letter and burn it up the next morning. The dream is on a Wednesday night. The Monday before, our dog, Gilbert, died in a kennel while I was at work. I had returned to La Jolla from a weekend in San Francisco and had not time to get him out of the kennel before I went to work Monday morning. I spoke to Carlo that night and told him Gilbert had died. He was very sad. He loved the dog very much and said he had hoped to see him when he returned from Spain.
>
> *Dream*: I dream I wake up in our bedroom because I hear Carlo tapping on the glass sliding door from the family room to the terrace in the back of our house. It is night. There is no one in the house but me. It is as if the children are just not there, it's like they don't even exist. All the lights in the family room are on, it is extremely bright, actually exceedingly brilliant. I am afraid of him because I know he is dead, but I know that I must answer his knock. I can't not answer. I get up and go into the family room. (The door is a sliding glass door which in reality we replaced with a french door several years ago, but in the dream it is the original sliding door. It is a door that could not be accessed from the street – only someone in the family would use that door.) I see Carlo outside in the darkness through the glass of the door. (Through a glass darkly!) He is wearing a sport jacket and tie as if he were going to the university to teach. I open the sliding door. He says, "You know I can't

come in." I answer that I know. [An acknowledgment by both that Carlo is dead.] We stand in the threshold of the door, he on the dark side and I on the light side. He embraces me and kisses me and says to me, "Everything is going to be all right now." I feel that all our worries and disagreements and anger are shed, that I am free of all negative feelings as they slide off me. An almost celestial feeling of love envelops us both. It is like the first kiss of a lover. Being "in love." I wake up from the dream sitting up in bed and hear myself almost shouting out loud, "I love you, I love you, I love you."

After the dream: I actually woke myself up by saying these words out loud. In the morning I wrote a letter to Carlo telling him about the dream and how immediate the love was for me and mailed the letter to him in Spain. I assumed the dream had to do with projecting Gilbert's death onto Carlo. The next Friday night – three nights later – Carlo was killed in an auto accident in Spain. I heard of this at 4 am Sunday morning with a call from the American consul in Seville. Of course Carlo never got the letter about the dream I sent him. I was reminded of a theme in German folk literature where death knocks three nights before taking the person. I thought of this immediately. My dream was three nights before Carlo's death. In the aftermath of dealing with the grief of his death, the dream seemed to be a gift from God. The message was of pure love and that everything would be all right. The dream was something I could always fall back on as I dealt with the grief and guilt and all that one must deal with in a death. It was a gift from him? from God? to help me.

In our discussions about her experience, Margaret informed me that at the time most of her awareness of psychoanalysis had been Freudian. She came to Jungian thought and analysis several years later. Reluctantly, I asked her if she had had her dream after she became familiar with Jung's concept of dreams, she might have taken the dream as premonitory and intervened with her husband. She said that she didn't know – the question was too difficult to contemplate in a meaningful way. She then went on to relate some other "coincidences" associated with her husband's death and its aftermath:

Coincidences (synchronicities?): By Monday afternoon I was in Seville with my two children and two step-daughters. While waiting for our flight in New York, Carlo's daughter phoned her husband, who told her that a postcard had come for her in that day's post from Carlo telling her about a wonderful evening of flamenco he had spent with some Gypsy friends, one of whom was Manuelo F. The post card said that Manuelo danced so beautifully "I want him to dance at my funeral." We found Manuelo. At the funeral the priest wouldn't let Manuelo dance, but he sang for Carlo at the graveside. Other Gypsy friends joined in with flamenco singing and clapping.

A second curious incident was that when I got to Seville, I remembered that Carlo was supposed to meet an American friend there who was coming from America, and that this friend would be wondering why Carlo didn't meet him; he wouldn't know what had happened. I realized I should try to find this friend, which would mean taking the phone directory and calling every hotel in Seville until I found him. It was mid-afternoon. The first hotel I called he was in his room and answered.

The third incident was that a friend brought Carlo's overnight bag from the car to me from the police station. In it was his watch that had stopped exactly at the time of his death. The hands simply wouldn't move, although the watch was not smashed. That night we were invited to dinner by the vice-president of Spain, who had been a close friend of Carlo and who had been at the bullfight with Carlo that afternoon just before Carlo was killed. The man gave me a present – a watch that he had planned to give to Carlo.[24]

From the standpoint of "intervention," we cannot know whether Carlo's and Margaret's unconsciouses' "intended" intervention to prevent Carlo's death. Certainly the question poses itself. It would appear that the emotional distress on both their parts was a clear message in Margaret's dream. Indeed, relief via the dream from that distress and the bonded love between them sustains Margaret to this day, years later.

Ellen

Ellen, a woman in her mid-50s, had had a mastectomy due to the discovery of breast cancer. A year and a half before, she had had the following dream:

> *Early morning dream*: A nurse was trying to give me some sort of medication through a needle in my neck vein. She was preparing me for a Cesarean section; I was to have a baby. Now, very late in my life. I said that I didn't think there was a baby; I'd never really felt it. Shouldn't I have had check-ups? "They" [the medical personnel] said – " *You're having a baby*." They also said I needed a transfusion.
>
> I began feeling around my abdomen. Hard knots, but not like a little foot. What was going to happen to me? The pumping in and out of the needle. I began replacing the nurse's tissues with fresh toilet paper. "You've undone my work." [protests the nurse.] All the other stuff had been sanitized.
>
> I was walking around. "Baby" wasn't going to come that fast. I worried most of all if baby, will he or she be all right? That hadn't even crossed my mind. The whole tone – I was not prepared for this, seemed almost reckless, I had hardly thought about it . . . not worried about it. Now I was in the midst of another health uncertainty.

The room was more like my internist's room than an operating room. But the nurse was not someone I knew. Would I be all right? Start my periods again?

The reference in the dream to, "Now I was in the midst of another health uncertainty," had specific meaning and references to Ellen. A few months after her mastectomy she went to a health center in another country. It was touted for its creative integration of alternative healing approaches with western allopathic treatment. Her primary goal in going to this health center was to build up her immune system and to avoid a reoccurrence of cancer. She and I had telephone sessions during her three-week stay at this health center. Ultimately she had found this health center quite aggressive in its approaches, insisting that patients follow their "suggested" practices. Ellen found the head physician – who was an allopathically trained physician – to be very aggressive and accusatory with her when she raised doubts and questions about suggested treatments and protocols. At one point during a meeting where Ellen was questioning him regarding certain conclusions he had proffered about her prognosis, he suggested that she *would* get cancer again if she did not cooperate with the "recommended" treatments. Ellen left shortly thereafter and considers her experience at that health center to have been very negative and one which heightened her fear of a return of her breast cancer – or another type of cancer.

Until the above encounter and particularly after the above dream, Ellen had been one who always accepted outer authority – sometimes even in cases where she knew the "authority" was wrong. It had been very hard for her to say no. Our work on this dream focused on what would make her contemplate that the medical authorities in the dream could be right about her having a baby in her 50s. And, having had three children, what would make her participate in going through these medical procedures for a Cesarean section when she was very aware in the dream of showing no signs of pregnancy whatsoever. We ended that session talking about her need to question (perceived) outer authority – especially medical authority – and to trust her own inner authority. It was not that outer medical authority should not be trusted. Professional physicians will welcome legitimate questions about health and treatment concerns. Ellen needed to learn that the issue was not *their* authority versus *her* authority. She was *entitled* to feel satisfied with the answers she received. If she weren't satisfied, she could and should pursue second opinions. Below are Ellen's notes around the above dream which she recorded the day of our session:

We talked of my doctor–nurse saying I'm having a baby. BUT in the dream I sense that I am not having a baby. About me and outer authorities, says Jerome. I kept going between the two – my sense that I had no baby inside, and I had daily lived that way, not thinking of any baby to protect in there or worrying about her health when born. I was more focused on me. How would I be? Why did they think I was having a baby? And the needle sucking in my neck – Aha, later I thought – a vampire – the outside authority is sucking my very life's blood . . .

And sure enough, by the dream's end I was in full vacillation. *I haven't been responsible about this baby, etc. vs. I'm not having a baby. At the very least, it's not coming soon, and I don't need a Cesarean OR this transfusion, and look, I'm walking around just fine. They must be wrong about some of this stuff.*

And the tissue scene – my taking control from the nurse of care for one of my most intimate body parts – where blood used to flow AND where it is still the sipapu – where life emerges and has emerged, and where sexual pleasure is most concentrated. The nurse and I were struggling over my control – her control of me. (Reminds me of Flinders writing of women being robbed, deprived of control over their very own desires and body.)[25]

Less than a year after the above dream, Ellen went for her annual physical examination. Her physician noted that Ellen had not had a colon exam and suggested that at her age and given her history of breast cancer, she should have her colon routinely examined. The physician offered Ellen a choice of a sigmoidoscopy which can examine the lower portion of the colon (about one-third of the colon length) or a colonoscopy, a much more thorough exam of the upper and lower portions of the colon (about two-thirds of the colon length). The latter is a much more complicated and uncomfortable procedure, usually requiring a local anaesthesia and someone to drive the patient to and from the procedure. Her physician said that since there were no indications of problems with her colon, she recommended the sigmoidoscopy which could be done in the physician's office.

Subsequent to this appointment with her internist, Ellen called to make an appointment for a sigmoidoscopy. However, when she spoke with her doctor's assistant who schedules appointments, she made a "Freudian slip" and said "colonoscopy" instead of what she intended to ask for, a "sigmoidoscopy." When she heard her slip, she thought to herself, "Oh! That's the more complicated procedure." She thought, "Well, then, since it came out of my mouth, I will do it" [act on my authority instead of the physician's recommendation], and she scheduled a colonoscopy instead of a sigmoidoscopy. She said that doing so felt like some kind of "large hurdle."

There followed a period of doubt about her "intuition" – after all, her physician had said that the sigmoidoscopy procedure would be fine. She went back and forth with herself. Recalling her dream and the issues it raised about outer authority versus her inner authority, she had decided to go with her body's intuitive feeling. As she approached the exam, Ellen had a fantasy that, "They would find a scary polyp. And they did." It was 4×5 centimeters in an area of the colon that could not have been examined by the sigmoidoscopy procedure. The polyp was biopsied and termed pre-cancerous. She was told that without removal of the polyp and surrounding tissue, that the risk was substantial that it would become cancerous within a year or so. Ellen subsequently had colon surgery to remove her ascending colon.

The synchronous events here were Ellen's dream alerting her to the issue of outer authority versus her sense of her own inner authority/truth, her "Freudian slip" when making an appointment to have her colon examined, her body intuition "telling her" to go with the colonoscopy, and her distinct fantasy of having a cancerous polyp in her colon, which had been neither diagnosed nor anticipated by her physician. Recalling that the factor that most distinguishes a synchronous event is the quality of the feeling associated with the event, it is not surprising that Ellen's intuition in this case seemed to come from her body. It was as if the dream prepared Ellen's body intuition to overrule the (perceived) authority of her personal physician (in the form of the physician's suggestion that a sigmoidoscopy would be fine) – something pointedly difficult for Ellen to do. In this instance, doing so on the basis of the synchronous interventions she experienced may well have saved her life.

In Chapter 15 I described people who indulge in a spiritual bypass by perceiving nearly everything as ordained – archetypal and synchronous. One way of distinguishing between them and individuals like those being described above is that the excitement of the *idea* or fantasy of synchronicity is what dazzles spiritual bypassers. In the people just described it is the quality of the feeling tone and its groundedness in the body. For clinicians trained to be sensitive to the possibility of synchronous intervention in clinical process, distinguishing between these two types of individual becomes more possible when these distinguishing characteristics are focused on. This is a crucial point since "spiritual bypassers" set themselves up to have their complaints and "intuitions" be dismissed by others, particularly those in the clinical professions. It is all the more important that clinicians – psychological and medical – go the extra step to make the above discriminations diagnostically when working with such individuals.

Ellen's dream symbols lend themselves particularly to a symbolic/subjective interpretation as contrasted with a more concrete/object level interpretation. The symbolic interpretation would focus around a new *intra-psychic* birth, the emergence of some kind of new energy, new direction, new phase in Ellen's life. Such interpretations, and there could be several layers of symbolic interpretation, would focus primarily on her intrapsychic process and would not focus specifically on taking the dream imagery literally and concretely.

A more concrete/objective "interpretation" (actually, in this instance I would prefer the term "listening" over the word "interpretation") would treat the dream more or less as I did, as addressing a current and concrete issue, probably having literally to do with Ellen's body – while simultaneously considering the symbolic. In using the term "listening," I mean, as therapist, listening with and through the body as much if not more than through the mind. Dreams of the sort that Ellen had with such powerful and graphic body imagery must be "heard" at the body level as well as on the mental level.

Jungian analysts Sylvia B. Perera and Edward C. Whitmont, in their treatise, *Dreams, a Portal to the Source*, observe that:

> The lysis . . . always points to the future, to what, while not yet in actual existence, is in the making, is possible or even likely. Crisis and lysis . . . hence may also be prophetic, not only subjectively but also on the object level.[26,27]

We must be careful not to overemphasize the subjective interpretation of dream imagery. On the one hand, all dream imagery is "symbolic" – the language of dreams *is* symbols. On the other hand the question remains, "to what do the symbols point?" What is the patient's *personal* association and relationship to a given symbol – notwithstanding an "objective" definition of the symbol?[28] Do they point to some kind of subjective inner psychological and emotional process that begs for more conscious light focused on it? Or/ and does it focus on critical events/issues taking place on the object level of the person's life? When the dream subject is the body, physical health, and life or death, the object level of the dream should *always* be a primary consideration, even when subjective meaning is evident. *Both* levels (objective and subjective) and import can be, and often are, operative at one and the same time.

In my view, the teaching and practice of dream interpretation sometimes reflects a subjective bias. Jung did suggest that "we analyze dreams not in order to learn about particular matters but to learn about the relationship of the conscious to these matters."[29] True enough *when these circumstances apply*. When they don't, then such a stance can be truly dangerous. Jung's quote above was intended as a general observation, not as dogma. He said:

> Dreams prepare, announce, or warn about certain situations often long before they actually happen. This is not *necessarily* a miracle or a precognition.[30]
>
> [Emphasis added.]

However, some dreams *are* prophecy. One such instance is reported by Jung himself when the dream of one of his patients foretold the manner of the patient's literal death:

> I remember the case of a man who was inextricably involved in a number of shady affairs. He developed an almost morbid passion for dangerous mountain-climbing as a sort of compensation: He was trying to "get

above himself." In one dream he saw himself stepping off the summit of a high mountain into the air. When he told me his dream, I instantly saw the risk he was running, and *I tried my best to emphasize the warning and convince him of the need to restrain himself. I even told him that the dream meant his death in a mountain accident.* It was in vain. Six months later he "stepped off into the air."[31]

[Emphasis added.]

In working with dreams, one has to take each dream *and the circumstances surrounding the dream* in its own contextual juices, which include not only previously covered dreams, symbols, and clinical material, but the emotions, feelings, and somatic field present in the temenos in which the dream is revealed. If the representation of a cigar is sometimes a cigar, then the body is sometimes the body, and death sometimes refers to the ending of one's physical life.

Molly

Molly was a woman in her early 50s. She was highly intuitive, and had had many years of therapy off and on in her adult years. Although she was very respectful of psyche and took her dreams seriously, she had not done major work on her dreams until our work together. Molly had had breast cancer and a mastectomy in her late 30s. We had begun our therapeutic work together about seven years after her cancer, which was still in remission.

As a highly intuitive person, Molly was not known for her organization in either her outer or her inner life. Indeed, the early phases of our work focused on grounding her intense energy and her propensity to be pulled this way and that by others' demands on her, her own creative personality, and her insatiable intellectual and psychological curiosity – all of which left her highly charged and struggling to bring order out of chaos in her life.

Recent research in cancer and psychoneuroimmunology indicates that stress can be a significant factor in the recurrence of some cancers. Psychologists Steven Maier, Linda Watkins, and Monika Fleshner, in their survey of interdisciplinary research in the field concluded:

[It] is clear that stress can alter immunity and that this can exert major effects on disease ... cancer patients who received psychiatric group intervention showed an increase in NK cell activity, compared with untreated control participants. Furthermore, this change was correlated with changes in anxiety.[32,33]

About four or five years into our work, Molly had a dream wherein she was visiting the hospital where she had had surgery for her mastectomy. It was as if she was being given a tour of the facility. Then she was taken to a different ward apart from the "tour," to what felt like the cancer ward in the dream. She was greeted at the door by a nurse who said to her, "This way please. We have a bed waiting for you on this ward."

Molly, of course, found this dream disturbing. The dream came at a time when her stress was very high and she was experiencing a great deal of anxiety. She was having great difficulty disengaging from an overwhelming number of "essential" commitments in her life. She was exhausted from the activity surrounding those commitments and in a high state of anxiety around some of them that were personally and legally conflicted. Indeed, the turmoil in her life was so great that she had missed her annual checkup with the oncologist at the very same hospital – something very uncharacteristic of Molly.

I reflected to her the implications of the dream, which I saw as confronting her with the demand that if she did not take effective action to reduce the "commitments" in her life and the attendant stress and anxiety they brought her, she was at risk of a recurrence of cancer. Indeed, she too saw the implications of the dream and took them quite seriously. She made immediate and radical changes in her lifestyle. As of this writing 13 or so years later, she is still in remission. We have had occasion to refer back to this dream several times throughout the several years of our clinical work together. Its mere mention – by either one of us – had clear meaning. In each instance, life adjustments would follow.

This dream and the attendant clinical intervention surrounding it represent a perplexing problem when dealing with "prevention," particularly in the context of psychological process and synchronicity. In short, if Molly's dream was a synchronous intervention on her behalf, since she heeded its warning, of course, "*nothing*" happened. In other words, oftentimes when there is successful intervention, there is nothing to show for it except for the clinical data (often transrational in nature), usually symbolic in its overt manifestation, which provoked the issue in the first place. In the context of the western model of healing, allopathic medicine in particular, non-statistical data do not suffice as valid "proof." Therefore, it is not possible, even inductively, to "prove" synchronous intervention. One is left with erring on the side of caution.

Nancy

Nancy was a woman in her early 30s. She and her husband had been trying to conceive a child without result. During the course of medical examinations to determine if there were an identifiable physical problem preventing pregnancy, Nancy began having "weird" body intuitions. These somatic intuitions, always vague, but always ominous, became progressively alarming to her. After reproaching herself for "being silly" over the course of several weeks, she spoke of them to her physician. Her physician, absent specific symptoms other than Nancy's intuitions, examined Nancy and pronounced her to be in good health. The exploratory procedures regarding pregnancy continued. Nancy's feelings/sensations of uneasiness persisted. She again conveyed these intuitions that something serious was wrong with her to her physician and was again reassured that she was in good health. Nancy felt relieved, but she could not sleep at night – her disquietude had shifted to a foreboding and she was haunted by her body's intuitions.

As Nancy's medical history unfolded, she was later diagnosed with ovarian cancer and died within a year and a half.

The essential clinical point here is for physicians to become more cognizant that a patient's foreboding can emanate from the patient's *body* and not "just"[34] from emotions/anxiety – even when there are no *apparent* objective data that points to pathology at the body level. In this particular case, the physician relied on *her* judgment in lieu of her patient's (body) intuition and the fact that there were no manifest symptoms with standard examination procedures. Consequently, she advised her patient that no further tests were needed.[35] There is significant likelihood that had Nancy been given an ultrasound, the cancer might have been detected early enough to have saved her life.

Janice

In a circumstance similar to the one described earlier in the case of Justin (whose son was scheduled for surgery), Janice's mother was the agent for a synchronous intervention with major health implications. Janice was scheduled to go on a ski vacation the following day. In a phone conversation her mother expressed a concern that Janice should be vacationing in a warm place, not going off to an even colder clime in the dead of winter (December). Janice protested that she had her reservations, tickets, etc., for her trip and that skiing was what she wanted to do. Her mother was uncharacteristically insistent and pushy. Janice protested once again. But her mother persisted. She changed her plans and the next day left for a vacation at a Club Med site in the Caribbean Islands.

Two days later she was sitting on the beach reading a book. A man came by and struck up a conversation with her. After getting acquainted he revealed that he was a dermatologist and also said that he noticed a dark spot on her upper back. Janice said that although she couldn't see it, there was a place there that itched all the time. The man said that she should get it checked by a dermatologist as soon as she returned to the States. As it turned out Janice was diagnosed with a malignant melanoma.[35] It was removed and she has had no recurrence of the melanoma.

About five years later, Janice was on her way to visit Nancy, the patient described above who had body forebodings and subsequently died of ovarian cancer. The two were casual friends. By this time Nancy was in the terminal phase of her ovarian cancer. Janice was wearing a new angora sweater. Being somewhat vain she reported that she consciously decided to not put on her seatbelt so as not to crease the rather delicate angora wool of the sweater. The route to Nancy's involved a ten-mile stretch of highway down a steep roadway which was two lanes wide in each direction with a grassy median between the north and south roads. The speed limit on this road was 55 mph. As Janice entered the roadway she had an uneasy feeling about not having put on her seatbelt. She continued to drive at the speed limit down this road for another minute or two. She reported that it was as if an internal voice was shouting at her to put on her seatbelt. She pulled over to the side of the road, stopped her car, put on her seatbelt, and resumed driving. In less than a minute, the driver of a car headed in the opposite direction had a fatal heart attack, crossed the median and hit Janice's car head on.

When the emergency workers came to extricate Janice from her car, she recalled that the first thing said to her by one of the EMT personnel was, "I'm not even going to ask if you had your seat belt on. You would be dead if you didn't!" I saw Janice in my office two days after the accident. It was quite amazing. She had no broken bones, just many contusions and a lot of bruising from the removal of a considerable amount of glass shards that had become imbedded in her face.

Clinically, I took the two previous events – her mother's intervention, and the "happenstance" meeting of the dermatologist on the beach – as two synchronous interventions aimed at saving her life. Viewing this last event, the car crash, from the same point of view, I asked myself the question of why Janice may have needed these events. What might be the deeper meaning to which they pointed? Translated clinically, I asked myself, and subsequently Janice, where else she might be setting herself up for disaster as she did when she decided to not wear her seatbelt. Although, as seen previously from the above discussion and clinical material, there is no *causal* link between synchronous events, it is prudent to explore the possibility of a meaningful *a*causal link between synchronous events and behavioral patterns of a patient.

So I pursued the question of why Janice's psyche may have needed to give her ego this "reminder" of her mortality. Much to my surprise, the discussion revealed that Janice had missed her last checkup with her dermatologist because she was "too busy." I was amazed at this revelation because Janice had had a near-phobic fear reaction to the possibility of recurrence of melanoma and had been "absolutely compulsive" (her words) about her quarterly follow-up examinations. Well, not so absolute, as it turns out.

This case example is particularly instructive for practicing clinicians. Synchronistic interventions, i.e. *acausal* meaningful events, are too readily overlooked by those to whom they occur and by clinicians as well. We are so biased – including myself – to place more value on "causal," i.e. statistical connection, that our tendency too often is to not pursue acausal, synchronous, psychic links beyond the events themselves. In my view, clinicians should always ask themselves and their patients what other dynamics a given synchronous event may point to. And, the clinician should be aware that the answer(s) to that question are more likely to lie in the patient's unconscious, than in her or his conscious awareness. In this context, the clinician should also be mindful to look to the patient's dreams as a source of information concerning the above question, particularly when the patient offers no conscious data or resists the question by dismissal, rationalization, or other defenses. Dream *content* is not subject to ego defense. What the individual *does* with his dream content is.

Likewise one could ask whether Janice set herself up for being hit by the other car had she not stopped to put on her seatbelt. The argument would go that in the minute or two that it took for her to pull over, put on her seatbelt, re-enter the highway, and regain driving speed, she would have passed the other car by the time the driver had his heart attack. While this is a reasonable question *in the context of cause and effect rational thinking and analysis*, the question is rendered irrelevant in the context of synchronistic *meaningful acausal connection*. These questions reflect parallel realities – one causal (rational), the other acausal (transrational). Such an event offers the opportunity of seeing through the lens of acausal connection to a different reality rather than losing that possibility by limiting our perception by seeing only through the traditional prism of causal connection. In the context of synchronicity the primary consideration is the *meaning* that emerges from acausal connection – most particularly if that meaning carries emotional and numinous potency and points to meaningful unconscious dynamics. In Janice's case, the car wreck – resulting or not, depending on one's (rational or/(and) transrational) point of view, from Janice's decision to stop to put on her seatbelt – pointed to a specific meaningful dynamic in Janice's psychology beyond the specific event itself. The danger in not seeing the existence of parallel realities, as in this case example, is that cause and effect thinking alone could lead the clinician into dropping the issue altogether once a direct causal link was established, i.e. a conclusion that Janice "caused" the accident by pulling over to the side and putting on her seatbelt. At the least, to my way of thinking this paradigm sets up a paradox that demands follow-up.[36]

We can see in the case of the Does, the World Trade Center victim(s) cited above, that there was a strong feeling reaction and connection for them as a result of their dreams. Unfortunately, that feeling connection did not reach sufficient threshold to spark them to take extreme action in the face of the connection that they did feel. My conjecture is that the force of our cultural left-brain, anti-transrational reality bias overruled what they themselves felt connected to. On the other extreme, in the case of Justin cited above, he never doubted the import of the synchronous connection that was forced on him.[37] The differentiating factor, which separates synchronous events from parapsychological events, is *meaning*. Thus, one – particularly the clinician, if one is involved – must learn to ask such questions as: "What does this experience mean to me ?" "What is it about my life that would call forth such an event(s)." "Why might I need this encounter?" "What might this experience point to?" "What makes it feel so important for me?" "What dreams or other experiences might relate to (amplify) this experience?" "What other experiences in my life feel like (carry the feeling tone of) this one?"[38]

In Janice's case (the patient with malignant melanoma), she did not associate her near encounter with death as a synchronous event per se. She was quite impacted by the "miracle" of her life "being saved" by having put her seatbelt on only moments before she was hit by the other car. It was in our subsequent sessions around this profound event in her life that the synchronous connections became evident. Together, we explored this chain of acausal links: The incident of the car accident, and her vanity that led her, contrary to her normal behavior, to decide not to wear her seatbelt; her mother's intervention in her vacation plans that led to the diagnosis of melanoma; her ignoring a place on her back that had itched constantly; her "forgetting" to get her regular dermatological check-up, a discovery that astounded her given her obsession concerning a recurrence of cancer. The pattern led us to a profound revelation: Notwithstanding her ferocious determination to survive, to live, there was a profoundly self-destructive – even suicidal – dynamic deep in Janice's psyche that she needed to be constantly aware of and guard against if indeed she was to survive. This chain of meaningful, albeit non-causal, events served to bring this destructive dynamic in her personality into the light of day. And, I can attest, as the clinician involved, it was no easy task. That dynamic in Janice's psyche resisted mightily being held up to the light of consciousness.

Role of the clinician

By way of introducing the topic, I wish to explore some clinical experiences with two therapists whom I have supervised over the years.[39]

The first therapist brought the case of a woman in her 40s. This woman was very resistant to virtually any interpretations of her behavior offered by her therapist. Indeed, in our supervisory work I had the sense that the manifest content, i.e. what the patient talked *about* in her sessions, was not the primary issue for this patient. My intuitive sense was that there was a self-destructive unconscious dynamic in this patient's defenses. The supervisory work turned to a focus on the patient's dream material, which seemed to focus on the same repetitive theme: The patient was in various contexts where she was going around in circles in a very dark and foreboding space. Although the venue changed from dream to dream, the theme was the same, and the setting became progressively darker and more foreboding with each successive dream. There was never any perceived external threat that made the dreams forbidding. That was the given of the setting of the dreams.

Oftentimes when I hear dreams – either in sessions with my patients or in supervisory sessions with other therapists – I try to both visualize them and feel them internally as if the dream were taking place within me. In the case of this patient, after three or four supervisory sessions with her therapist, I had the distinct feeling that this patient's rigidity and extreme resistance to change in her life set her up as a prime candidate for cancer. During at least two of the therapist's presentations of her patient's dreams, I had two nearly identical images coming out of her dreams: Those images were of a black car in a very dark – eerie – setting driving down a street at furious speed, aiming at a concrete wall. Psychologically and symbolically I tend to see cancer as an autoimmune disease. In other words, I had the strong feeling that this woman's narcissism and resistance to growth in her life was of such severity that it rendered her toxic to her own life force. Kalsched, in describing Leopold Stein's concept of "archetypal defenses", observes:

> Stein . . . used the analogy of the body's immune system to support his contention that "the self . . . as a 'commonwealth of archetypes' . . . carries out defence actions on a much more basic level [than the ego.]" Stein proposed the fascinating idea that the extreme negativity and self-destructiveness present in people who are primitively defended, might be understood as an attack by the primal Self on parts of the ego that it mistook for foreign invaders. He points out that proper immunological response depends on the ability of the body's immune system to accurately recognize not-self elements and then attack and kill them. Similarly, for the psyche, Stein proposed that in defenses of the Self, parts of the personality were mistaken as not-self elements and attacked, leading to self-destruction in a kind of autoimmune disease . . . of the psyche.[40]

This is exactly the hard place for me as a clinician. I had *no* data in the statistical sense of the word to support the clinical position that I came to regarding this patient. And, she wasn't even my patient. How could I possibly make such a suggestion of the possibility of cancer to her therapist? I knew nothing about her medical history; nothing about her family's medical history. I was talking about a medical "diagnosis" based primarily on the patient's seemingly murky dreams and a feeling quality in the nature of her resistance to interpretation in her sessions as reported to me by a third party. Thus, my convictions felt like the definition of hubris *to me*![41] Yet, the clinical picture seemed strong to me. At a feeling level, the only ethical position for me was to tell my supervisee what I honestly thought regarding her patient. What she would decide to do would be her decision. But in my role as supervisor I felt ethically bound to convey my convictions. I did so.

The therapist, after exploring with me the "data" that brought me to my position regarding her patient, came to a view that something indeed was dark, menacing, and potentially threatening to the well-being of her patient, possibly her physical health. In a subsequent session with her patient, where the patient brought yet another dream similar to those described above, the therapist expressed her concern to her patient including the possibility of some kind of medical complication. The therapist did not mention cancer or any other specific medical possibility, but pressed the foreboding nature of the patient's dreams and the patient's unwillingness to explore what those dark areas of her life could be. The patient would hear none of it. She began to tell the therapist what she wanted to hear (e.g. how to deal with this or that problem in her marriage) and what she did not want to hear (e.g. talk about unconscious contents in her psyche). She became irate and summarily quit the therapy. When the therapist conveyed the outcome to me I questioned myself about the stance I had taken in the supervision. At the same time I was concerned for the health of the patient. My "guidance" in this supervision resulted in the loss of her client for this supervisee.

About a year later, I heard from the patient's therapist, my supervisee, that the patient had indeed come down with ovarian cancer and that she had had surgery and was currently undergoing treatment. The therapist learned this information through encountering her former patient at a social event in the community. The therapist had no further professional contact with the patient. I have no information as to what conscious role the patient's therapy had in her diagnosis, if any. It would appear that the patient was still angry at the therapist for speaking an unwanted and frightening truth to her since she made no effort to contact the therapist regarding subsequent events that had unfolded in her life.

Whatever one's fantasy about psychological work, it is weighty and often self-doubting work indeed. One of the hardest points for me in my clinical work is to come to a conviction about a patient that feels strong and true – and that is totally unwelcome to the patient. Sometimes the unwanted information is resisted fiercely. Sometimes it is appropriate for the clinician to back off somewhat until the patient is more ready to hear the unwanted "truth."[42] Sometimes, the matter is of such urgency, that the ethical position, clinically, is to force the information on the patient in spite of furious resistance, including the risk of sacrificing the therapy itself by insisting that the patient deal with the issue at hand.[43] And sometimes all such efforts prove futile. In these instances the therapist can only trust to the gods that the work ultimately will seep to the deeper layers of the psyche and light a spark of awareness.

In my supervisory work with another therapist, in this case in a supervision group, the following dream was presented by a woman patient's therapist:

Week of July 1990
Jeff, my brother, is a baby. The bed becomes a convertible white car. Real cars start flying by the windows. The room tilts on its side. We fly through the window and side of the house. The bed is shaking and swerving. My house is sinking and swaying. My brother becomes a baby in my

arms. I put my hands over his ears and start singing. The car is flying but starts heading forward. The swirling whole. The dream ends.

When I ask Vanessa about the dream and ask her to draw the dream, I got the picture you see in Figure 16.2. She told me the winds were like two tornadoes and the car flew into the first tornado where you see the black rectangle.[44]

After hearing the content and looking at the drawing of the dream my instant reaction was that this patient should get a physical examination as soon as possible. The patient's therapist, formerly a registered nurse herself, agreed with me and suggested to her patient that she get a physical examination. The exam did reveal a lump in the patient's breast, which was excised and found to be benign. No further treatment was necessary. My recollection is that the patient's therapist and I did not process this case further. However, I did retain a copy of the dream and drawing as written out by the patient. During the ensuing 13 years, I have pondered why I have held on to this drawing. I also pondered what the second tornado represented in the dream – the first, dark with the rectangle, clearly reflecting the tumor in the patient's breast. But what of the second tornado?

In order to obtain permission to use her dream material for this book, through the therapist I contacted the patient. She chose to speak with me personally, which we did by telephone. In the course of our discussion she offered the following additional information which she subsequently put into writing via email and which is presented unedited (except for added emphasis) below:

In the summer 1998 I was pregnant with our first child. I had had a doctor's appointment on Thursday and all was well. Saturday night I had nightmares all night. My husband said I tossed and screamed and moaned in my sleep. I remember in my dream that there was death and dying and blood. I woke up with a start on Sunday morning and I knew the baby was dead. I called a friend of mine who was a midwife who was to assist me at the birth of this child and told her I had this terrible dream and I knew the baby was dead. She said it was not unusual for new

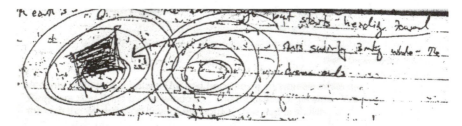

Figure 16.2 Drawing of the dream.

mothers to have nightmares about the loss of their babies but that I was fine. I had no pain, cramping, bleeding, no symptoms, nothing. I told her that she needed to listen to me and that I was not pregnant and that the baby was dead. She said to keep in touch with her during the day. Although she was reassuring and calming I remember feeling a stone, bone-chilling cold and that the baby was gone. We were at the beach and driving back home, a 7 ½-hour trip. I told myself to make a "miscarriage kit" of an extra change of clothes and pads and to wear a large loose fitting dress. Twelve hours later, about midnight, I delivered the baby along the side of the interstate in a truck stop. I had never been pregnant before, had not read about miscarriages, but I had a sense of how to get ready and deliver this little baby. We had a funeral three days later.

In the summer of 1999 I was pregnant for the second time. Again, I had a nightmare and in it we were rushing to the hospital to save this beautiful little baby girl whose breath was all gone but once we arrived the doctors said there was nothing they could do to save her and she died. Again I woke up and realized from the dream that the baby was dead. I called my friend who was a midwife (the same midwife from the previous summer) and I told her the baby was dead. Again I had no symptoms. She said to keep her posted. I began miscarrying nine hours later. She came and spent the next five days with me.

In the summer of 2000 I was pregnant for the third time, this time with twins, a boy and a girl. At this point in the pregnancy the babies had been kicking and swimming and moving for some time and I could always tell which movement belonged to which baby. The little girl had stopped moving for 48–72 hours. I went to sleep and again had another nightmare. (Just a note – I do not have frequent nightmares. As I view them, I only have them when I need to "wake up" and pay closer attention, change something, take a stronger action in some area of my life or when others close to me are ill, dying, or in danger.) I don't remember the specifics but I woke up and was terrified that something was wrong. I called my doctor's office and explained that I had had similar nightmares prior to the loss of the other pregnancies and that something was wrong. *My doctor got me in immediately, and before we did the ultrasound I again explained that I was thankful that she had gotten me in and I hoped she didn't think I was crazy but I needed to listen to my dreams.* She explained that that was okay because my only experience with pregnancies had been death so it was natural for me to feel that way. She did the ultrasound and saw that both babies were moving.

As I was an "older" mother, the twins would be born after my 42nd birthday, and had lost several pregnancies and as I was carrying twins, she referred me to a high-risk obstetrician for additional monitoring. That doctor found a cyst on my daughter's brain. When I saw the cyst on the ultrasound I just knew I was right again. The doctor said there was

1% chance it would be fatal within six weeks of her birth and a 99% chance it was not. I called all my friends and churches and got these babies, especially my daughter's brain and cyst, on everybody's prayer, energy, and meditation lists. At the 26th week of my pregnancy the ventricle in her brain absorbed the cyst, it was gone. Whew!! That was an incredibly long four weeks from detecting the cyst until the brain reabsorbed it. I don't even remember sleeping those four weeks, much less dreaming. My doctor said that some cysts are like that in prenatal development and once a certain part of the brain reaches its next growth spurt you will see cysts reabsorbed.

I hope these have been helpful. As I read these dreams and events again and spend some time with them, I am sad. But it just reminds me to live and dream with an "open eye" as B. [her therapist] used to say. I used to think I was crazy for dreaming and knowing things and so I discounted all that incoming information. B. was able to show me and assure me that that was not the case. Thanks for writing a book that helps people wake up and pay attention to the incoming information they receive and for medical providers to trust their patients additional info. I wish the best for you in your new book.

Sincerely,
Vanessa
(Mother of twins. Yippee!)

As Vanessa and I talked on the telephone, I could hear the hubbub of one-year old twins in the background, raucously exploring life.

From the standpoint of scientific causality, i.e. connection in *replicable events*, we are at a loss. What caused what? As von Franz observes, "acausal orderedness can be investigated experimentally." The key, in the case of Vanessa, is the relationship between her dreams and her medical status. There is an identifiable connection between her dreams and her body while the "causal connection," in the (statistical) scientific sense of the word, is unknown, *if there is one at all*.

Which takes me back to July 1990. I have always wondered why I held on to Vanessa's dream. The second tornado felt like unfinished business to me. But what kind of unfinished business and what might that have to do with me?

After speaking with Vanessa on the telephone, the pieces, i.e. the *acausal connections*, came together for me. Vanessa's encounter with her first tornado – her dream and the detection of her breast tumor via her dream – gave her the imperative, in her own words, "to listen to my dreams." Her tumor was benign. But her swift action in the wake of her dream regarding her (twin) daughter and getting to a high-risk obstetrician who prescribed special care during the remainder of her pregnancy, may well have saved her pregnancy, given her previous history. The second tornado, although intersecting with the first, has no dark center. In isolation it looks like a normal breast. When she took the initiative with her obstetrician, even in the face of her fear of being thought to be seen as crazy, and insisted that her dreams be listened to, she did the work of separating the clear/clean breast from the threat and intrapsychic gravitational pull of the dark aspect of her femininity.[45] In other words, Vanessa's work, in her therapy and intrapsychically, was to learn to trust the role of her dreams in monitoring her mental and physical health.

The second consideration here is the role of Vanessa's therapist and my role as supervisor. Her therapist's instincts were well attuned when she asked Vanessa to draw the dream. I might not have intuited the tumor without the drawing. Her therapist's psyche/soma sensitivity and attunement was important in taking seriously my concern that Vanessa obtain a physical examination. The direct acausal connection is highlighted by the fact that there was no other indicator of a tumor besides her dream. This experience imprinted on her psyche the psyche/soma connection and the role that dreams can play in early detection and diagnosis. As I think of it, the immune system[46] is where psyche and soma meet, connect, and dialogue. This did happen in Vanessa's case and her dream was the symbolic "report" emanating from that dialogue. Of course, none of this would mean anything without a receptive ego attitude. And this was the crucial role played by Vanessa's therapist in supporting and reinforcing a balanced and appropriate ego attitude – an attitude of an "open eye" as her therapist put it – towards Vanessa's dreams and their validity as a source of information regarding the state of her physical health. In Vanessa's own words, "[my therapist] was able to show me and assure me that . . . I was not crazy for dreaming and knowing things . . . Thanks for . . . medical providers [that] trust their patients' additional info."

Of course, the facts presented here relate to those instances where the transrational data in dreams proved to be uniquely addressing actual medical conditions – in some instances allowing life-saving interventions. I haven't presented data regarding those instances where the clinician thought that dreams presented data on medical conditions that failed to prove to be the case, i.e. false positives. In my own personal experience, synchronous experiences (i.e. dreams, body intuitions, etc.) are rare – perhaps occurring two dozen times in my nearly 30 years of clinical experience and perhaps six to eight times in my role as supervisor over the same period of time. I know of no instances where such experiences proved false, i.e. where there was no subsequent medical problem that became apparent. And even here, the synchronous intervention is not false; just the suspected medical condition isn't *currently* evident. In circumstances like that of Molly, the patient who had the dream about being invited to occupy a bed in the cancer ward described above, where *preventive* action in the face of health-threatening indications, *is successful*, then "nothing" happens. Prevention often is not provable – unless one has a large statistical sample in double-blind studies.

Transrational data in the context of allopathic medicine

I have endeavored to portray how transrational data – in this context psychological data emanating from dreams and mind/body awareness – can be a profound, or only source of data regarding medical and other life-threatening conditions. In previous chapters I have asserted that as Borderland consciousness becomes more prevalent as a result of evolutionary process emanating from the collective unconscious, such sources of transrational data are becoming more commonplace. They serve as a potential major adjunctive source informing clinicians of all types regarding the medical circumstance of their patients – and even of their diagnoses and treatment.

At the same time, I am certainly not suggesting that physicians must become adept at dream analysis and other skills associated with the psychological professions. For one thing, dream interpretation is as much an art as a skill and it takes many years and hundreds of dreams analyzed before most clinicians become adept at it. And, not all therapists have the innate attributes to become proficient at dream analysis. My primary point here is to make the physician aware of another *source* of valid clinical data, albeit a transrational one. Most physicians are predisposed to valuing cause and effect relationship as the *only* scientific and valid source of data, while acknowledging their sometime reliance on their own clinical intuition.[47] But even that clinical intuition, more often than not, looks for cause and effect relationship, and certainly for something sensate, or at least for some indicator that can be validated by laboratory tests. Seldom is their intuition screening for transrational data such as those presented in dreams and other *unconscious* sources of mind/body data. And more often than not, when such data are proffered, the physician either does not consider them a valid source of information or discounts them for lack of knowing what to do with them.

I am suggesting here that physicians be trained to know that there are other – transrational – potential sources of valid data on their patients' medical status. I would want them to know that dreams *can be* a primary source of such information. I would hope that they would be trained to ask patients if they had dreams that they thought might bear on their medical condition, particularly when there are vague and lingering symptoms in the absence of conclusive data familiar to the physician. Ideally, a physician would have a psychological consultant, a practitioner of dream work to whom he could refer a patient for consultation.[48] At the least I would hope that he would ask the question and suggest to those patients whose responses were in the affirmative to seek such counsel. Such counsel is not readily available in the clinical world,[49] but it is there to be found for those who are compelled to seek it out. These types of synchronous event – situations where the patient's dreams, body images, and intuitions – present the physician with a dilemma that challenges him to act *contra naturam*, contrary to what seems natural and right to his own training, i.e. the challenge to take seriously *and as potentially clinically valid* transrational data presented by the patient. This challenge is but one of a number being constellated by Borderland consciousness in the evolutionary transition now taking place. Ultimately, the art in these challenges is to be open to the possible in what does not make rational sense.

Notes

1 In this quote, Stephen Hawking (Isaac Newton chair in Physics, Cambridge University) is implying that time is circular and that many events are not necessarily causal, no matter how we may perceive them.

2 Spiegelman, 2002: 70.

3 I am aware that the following material on "synchronicity" is difficult to read and to digest. I have struggled to make it less so. But as Spiegelman asserts, the intrusion of both psyche and acausality into science is ultimately "paradigm-shaking." These relatively new concepts are very difficult to integrate and metabolize into our left-brain manner of thinking. I would encourage the reader to comprehend this material as well as possible after a reading or two, but to rely more on the clinical examples that follow to amplify the conceptual discourse on synchronicity.

4 Spiegelman, 2002: 67.

5 Spiegelman, 2002: 69.

6 The *Psychiatric Dictionary* defines "parapsychology" as: "The branch of psychology that deals with paranormal behavior and events such as telepathy, precognition, and clairvoyance, that are not explicable by present-day 'natural' laws" (Campbell, 1996: 515). This definition and Spiegelman's discussion of it are consistent with the *historical* view and exploration/experimentation of parapsychology by J. B. Rhine and others. In my view while parapsychological and synchronistic phenomena have been historically distinguishable by these categories, it appears to me that there has been and continues to be varying degrees of convergence of such phenomena – in part as a function of the evolution of Borderland consciousness. For example "clairvoyance," "projective introjection," "psychic induction" (as occurs in projective identification), and some of the synchronistic experiences I will be describing below have some common characteristics. I will continue this discussion based on the historical older model of these phenomena rather than engage in a more refined differentiation which will detract from the focus of this chapter and which is a complex discussion in its own right.

7 The case of the Does cited below is one case in point. John told his wife about his synchronous dreams prior to the events that they depicted. There are many instances of synchronous dreams recorded in writing and otherwise witnessed to numbers of people prior to the events that they address.

8 Spiegelman, 2002: 71.

9 Unfortunately, an "opportunity" was lost when there was no timely attempt to mount a project to collect and record dreams of those who did work at the sites of the terrorist attacks in the wake of 9/11. Oftentimes, human drama leaves little room for timely scientific planning or research design.

10 July 14, 2002.

11 I use the term "intervention" here because were the individual to heed the message of the dream *and act on it*, then not only their lives would have been altered, but also, literally, the future – theirs and their progeny and all connected with them.

I would also point out that not all such intervention is "positive." Adolf Hitler was reported to have had numerous synchronistic "interventions" in the form of synchronous events and his own intuitions regarding specific assassination plots set for him. (To my knowledge, no information is available on Hitler's dreams.)

12 Hopcke, 1988: 56.

13 Rudolf Otto (1923/1958) introduced the word "numinosum" to describe the heightened psychobiological states of arousal that are characteristic of all original spiritual experience. In this instance the word "spiritual" is synonymous with "transpersonal."

14 Hopcke, 1988: 56. (Emphasis in original.)

15 Unless otherwise noted, all dreams are reported in the words of the dreamer. As any clinician skilled in dream analysis knows, there are layers of meaning – and thus interpretations – contained in any one dream. For purposes of the focus of this chapter, I will not be exploring or interpreting presented dreams beyond a focus on those dream contents addressing what I have called "synchronous intervention," with specific emphasis on dreams as a source of transrational information on critical health, and life and death issues.

16 Shulman, 1997: 126.

17 Jung, 1961: 198; para. 449.

18 Dreams seem to be the primary language of the unconscious. (Some other "languages" of the unconscious are fantasy, spontaneous imagery, intrusive thoughts and sensations, hypnogogic states, etc.) It is crucial to remember that Jung's concept is of the dynamic Self and refers to an observing unconscious that knows more about the individual than the individual knows about it. Central in Jung's theory and model of psychoanalysis is the notion that through the establishment of the ego-Self axis (discussed previously) a dialogue becomes possible between the ego and the Self, between the conscious individual and an unconscious which at one and the same time informs the individual transpersonally as well as personally.

19 In my years of experience dealing with these questions, I find no rhyme nor reason in *who* is chosen for intervention. One might think that years of analytic work and the establishment of an ego-Self dialogue would increase availability to synchronous intervention, particularly through the medium of one's dreams. I personally have not experienced such a correlation. People in analysis by definition tend to be more focused on their dreams. At the same time, I have heard numerous tales of people who have not done analytic work whose dreams reflect synchronous intervention. (Whether the individual heeds those dreams or not is another consideration.)

20 Levine, 1997: 2–3.

21 Jung called the "psychoid dimension" the bridge between mind and matter. Robertson, 2002: 103; Rossi, 2001: 82.

22 The Does obviously paid attention to their dreams – and to these dreams in particular. However, it is not known whether either of them had received therapy or worked on their dreams with a professional.

23 One's typology could be terribly important here. For example, might a feeling type be more inclined to take such synchronous dream experiences more seriously than a thinking type or likewise a sensate type more than an intuitive? To my knowledge, no research on this kind of typological question in conjunction with synchronous events has been conducted.

24 Over the years I have heard innumerable stories about clocks/watches that stopped within a few days before, at the time of, or immediately after death. Death seems a profound stopping of time, *kronos*, in the earthly realm, both literally and symbolically. I consider these events synchronistic and not parapsychological as described above. The defining criterion is connection through meaning as opposed to meaningless connection of the latter.

25 Emphasis is in the original as Ellen wrote it.
26 The *Shorter Oxford English Dictionary* (1996) defines *lysis* as: "A gradual resolution of a disease [condition] without apparent phenomena."
27 Whitmont & Perera, 1989: 78.
28 Edward (Christopher) Whitmont once shared with me the following account: Several years previously a woman came to him because of a dream that disturbed her very much. She had seen at least two analysts prior to coming to Whitmont, terminating the relationship with each of them because of their treatment of her dream. The central – and particularly disturbing to this patient – symbol in the dream was that of a butterfly. In the dream the butterfly was flitting between plants and landing on them. Whitmont's initial statement to the woman was that he did not understand why she was so disturbed. A butterfly symbolizes the psyche and the dream imagery seemed to imply that some kind of pollination was taking place – a positive image and a seemingly healthy internal psychological and spiritual process. The woman responded with some irritation that she was a (professional?) gardener, that *for her* butterflies were predators – they induced cross-pollination, which was destructive to some of her plants and the type of garden she so diligently strived to achieve. She insisted that he take the image of the butterfly as being a predator. When Whitmont did so, the entire picture of the dream changed as did the psychological picture that this woman brought to her analytical process that continued for some years.
29 Zabriskie, 2002: 10.
30 Jung, 1961: 208, para. 473.
31 Jung, 1961: 207–208, para. 471.
32 Maier, Watkins, & Fleshner, 1994: 1010. Also, Keller, 1999.
33 NK (natural killer) cells are a type of lymphocyte that does not have to be activated for it to be able to destroy cells and responds in a relatively nonspecific way to a variety of tumor and virally infected cells. Their effect can be beneficial as in the destruction of cancer cells, or deleterious in the case of a non-discriminate killing of cells essential for health resulting in such autoimmune diseases as leukemia or multiple sclerosis.
34 In my own clinical practice, I have learned to be forewarned of some lurking unconscious shadow dynamic *and* of the patient's *or the therapist's* denial of a probable unwanted truth *anytime* the word "just" is used in a clinical session. In my experience, clinical suspicion of that word is warranted in over 90% of instances of its use.
35 The technical diagnosis was malignant melanoma, Clark Level 3, with an 80% probability of recovery – if excised and treated at that stage of development.
36 And, the other end of this paradox is that had Janice not been involved in the car wreck, her recklessness regarding her follow-up exams in the wake of her melanoma may not have become focused on, thus posing a life-threatening risk to her health and well-being.
37 Justin reported that although he had been in Jungian analysis he was not familiar with either the word or the concept of "synchronicity" at the time of his son's surgery. He became familiar with it in the wake of this profound encounter with synchronicity.
38 Some of these questions will be amplified below in the discussion of the role of the clinician.
39 Both therapists were supervised during my clinical practice in Washington D.C. It is common practice for even established clinicians to seek supervisory counsel from senior and peer colleagues. In a supervisory relationship the supervisor does not know the identity of the case that is brought to the supervision. The

supervisor knows only the clinical information brought into the supervision by the patient's therapist.

40 Kalsched, 1996: 101.

41 It still does when I come to such conclusions. The resistance I have to overcome in myself to take my clinical intuitions and insights seriously becomes incrementally more manageable each time I have found myself in such situations. At the same time, I do not want to be without that doubt and internal challenge. It forces me to explore my own clinical process with patients and supervisees more deeply, and plays a crucial role in holding me back from those tendencies towards inflation and hubris that I may in fact harbor.

42 For the clinician reader, the dynamics of this case called for working for some period of time through a "mirror transference" before interpretive/analytic work was engaged. (Kohut, 1971.)

43 In this regard, I am reminded of a man in his early 30s who had repeated dreams with themes of self-destruction. In his outer life he was highly "accident prone" as he called it. The theme of his dreams became increasingly life threatening. I kept pressing my concerns on him which he took "politely" as he dismissed them. In two successive sessions in two successive weeks he came to his session with sports injuries, in one case, arriving at my office bleeding from one of them. During that session I questioned him in minute detail about his actions from the time he left his house. When he said he drove to work, I asked such questions as "What did you take with you?" "What route did you take?" "What did you do while you were waiting for the red light?" These questions revealed that he was reading a report for his work as he was actually driving. I ended up shouting and shaking my finger at him that he was courting extreme physical danger to himself and to others. He politely informed me that he would think about what I had said. The next week he reported that on the way to work he stopped at a convenience store and while driving out came within an inch of hitting a child walking behind his car. He was glancing at the newspaper and sipping the coffee he had just bought while he was backing out of his parking space. He said that he was beginning to listen more seriously to what I was saying and what I pointed out that his dreams were saying.

Also see the dream of one of Jung's patients – the mountain climber – and his response to it as recounted above, pp. 185–186.

44 I have presented the dream here as written out by the patient's therapist, my supervisee. The drawing of the the two tornadoes in the dream was made by the patient herself.

45 It should be remembered that *all* archetypes are bipolar, having a positive and a negative pole at the extremes. All mythology is replete with mother figures who are both nurturing and devouring of their offspring. I stress here that I am not speaking of the ego, i.e. Vanessa's ego. The archetype is impersonal and each pole is more or less active in *every* individual. When one is vulnerable to an impersonal archetypal dynamic intrapsychically, sometimes all that one can do is to become aware of the dynamic, learn to identify it, and to take appropriate defensive measures in the face of it – as did Vanessa.

46 The immune system, medically speaking, is really a complex of biochemical processes, which, acting in concert with one another, comprise what we call "*the* immune system." It is my contention that the psyche is as much part of the individual's immune system as are the biochemical processes. For purposes of simplifying our discussion, I use the phrase "the immune system" as if it were a single complex dynamic operating in defense of the organism.

47 Intuition itself is a transrational phenomenon. Intuition is a gestalt, a knowing,

not a *process* of discovery. The intuitive *starts* with a conclusion and then figures out how he got there. That is the nature of intuitive process.

48 How to get coverage under managed care for such "dream consultations" is a whole conundrum unto itself and would make for a humorous sit-com were the stakes not so serious.

49 As suggested above, dream interpretation is an art. Typically it is one developed in psychoanalytic training – a specialty within the psychological professions. And, of course, not all psychoanalysts are adept at dream analysis. But many are. Perhaps with greater demand, there will be more. And perhaps, with demand, a new class of specialists in dream analysis regarding the psyche/soma connection will develop.

Chapter 17

Environmental illness complex[1]

Ironically, the idea that the body expresses thoughts and feelings hidden in the mind preserves an odd duality, as if the body did not think and feel . . . Histories of sorrow enter flesh and bone at the same time as they enter the mind. Grief and fear move directly into flesh.[2]

The exhaustion of chronic fatigue immune dysfunction is almost unimaginable. It is like having your wind sucked out by a vacuum cleaner and your skin peeled off. Any stimulation, from a slight sound to the knowledge of another person in the room, makes the body feel as though a knife is slicing through it.[3]

There is nothing imaginary or simulated about the patient's perception of his or her illness. Although the symptom may be psychogenic, the pain or the grinding fatigue is very real.[4]

Approaching the topic of environmental illness is both challenging and daunting. In the area of clinical treatment, be it medical or psychological/psychiatric or the various alternative disciplines, seldom have I encountered more consternation and frustration, more conflicting attitudes and convictions held with such passion regarding what the very syndrome *is* that is being addressed. Indeed, as outlined below, there still is not consensus as of this date in some treatment circles – particularly allopathic medicine – that a syndrome of "environmental illness" exists at all.

So how does one address an illness that for many practitioners is merely a phantom of something else, or at the deepest level of cynicism is considered a hoax? My answer is, "Slowly, carefully, and with respect." Therefore I will spend some considerable time discussing what environmental illness appears to be – to me, at least – before addressing the Borderland dynamic that I think is a core shadow component, negative and positive, in this perplexing and confounding syndrome.

Environmental illness is a dreadful affliction. The National Institute of Environmental Health Sciences (NIEHS) defines environmental illness (EI) as, "a chronic, recurring disease caused by a person's inability to tolerate an environmental chemical or a class of foreign chemicals."[5] It goes on to say:

> [Environmental illness] represents a complex gene–environment inter-action, the true cause of which is currently unknown. There is always a precipitating event, usually associated with the smell of a chemical, and a response involving one or more organ systems. Once the initial event has passed, the same response or even an exaggerated [response] occurs each time the stimulus is encountered again. Often the initiating stimulus is a higher dose or an overwhelming dose, but subsequently much lower doses can trigger the symptoms. A number of unrelated chemicals (e.g. insecticides, antiseptic cleaning agents) might precipitate the same response. Because the syndrome is similar to certain allergic conditions and to certain organ–system responses caused by emotional disturbances, [it] has often been confused with allergy (atopy) or psychiatric illness.

NIEHS identifies six criteria that "qualify" the patient from a medical standpoint as "truly having" environmental illness:

1. Symptoms are reproducible with repeated (chemical) exposures.
2. The condition is chronic.
3. Low levels of exposure (lower than previously or commonly tolerated) result in manifestations of the syndrome (i.e. increased sensitivity).
4. The symptoms improve, or resolve completely, when the triggering chemicals are removed.
5. Responses often occur to multiple chemically unrelated substances.
6. Symptoms involve multiple-organ symptoms (runny nose, itchy eyes, headache, scratchy throat, earache, scalp pain, mental confusion or sleepiness, palpitations of the heart, upset stomach, nausea and/or diarrhea, abdominal cramping, aching joints).[6]

In addition, other medical conditions are associated with or considered by some to be an integral component of EI such as sick-building syndrome, food intolerance syndrome, Gulf War illness, chronic fatigue immune dysfunction syndrome (CFIDS), fibromyalgia, irritable bowel syndrome, atypical connective tissue disease, chronic hypoglycemia, drug-induced autoantibodies/ hepatitis (liver toxicity), illness while living near a toxic waste dumpsite, and a number of others.[7]

The disease is also known as "multiple chemical sensitivities (MCS)." There are many who struggle with environmental illness who are quite adamant about MCS as a designation for their illness, and who are passionate in their rejection of the term "environmental illness." I choose the latter because it includes the specific syndrome referred to by MCS, i.e. accumulated chemical exposure in the environment, and a physical toxic hypersensitivity to various substances, as well as a number of other syndromes and dynamics, including Borderland dynamics, which can be part of this illness complex. These will be discussed further in this chapter.

The NIEHS statement, while using the term, "multiple chemical sensitivities syndrome (MCSS)," says that the preferred medical term is "idiopathic environmental intolerance (IEI)." Without going into the arguments pro or contra regarding this term, I will continue to use the term "environmental illness" and "environmental illness complex" throughout this chapter.

In my review of the literature and in interviews of a dozen or more individuals who suffer environmental illness, as well as practitioners of relevant disciplines, I encountered profound frustration on the part of practitioners who treat EI patients.[8] This frustration can be so intense as to condition medical practitioners to dread, even to disdain, patients who present symptomatic patterns that suggest EI. They are confronted with confusing and sometimes life-threatening symptoms that seem to defy, even taunt, their repertoire of knowledge and diagnostic skills. In their frustration, some practitioners, having exhausted their best efforts to diagnose and treat EI, refer these patients from one clinical discipline to another: From dermatologist, to neurologist, to psychiatrist, to endocrinologist, to infectious diseases physician, to alternative healer, and back again. A "Special Report" of the *Psychiatric Times*, states that despite profound and obvious debilitating symptoms, patients' toxic hypersensitivity is often seen as secondary to an unknown primary cause, e.g. psychiatric disorder, sexual and emotional abuse, or posttraumatic stress disorder (PTSD). The report asserts that, "Taken together, the specific phenomenological and psychophysiological evidence in MCS indicates that affected individuals diverge from the clinical pictures of typical psychiatric patients,"[9] conceding that "people who become ill from low levels of environmental chemicals may be individuals who are unusually sensitizable individuals to a wide range of exogenous influences such as chemicals, drugs, foods, noise, and stress."[10] Clearly, EI is a conundrum of symptoms, conflicting and contradictory research findings, and frustration. Reflecting the enigma of EI is the fact that medically, there is no acceptable diagnostic designation for either MCS or EI. In order for some of their patients to obtain insurance coverage, many physicians are compelled to use other diagnostic categories such as "chronic allergic sinusitis," "seasonal rhinitis," "toxic encephalopathy," "peripheral injury to multiple nerves," etc. – diagnostic categories that are in the AMA *Manual of Diagnostic Codes.*[11] Such subtle coercion flies in the face of physicians' clinical experience, which is that EI is a complex of syndromes that needs to be diagnosed and treated as such, as well as requiring the treatment of the individual symptoms presented by their patients.

The *Psychiatric Times* indicates that EI affects 6% of the population, at a lost US worker productivity estimated at $10 billion a year.[12] And one could go on and on with statistics and seeming nitpicking over diagnostic terms in this no man's land of frustration and sometimes despair for both those who suffer this illness and for those who strive to treat it. In the last analysis, however, it is arrogantly insulting as well as injurious to the health of those with EI to have their very suffering denied.

Many individuals with EI are environmentally poisoned. They may live on or near a chemical dumpsite or are hypersensitive or allergic to the pollen of specific plants and trees, or to mold, dust, particular foods, and industrial products such as pesticides. Often treatment consists of detoxification and desensitization to the extent this is medically possible. In some cases these actions do help, if not by curing the illness, at least by alleviating symptoms.

The typical EI patient is profoundly ill. The reaction to toxins, be they natural (pollen, food) or manufactured (pesticides, fertilizers, auto exhaust) can be of such magnitude as to render them unable to eat more than five or six specific foods, or unable to live in a certain house, and in some cases, unable to live in any house at all.[13] In extreme cases, some have lost their vision through malnutrition, resulting from their inability to eat most foods. Others live in chronic pain. Still others require excessive amounts of sleep that neither refreshes nor heals. Some are so weak with fatigue that they can barely tend to their most basic survival needs. Many are so mentally depleted that they cannot concentrate sufficiently to make a grocery list; hence they could not benefit from psychotherapy were it available to them.

Many who have been stricken with EI have been forced into homelessness, living in the outdoors summer and winter in a tent, a car, or a mobile home or trailer. These last sometimes require a ceramicized or stainless steel interior to avoid potentially contaminating manufactured materials. Some have been able to find safe air to breathe only in the most remote, isolated parts of the country, creating a silent and invisible diaspora of the afflicted.[14] In such places employment is virtually impossible, and poverty is a certainty for those without independent means of support. These EI exiles are not unlike the invisible leper colonies of the Middle Ages, forced to live in near-total isolation with few friends or community. In its extreme, EI is an illness that brings spiraling depression, desperation, despair, and death.[15] Although there are no definitive statistics, anecdotal and clinical reports show that the incidence of suicide is high.[16]

Herein lies another arcane and sometimes deadly dimension of EI. One would *expect* those who suffer specific allergic reactions to substances to avoid those toxins and places of potential contact. In the case of a toxic wastesite such as Rocky Flats in Colorado, Love Canal in New York, or the vicinity of the power plant in California featured in the film, *Erin Brockovich*, this decision appears obvious enough. However, what if the allergic substance is perfume, or paper, or plasterboard? How does one avoid these substances in any kind of communal setting where one has little or no control over the environment?

Avoidance model of diagnosis and treatment

For some individuals with EI, the "avoidance model" of treatment can become a problem in its own right, contributing to a downward spiral of progressive isolation that contributes to depression, which, in turn, exacerbates symptoms, which heightens a need for further avoidance. While it *is* sometimes necessary to eliminate the individual's contact with allergenic substances and to systematically eliminate and reintroduce food in the patient's diet to determine allergic reaction, avoidance itself becomes the "model" of treatment. When this is the case there is danger that the treatment structure may become primarily fear based, one that progressively closes off other alternatives, subtly becoming self-reinforcing. Such a progressively defensive system would tend to encourage further symptom development to "prove" somatic reality in cases where the individual did not feel that the symptom pattern was medically accepted. And ultimately, such a treatment structure (system) based on extreme avoidance can diminish or even exclude the patient's own determination to contribute, psychologically and physically, to her[17] own healing process – leading to a kind of collapse into victimhood. Healing can become perversely subordinated to the pursuit of validation of somatic illness. Yet at the same time, how does one heal an illness that, on the one hand, leaves the individual desperately ill, and, on the other, does not permit her to own, since it is repeatedly denied by medical practitioners? This dilemma of "avoidance models" of diagnosis and treatment in conjunction with EI was voiced by several people whom I interviewed for this chapter, both individuals with EI as well as clinical practitioners.

Presented below is a composite story drawn from individuals who, operating out of such an avoidance model of treatment, turned away from this model in the course of their recovery from EI.

Usually there was a dramatic onset – resulting from medications taken, a profound encounter with a healing discipline, or a traumatic event – pesticide or other chemical poisoning – which was perceived to serve as a trigger for the onset of "classic" EI symptoms. The patient's symptoms typically were either gradual or sudden onset anxiety, loss of energy, mental confusion, and sensitivity to substance(s), including, in the extreme phase, food. There was progressive withdrawal from the kind of life engagement that preexisted onset of EI symptoms, often including moving to a new geographic area of the country. This would be followed by various medical treatments (allopathic and alternative), most, or all of which, did not provide significant relief from symptoms. This "defeat" would then be followed by further withdrawal and depression, and a heightening of symptoms.

One respondent, a man, reported that one day he walked into a large department store. Suddenly he found himself near the cosmetics counter. Immediately he began to feel ill. There was the thought of flight simultaneous with feelings/thoughts of fainting and other mental confusion. In that moment of encroaching panic, he experienced an inner voice that said, "So what. So what! *So what!*" That inner voice shouted at him, "I refuse to in any way be controlled by this illness. I don't care anymore. If I'm symptomatic, who cares! I'm not going to get sick – no matter what! I've got to work. I can't afford this crap! I want to enjoy life. I'm *not* going to isolate myself in a sterile environment."

These experiences, where, from a clinical point of view, the Self rose up in literal defiance to challenge the message of victimhood at the base of a downward spiral into the ultimate despair of severe EI, became dramatic turning points in the life of this man. I heard similar stories where the Self defiantly challenged a freefall of the ego into despair and victimhood. Each has experienced varying, but substantial, degrees of recovery from the illness.

At the same time, it is significant that in no instance did any of these individuals deny the somatic experience of the illness. All would acknowledge having become physically sick; all still carry some degree of sensitivity to various substances, including foods. *None* is disabled by the illness. Thus, the question is not whether they became ill with EI. They did. Severely so. However, it is as if the somatic self alerted the somato-psychic self – not the psychosomatic self – that it was about to plunge to the depths. The somato-psychic self became mobilized and asserted a dominant intentionality over the psychosomatic self – in Jungian terms, it activated the archetype of healing in defense of the somatic self.[18]

Joyce McDougall, renowned psychoanalyst and authority on psychosomatic illness, points out that psychosomatic literature stresses the unavailability of affect, the lack of imaginative capacity, and particularly, the difficulty in verbal communication. She also acknowledges that psychoanalysis itself, as a treatment modality, has "privileged the role of language in the structuring of the psyche and in psychoanalytic treatment." And she further points out that, *"not all communications use language"* (p. 11; p. 101 emphasis, in original).[19] In other words, psychosomatic literature and medical/ psychoanalytic practice contain a bias that, however subtly, demands a verbal facility on the somatic level of experience in order to partake of the treatment. However, the body has its own language – somatic language – which *in the pathological model of western medicine, i.e. deviation from the norm of measurable (somatic) variables*, becomes immediately pathologized, rather than just *listened to.*[20] Thus, notwithstanding McDougall's creative and effective use of psychoanalytic theory in the treatment of psychosomatic illness, wherein *she* can relate to both the positive as well as the negative pole of psychosomatic dynamics, it is my observation that the term "psychosomatic" has become so contaminated through negative and pejorative connotation as to be affectively and effectively spoiled.[21] Therefore I prefer to use the term "somato-psychic self" or the somatic self in referencing the *positive* activation and mobilization of the psyche in defense of the body.

Other comments regarding the "avoidance model" made by some practitioners as well as those struggling with EI were:

- The message of a tightly held diagnosis of MCS *to the exclusion of any consideration than that of toxicity as the **sole** basis of the illness*, is, "If I avoid, I'll get better."
- The allopathic treatment response (avoidance and desensitization as the sole form of treatment) to MCS is destructive.
- Most people with severe MCS won't see a psychotherapist. There is almost always a psychological component, even when toxic poisoning is known and laboratory confirmed.
- Many people with severe MCS have a history of traumatic experience in early childhood.
- EI, because of pollution of the environment by big corporations, is like a religion. It can become a way of life. It is as if to say that when corporations are eliminated/prosecuted/condemned, or if they apologize and admit their role, I can heal. It's not that the assertion of corporate responsibility or complicity isn't true; the way to heal is not to isolate, but to assume authority for one's own healing and to adapt.

Perhaps most wounding of all are the more subtle factors attendant to this illness. There is still major controversy as to whether EI exists *at all*, and if it does, whether it is "truly" a physical ailment or "just" a psychiatric disorder. Ann McCampbell, a physician struggling with EI, states, "Many chemically sensitive people experience symptoms that are vastly different from typical toxic reactions. This unpredictable and exquisite sensitivity is such a baffling phenomenon that many scientists and doctors find it hard to accept it as real."[22] The National Institute of Environmental Health Sciences reports that in an environmental health sciences meeting in Brisbane, Australia, some years ago, "There was an old-fashioned debate on MCS, and the proponents who believed that it was *simply* a psychiatric disorder won the debate"[23] (emphasis added).[24] McCampbell says that, "MCS remains an almost silent epidemic because of the political and medical divisiveness over the illness."[25] In addition to being told that "It's all in your head," some individuals suffering EI are accused of malingering in order to obtain disability benefits.[26]

Notwithstanding the above, many individuals, including some I interviewed in conjunction with this chapter, with the help of traditional and non-traditional medicine, and, importantly, their own sense of their illness, have healed significantly, albeit if not completely.[27]

Environmental illness complex

I have coined the term "environmental illness complex" (EIC) to title this chapter, because, notwithstanding significant protest from individuals who struggle with EI, it seems apparent that EI, more often than not represents a complex of interacting syndromes and dynamics even when specific toxins or toxic effects and their source can be identified.[28] Those who protest such designations/explanations argue that multiple chemical sensitivities are just that – hypersensitivity to substances, manufactured or natural, through a combination of genetic predisposition and exogenous poisoning – *and nothing else*. They insist it is not the result of other factors such as complications secondary to other diagnoses, physical or psychiatric, e.g. infectious disease, psychosomatic disorders, trauma (PTSD), neurosis, or other, particularly psychiatric, conditions. Thus their insistence on the designation, "multiple chemical sensitivity," rather than "environmental illness." The latter designation opens the door to a broader etiology than solely chemical toxicity of one kind or another. At the same time, the stricter (MCS) interpretation is already blurred by the association of EI with such conditions as chronic fatigue immune dysfunction syndrome (CFIDS), fibromyalgia, irritable bowel syndrome, and atypical connective tissue disease, among others, even though it is not clear whether they represent manifestations of MCS or are distinct diseases.[29] In my exploration of EIC, both with people who are ill and with practitioners (some of whom suffer EIC), it seems apparent to me that in virtually all cases a complex of syndromes are involved – physical, psychological, and Borderland. *However the onset of EIC may have occurred, it soon devolves into a complex of syndromes that must be treated as a whole as well as individually,* and *one in which the patient is seen as an active part of and contributing member of the treatment team.*

Mind–body split in EIC

The sensitivity of those with EIC concerning psychiatrically related diagnoses is of particular note, and with some real justification. Since the time of the Greeks, psyche and soma have been viewed as separate, and even the mind and brain were viewed as separate and distinct. The current *emerging* view is that the mind and brain are inseparable and are "joined as the psyche."[30] The recent work of Daniel Siegel, Allan Schore, and others formulates how neurobiology influences *and is influenced by* interpersonal relationships, attachment, grief, early life experiences, and the intersubjective dimension of relating.[31] This recent and on-going research, much of it backed by clinical data (CAT scans, PET scans, SPECT scans, FMRIs, and controlled behavioral studies), is already revolutionizing thinking around clinical diagnosis and treatment based on the "archaic" medical model of a split between psyche and soma. However, more than not, current clinical practice remains based in that classical model.[32] Consequently, patients have been trained to think of health and sickness in terms of a split between psyche and soma, and so have most of the practitioners who treat them. This view of health, illness, and the mind–body relationship is reflected and reinforced at all levels in our culture, i.e. movies, TV, electronic and print media, our legal system, commercial advertising, our schools, among others.[33]

With regard to the diagnosis and treatment of EIC, the process too often becomes a conundrum that feeds on itself. Patients who *ultimately* will be diagnosed as having EI – *if they receive that diagnosis at all* – typically present vague symptomatology that could be associated with a host of maladies and diseases. Some present with "clear" clinical data such as abnormal liver function scores, high white or red blood cell counts, toxic levels of foreign matter (e.g. mercury, pesticides), fever, neurologic dysfunction, and other, sometimes dramatic, symptoms. Others present without any dramatic symptoms other than the way they feel, e.g. chronic low energy, confusion, and "hypersensitivity." The clinician to whom they are presenting their symptoms typically is not an environmental physician, but is their medical internist, or their psychotherapist, neither of whom is likely to be familiar with EIC as a clinical entity, and certainly not with the subtleties of diagnosing this difficult and elusive syndrome. If they get to an environmental physician at all, it is likely to occur after a seeming desultory journey from one specialist to another to another, perhaps over a period of years, with spiraling frustration, depression, and financial depletion. Too often, pinpointing a diagnosis of EIC is akin to trying to grab hold of quicksilver – ever elusive, almost never pin downable.

Moreover, the problem of the prevailing medical model based on a split between psyche and soma is more than just semantic. Even when the treating physician/practitioner perceives that a more holistic view of treatment is in order, she is limited by her training, which is based on that split – as is much of medical technology. Typically lab reports do not indicate the patient's emotional reaction to toxins and the impact on the patient's immune system of that somato-psychic interaction.

Symbolically and somatically, we can imagine the immune system as being the interface between the nexus of psyche and soma.[34,35] Notwithstanding progressive views of the interaction of psyche and soma *within the patient*, medical and other practitioners still are faced with the limits of their training and medical technology, which impinges on their clinical intuition and vision. They still tend, consciously or unconsciously, to force symptom patterns into familiar categorical clinical models that, too often, in the case of EIC, don't work. Even the American Academy of Environmental Medicine, which views EIC as a diagnostic complex, is forced to make reference to *categories* of treatment, psychological or endocrinological, for example, because clinical resources are so structured – psychologists/psychiatrists for "psychological dysfunctions," and endocrinologists for endocrine problems.[36] Interface and coordination between these disciplines with regard to a given patient typically are limited, if present at all, and usually occur during an acute phase of the illness when the patient is in a hospital setting. Or, as is often the case, in their frustration in the face of continued "failure" to diagnose the patient's problem, practitioners of all kinds "send the patient on" – often thinking, "It's all in their head!," i.e. not "real" – to yet another specialist for another round with similar outcome.[37] Thus the sensitivity of EIC patients to psychiatric diagnoses, even when the diagnosis, e.g. psychosomatic disorder, may be all or partially valid.[38]

In a book entitled, *From Paralysis to Fatigue: A History of Psychosomatic Illness in the Modern Era*, Edward Shorter, a medical historian, offers the following observation:

> The psychotherapy paradigm triumphed because it seemed to offer physicians a sensible explanation of why patients somatize and how to treat them. But the advocates of all of these therapies underestimated the deep terror with which patients contemplate physical symptoms. No therapeutic approach would succeed that did not reassure patients of the reality of their symptoms. No therapy that forthrightly assumed the non-organic nature of the symptoms would be accepted by the patients.[39]

The above quote, a profound truth in its essence, ironically lends itself to the contentious epithet of, "It's all in your head!" *Some* of "it" no doubt *is* in the patient's head, i.e. the psyche-not-split-off-from-soma. But the derision accompanying the epithet and the branding of the patient as a "psych case," meriting no further consideration of somatic illness, adds insult to real suffering. For the psyche not split off from soma, it is never "either/or," black or white. In her poignant book, *What Her Body Thought*, describing her own struggles with EIC, Susan Griffin insightfully sums up this dilemma:

> [T]hough the new psychosomatic approach has yielded insight and healing, it also has had the opposite effect. Instead of weaving mind and body together, the approach has been used to deny illness and even the force of physical experience . . . Repeatedly, the psychosomatic understanding of illness has been used to blame the ill for their suffering. As Susan Sontag writes, "Patients who have unwittingly caused their disease are also being made to feel that they have deserved it."[40]

This misuse of the medical model and medical authority, however inadvertent, can wound or even traumatize the patient as well as activate and exacerbate trauma that the patient may bring with her, consciously and unconsciously. It can play into the trauma model depicted by Donald Kalsched in *The Inner World of Trauma*, wherein the terror of having one's somatic reality denied sets off primitive and dissociative defenses within the patient that "both *characterize severe psychopathology* and also . . . *cause* it." This violation of the patient's inner core of experiential truth (i.e. the somatic symptoms that assault her) is beyond the imaginable for the patient. And as Kalsched rightly points out, "The violation of this inner core of the personality [of the individual's somatic reality] . . . [can set off] archetypal defenses [that] will go to any length to protect the Self – even to the point of killing the host personality in which this personal spirit is housed (suicide)."[41] In the case of individuals with EIC, this can mean starvation, because of severe allergic reactions to food, to the point of organ failure and the rejection of any treatment approach, however efficacious, that does not validate the individual's somatic reality.[42]

The psychoanalytic model of trauma developed by Kalsched and how it can trigger destructive defenses in the individual, is given neurobiological support in the work of Daniel J. Siegel. Siegel points out that:

> [B]ehavior itself alters genetic expression which then creates behavior. In the end, changes in the organization of brain function, emotional regulation, and long-term memory are mediated by alterations in neural structure . . . Experience, gene expression, mental activity, behavior, and continued interactions with the environment (experience) are tightly linked in a transactional set of processes. Such is the recursive nature of development and the way in which nature and nurture, genes and experience, are inextricably part of the same process.[43]

I propose that what Siegel refers to as "environment (experience)," applies as well to the literal environment, i.e. nature. Although Siegel is here describing the developmental process in parent–child relationship, these truths apply on the adult level as well, and to the inner "traumatized" child that is cringing, sometimes defiantly, in the deep psychological and emotional layers within many who have been afflicted with EIC.

Environmental illness complex and the Borderland

So what does all of this have to do with the Borderland?

We have seen in earlier chapters that those individuals connected to the Borderland through whichever portal(s) they make that connection, routinely experience what I have called transrational reality. Borderlanders predominantly experience that connection, particularly their bond with nature, as being transcendently positive and nurturing. Although for some Borderlanders their connection with nature can be a conduit for deep pain – the 6 year old and the "sleeping jar," for example. The child's Borderland connection resulted in the experience becoming traumatically "real" for her on a somatopsychic level.[44] It was not the Borderland itself that was the source of pain or trauma, but rather individual human action.[45]

The vast majority of those with EIC ultimately come to encounter the strange paradox of nature inherent in the illness. EIC thrusts them into a perverse connection with nature. Individuals with EIC ultimately come to fit the profile of those whose connection with the Borderland is through the trauma portal. I say "ultimately," because even if they began their Borderland journey through one of the other two portals, ultimately EIC itself, once it becomes chronic and/or acute, becomes their trauma. For them, the Borderland is not just a conduit for traumatic experience, nature herself is the source of the trauma. It is *in* or *through* nature that they experience their illness, i.e. through pollens, polluted air and water, pesticides, contaminated food, etc. The distinction between nature itself, and "*in* or *through* nature," becomes progressively blurred as they become more desperately ill, until there is hardly any distinction at all on an unconscious, if not a conscious level. The point is that nature is *experienced* as the source of their poisoning.[46]

One of the most perplexing questions concerning those with EIC and the professionals who treat them is why some individuals are so horribly intolerant of even minute traces of a substance and others are not. Is it all in the genes or perhaps is it some other dynamic at work as well? I have suggested above that some of those with EIC eventually come to resemble, psychodynamically, those individuals who enter the Borderland through the trauma portal. Siegel, in discussing studies of early trauma, suggests that the brain itself can be severely affected by trauma, thus impacting the brain's capacity to adapt to stress. Given that EIC ultimately comes to look like a characteristic trauma pattern, this may point to a neurobiological basis for the chronic and unrelenting nature of EIC.

I have suggested in earlier chapters that for Borderlanders, nature can become the positive, if not life-saving, "primary caregiver," when the interpersonal dimension of treatment and healing have been spoiled.[47] Schore quotes Davies and Frawley regarding parent-inflicted abuse: "The continued survival of the child is felt to be at risk, because the actuality of the abuse *jeopardizes [the] primary object bond and challenges the child's capacity to trust* and, therefore, to securely depend." In this regard, Laub and Auerhahn assert that the "essential experience of trauma [is] an unraveling of the relationship between self and nurturing other, the very fabric of psychic life" [Italics added].[48] Siegel asserts that: "Early life histories of absence of any attachment experience (as in severe neglect) or the experience of overwhelming trauma (as in physical, sexual, or emotional abuse) may markedly alter the neurobiological structure of the brain *in ways that are difficult if not impossible to repair*" (emphasis added).[49] I suggest that for some individuals with EIC, the "irreparable damage" is to the interpersonal dimension of relationship as a whole, and that the Self facilitates an "attachment" to impersonal nature in lieu of a personal primary attachment figure – in this case a healer(s) – in an attempt to repair body, psyche, and soul.[50]

For the insecurely attached, trauma often provokes an attachment crisis, both interpersonally with others and between the individual and his/her own body experience.[51] Siegel, in speaking of "attuned communication" says:

For the nonverbal infant, this intimate, collaborative communication is without words [and] this need for nonverbal attunement persists throughout life . . . Infant attachment studies remind us of the crucial importance of nonverbal communication in all forms of human relationships.

(p.71)

Although attachment behavior is seen primarily in children, adults continue to manifest attachment [behavior] throughout the lifespan.

(p. 68)

We have discussed the sustaining and positive nonverbal attunement between the Borderland personality and nature, as reflected in the various stories and testimonials presented by "Borderlanders." However, this can also lead to a profound paradox: That which can heal, can also render us sick. Susan Schmall, a clinical psychologist and former clinical director of Southwestern College in Santa Fe, New Mexico, wrote:

> Immune system disorders . . . are proliferating because of the destruction of the earth. We can not keep believing that only water, land, plants and animals are affected by pollution and destruction of the land. These insults have a profound effect on human beings as well. Those of us who are sick are the first of many to voice earth's pain.[52]

Siegel makes a strong *neurobiological* case for the role of attachment in the overall developmental emotional and psychological health of both children and adults.[53] Several practitioners who treat people with EIC have asserted that many carry the characteristics of early trauma. This would be consistent with serious attachment problems in childhood. To my mind this would imply the need for in-depth work on attachment with some people with chronically disabling EIC, particularly in individuals who are treatment resistant. Siegel says:

> Studies of early trauma and neglect reveal that neural structure and function within the brain can be severely affected and lead to long-lasting and extensive effects on the brain's capacity to adapt to stress.[54]

Although he was not speaking specifically of EIC, the implications for the somato-psychic self seem obvious. In this case, the "attachment work" would be on the transrational level – not in the interpersonal realm as much as in the *impersonal* realm with nature. Or another way of putting it, if attachment on the *interpersonal* level is to become efficacious, in some cases of severe EIC it would have to be approached through the transrational, i.e. the Borderland dimension. Those who are attuned to the transrational as a legitimate dimension of experience and who have worked with individuals with EIC, often can feel and intuit, if not "see" directly, transrational dynamics (i.e. the Borderland) operating in the background.

It is noted as well that not all individuals with EIC have experienced trauma prior to the onset of their illness. A number of these individuals may have had at least one foot in the Borderland and thus in the transrational dimension prior to the onset of their illness. However, if they have a pro-longed experience with EIC, the illness itself ultimately becomes their trauma and most of them pass through the trauma portal into the negative dimen-sion of the Borderland. This was the uniform clinical impression that I received from those I interviewed, including clinical practitioners, as well as from much of the literature on EI which I reviewed.

But a two-way street *is* a two-way street. *That which can make us sick, can also heal.* There is potential for connecting to the positive pole of the Borderland *if the Borderland connection is not pathologized.* Dr. Schmall recounts:

> My healing is completely related to the healing of the earth. Progress has come for me only as I have come more and more to develop a natural way of living. I have seen this for others also afflicted with immune system disorders. During the year I was becoming ill, my dreams con-sisted mainly of nightmares of massive proportion – earthquakes, tidal waves, nuclear war . . . I have found that global dreams are not uncom-mon for people experiencing immune system collapse. When I was finally bedridden my dreams stopped completely. But not before I had a vision of a Native American woman who said to me that what I needed to do was just sink into the earth. She would stay with me and show me the land.[55]

In other words, not only is it counterintuitive to attempt to get the EIC patient to "see" that they have identified with the negative pole of nature, such an approach can "spoil" the healing potential of the Borderland itself in a manner similar to the way in which the interpersonal dimension has been spoiled. One can *experience* the positive pole of nature without having to *choose* to disidentify with the negative pole. (Obviously, individuals with EIC do not feel that they have that choice.)

One environmental physician whom I interviewed for this chapter, who herself is recovering from EIC, informed me that one of the many treatment approaches used with her patients is to have the individual spend several hours a week lying spread-eagled on the ground with as much of the person's skin touching earth as possible. This treatment, seemingly unorthodox, if not "kooky," actually is aimed at activating the positive pole of a "virtual other," i.e. earth.[56] Some with EIC know the positive pole of nature *as an idea.* Yet their somatic *experience* is exactly opposite. Whatever they may *think* about nature and its nurturing qualities, their *somatic experience* is highly negativized.[57] For those with severe EIC, often they feel forced to withdraw into a deeper isolation where they are increasingly alone with – nature.[58]

A treatment that calls for the individual to spread-eagle on the earth is unorthodox, to be sure. But it is far from "kooky," when one takes into consideration some of the more recent research on the neurobiology of mind–body development. One individual recovering from EIC stated, "If the earth has a voice, I was one of its voices. I was one of its nerve endings." Of course, this could be a reflection of either the positive or negative pole of the Borderland. For this individual, it was life saving. By way of contrast, Susan Griffin provides a graphic and moving description of the negative pole of the Borderland:

> The irony is that though a psychosomatic approach to medicine has the potential to heal not only individual illness but, in its wider implications, our shared alienation from nature, the denial that commonly infuses this perspective blends almost imperceptibly with another unconscious belief, the illusory sense that human beings are neither dependent on nor really part of life on earth. But we are part of the earth, and the effects of ecological damage can be seen in the human body.
>
> While I suffered the derangement of various systems in my body, I began to think of myself as a canary in the mine . . . I felt as if the destruction of the environment were occurring in my own cells.[59]

Notably, of the practitioners whom I interviewed for this chapter, when given the Borderland concept and asked if they thought there was a transrational and spiritual dynamic to the nature of the illness, *all* answered in the affirmative. When asked if they thought that consideration of transrational and spiritual dynamics in the treatment of EIC was essential, once more, all answered in the affirmative.

I am not suggesting that a transrational approach in the treatment of EIC should be in lieu of more traditional and rational approaches. I see environmental illness as a disease "complex," and therefore creative integration of various available therapies, orthodox and unorthodox, need to be employed.[60]

It is important to note that many individuals with EIC do heal. They are not necessarily cured – but they are healed. In Susan Schmall's words:

> As I begin to come out of this illness I no longer feel like an individual. I no longer call myself sick although I still experience a host of symptoms. I feel like a piece of the living earth, being molded and shaped to do her work, just like the trees, the mountains, the canyons and all other living things.[61]

I have heard similar statements from many of those I have interviewed, and one can find such statements in the personal testimonial literature of those with EIC, such as Susan Griffin's book, *What Her Body Thought*. The above quote by Dr. Schmall might be interpreted as evidence of a dissociation or other pathological condition from the perspective of psychotherapies that do not accord legitimacy to transpersonal reality. In the final analysis, the ultimate test of healing is not in the doctor, but, except under the most extraordinary circumstances, in the patient.[62] As clinicians we need to heed the experience and the wisdom of our patients.

Ahead

Given the theoretical framework regarding the evolution of the western ego posed in Part I of this book, it would follow that the incidence of EIC is likely to increase significantly in the decades ahead. When one considers degradation of the environment and its impact on the ecology, this "natural" increase in the incidence of EIC would be further accelerated.

It would appear that EIC is a syndrome that demands a radical reassessment of diagnostic and treatment models that directly or indirectly operate on a paradigm of a mind/body *and rational/transrational* split. One way of looking at EIC is as if it were the first identifiable "Borderland syndrome" that can be understood only through a lens that embraces the transrational (Borderland) dimension of the mind/body unity.

Some individuals with EIC will evolve to a positive Borderland consciousness; for others the Borderland will become a negative, destructive consciousness, that one must hope will be addressed through the recognition by western and traditional[63] medical/psychological practitioners of the complexity of this emerging phenomenon.

Notes

1 I wish to emphasize that the observations that follow are not comprehensive or meant to be a definitive statement on what I have come to call "environmental illness complex." My intention is to bring a clarifying dimension – the Borderland – to bear on a profoundly perplexing syndrome.
2 Griffin, 1999: 204–205.
3 Schmall, 1997: 2.
4 Shorter, 1993: ix.
5 Nebert, 2003: 1.
6 Nebert, 2003: 1–2.
7 Nebert, 2003: 2.
8 As with many illnesses, physical and psychological, some practitioners who treat EI have suffered and are recovering from the illness themselves. They too find the illness confounding and frustrating, albeit with a different perspective and tolerance for its perplexing nature.
9 Bell, 2003: 1.
10 Bell, 2003: 2.
11 AMA, 2003.
12 Bell, 2003.

13 Hypersensitivity to "natural" substances such as food is complicated by possible contamination by other substances e.g. how food is grown (organic or with chemical pesticides and fertilizers) to how it is cooked.

14 Zwillinger, 1999: 84.

15 Elliott.

16 Zwillinger, 1999.

17 I will be using the pronouns "she" and "her" throughout this chapter since the incidence of EI is known to be considerably higher in women than in men (McCampbell, 1998: 3).

18 I am aware that the language here, i.e. somato-psychic self, somatic-self, and psychosomatic self, is awkward, even confusing. But since we have no language that reflects mindbody unity we have the choice of adapting what seems to me to be archaic language that tends to split mindbody no matter how much we clarify, or to coin new terms that go beyond past meaning. If nothing else, they do get us to reflect upon what we mean.

19 McDougall, 1989: 11, 101.

20 Griffin, 1999: 204–205.

21 Erskine, 1994: 1–2.

22 McCampbell, 1998: 1.

23 Nebert, 2003: 1.

24 One wonders what a "simple" psychiatric disorder would be in the face of such profound and chronic illness. The implication of the word, of course, is, "not real."

25 McCampbell, 1998: 3.

26 Although officially not a syndrome recognized by the International Classification of Diseases, in the AMA *Manual of Diagnostic Codes*, MCS is sometimes recognized – although recognition is extremely difficult to obtain – by the Social Security Administration as a disability under SSI.

27 Reliable statistics are sketchy. Data on treatment and healing are primarily anecdotal – both from patients and practitioners. In 1998 Ann McCampbell wrote that "There is no cure for MCS [EI], but there are many treatments that have helped people . . . reduce their symptoms and improve or restore their health" (McCampbell, 1998: 9). Apparently, this clinical picture has not changed significantly since then.

28 The formation of the American Academy of Environmental Medicine in 1965 was a concrete manifestation of this recognition. The Academy (2003:1) defines "environmental medicine" as "the comprehensive, proactive and preventive strategic approach to medical care dedicated to the evaluation, management, and prevention of the adverse consequences resulting from environmentally triggered illness*es* (ETI*s*)." Currently there are 250–300 members of the AAEM.

29 McCampbell, 1998: 2; Nebert, 2003: 2.

30 Swedo, 1996: 22–23.

31 Schore, 1994; Siegel, 1999; Tyminski, 2003: 39.

32 Erskine, 1994: 1–2.

33 Shorter, 1993: 2–3, 295.

34 McDougall, 1989.

35 A further complicating factor is that, based on clinical reports, many individuals with EIC are known to have defects with symbol formation and symbolic understanding. Consequently, the expression of fantasies and affects remain stuck in body processes (Feldman, 1995: 176). Difficulties in symbolic process can be disruptive to healing dynamics between psyche and soma since symbolic *process* (not words or even images, necessarily, but the *imaginal*) is *a* "language" through

which each dimension, i.e. soma and psyche, communicates to/with the other. In short, one has to be able to imagine healing in order to heal. Also see McDougall, 1989: 19–20, and the syndrome "Alexithymia," pp. 24–25, as well as Chapter 2.

36 2003: 3.

37 To some this statement may seem glib. However, I have personally heard this literal statement from two medical practitioners vis-à-vis EIC.

38 Of course, there are notable exceptions to this picture within all categories of clinical practice. For an exceptional example in this regard, the reader is referred to the paper, "On Depression," by Erica M. Elliott, a practicing environmental physician, who herself is recovering from EIC. This paper, containing two case histories, as well as a roadmap for differential diagnosis and treatment across disciplines in the identification and treatment of environmental illness complex is a model for approaching this very difficult syndrome from within the illness itself, adjusting medical discipline and resources to the requirements of the illness rather than vice versa (Elliott).

It should also be noted that some of the most creative and successful practitioners in the treatment of EIC have been individuals whose orientation and training have been far out of the mainstream – from unlicenced body workers to shamanistic healers.

39 Shorter, 1993: 266. See also "Witnessing as clinical tool" in Chapter 14.

40 Griffin, 1999: 93.

41 Kalsched, 1996: 1–3.

42 This "trauma" can be viewed as a malfunction – a metaphorical "stuckness" in the "on" position – of what Daniel Siegel calls "implicit memory." Implicit memory, present by age one, *is*. It cannot be turned on and off through conscious focus. Although research has not yet explored the neurobiology of somatosensory memory, Siegel believes it to be an integral aspect of implicit memory. When focal attention is blocked – the kind of emotional splitting off/dissociation that happens in cases of trauma – "items are not encoded explicitly . . . [but] implicit memory is intact." In essence, the *body* "remembers" but the mind does not. *Thus, from the subjective reality of the patient, it is a somatic reality* (Siegel, 1999: 29–30, 39, 50–55, 60). Also see Chapter 2.

43 Siegel, 1999: 19.

44 One could argue as to whether the injury/trauma to this little girl was on a somatic level or on a psychic/emotional level. Obviously it was both. Again we get into the conundrum of the psyche–soma split in western culture. I have chosen to say that for her it was "real" on a somato-psychic level because her experience of the transrational left her *hearing* the cries of the butterflies and other bugs.

45 See Chapter 10.

46 *Experienced*, as opposed to "perceived" which would imply a more conscious and focused awareness. It is because of this blurring of the boundaries that a Love Canal or a Rocky Flats is experienced as being the source of toxic poisoning in/through/by nature when in fact the earth in those contexts, is it self victim of human poisoning.

47 See pp. 115–116.

48 See Chapter 11.

49 Siegel, 1999: 86.

50 See Chapter 11. In saying this, I do not mean that these individuals cannot relate and do not have meaningful, loving relationships. I do mean that the damage is on an interpersonal level specifically in terms of their capacity to be healed through a transference-like relationship with a primary healer(s). For purposes of our discussion here, relationships with medical doctors and alternative healers, as

well as psychotherapists, constitute a transference relationship of one kind or another.

51 Daniel Siegel discusses four categories of attachment: secure, avoidant, ambivalent and disorganized/disoriented. See Siegel, 1999: Chapter 3.

52 Schmall, 1997: 3–4.

53 Although his research is primarily on the developmental process in children, he does address related dynamics in adults as well.

54 Siegel, 1999: 120.

55 Schmall, 1997: p. 4.

56 Patient feedback indicates that this treatment is efficacious. Other practitioners utilize related "nature" treatments such as talking to trees. One of my own patients reported that she had a devastating headache accompanying a sudden onset of episodic depression. She tried to alleviate her symptoms with medication to no avail. Instinctively (she told me about the experience after the fact and I had no role in it) she sought out her favorite tree and sat in front of it for an hour or more and suddenly realized her symptoms were gone. *It is vital that we not force these unorthodox measures into standard medical models of practice, i.e. the "placebo" effect (which I take as a medical term for, "we don't know" the nature of the healing dynamic) or some other answer comforting to our left-brain rational bias. We need to take these transrational experiences and treatments **on their own terms**. It behooves us to adjust our thinking rather than to "adjust" the experience to fit treatment models with which we are comfortable.*

57 This "split" between the individual's mental idea regarding the nurturing aspects of nature versus their somatic experience of nature could be explained by Siegel's differentiation of "explicit" versus "implicit" memory. See Siegel, 1999: Chapter 2.

58 Zwillinger, 1999.

59 Griffin, 1999: 96–97.

60 For Susan Schmall, it was a combination of many treatments and therapies that brought her healing: Macrobiotic diet, acupuncture, religious and spiritual practice, and the "process-oriented therapy" of Arnold Mindell. The last uses a method of working with bodily symptoms in which the symptom itself is amplified until the message in it is heard.

61 Schmall, 1997: 2.

62 In the case of Dr. Schmall, I personally interviewed her and saw no evidence of dissociation, as did not other highly trained clinicians who have known her over a period of years.

63 I prefer the word "traditional" to "alternative."

Chapter 18

Further reflections

We have so much control in proportion to the amount of our consciousness.
We have to learn how to live in the universe on its terms, instead of ours.[1]

The reader may have registered that nowhere in the text of this book does the phrase "New Age" appear. The New Age movement is defined by mainstream culture as a "broad-based amalgam of diverse spiritual, social, and political elements with the common aim of transforming individuals and society through spiritual awareness. *The New Age is a utopian vision, an era of harmony and progress*" (emphasis added).[2] Whatever the intention of those who consider themselves part of the New Age movement, the above definition reflects a perception of it as a "utopian vision," i.e. idealistic *and* not grounded in (rational) reality.[3] This perceptual attitude reflects an antagonism between mainstream culture and the New Age movement. Whatever else might be said of each party, with the exception of the energy each invests in disdaining the other, they go their separate ways with self-proclaimed clarity of vision. And of course, there is *some* truth on both sides of the fence.

From my perspective, as reflected in this book, the problem is that there *is* a "fence." In addition to a plea for consideration of transrational reality, particularly in clinical circles, I would hope that I have conveyed my conviction that the "Borderland" represents that dimension where there is no "fence" but rather a dynamic tension pressing for a confluence of some of what is alluded to in the New Age movement and mainstream culture – one that would evoke what Jung referred to as the "transcendent function."[4] There are a number of metaphorical representations of this dynamic which I have proposed *is* taking place, such as a "meeting of left-brain reality and right-brain reality." For myself, I see the Borderland as the dimension in which a new consciousness is emergent and evident, one that incorporates transrational reality. This book is about that new consciousness and how it is manifest(ing) – in the culture at large and particularly in clinical contexts.

In the clinical realm, contemporary brain research, some of which is discussed in this book, is bridging the split and the polarities that have long existed in the clinical disciplines. That research is rapidly linking left-brain/ right-brain thinking/experience for a more unified, more holistic, approach to medicine and healing. The "hard science" of medicine is now validating much of the "soft science" of psychology, most particularly some of the fundamental pillars of psychoanalytic theory.

However, given the emergence of more holistic possibilities in the clinical disciplines, I believe we can look toward transformative approaches to some areas of treatment of some disorders that historically have been particularly confounding, such as psychosomatic disorders, autoimmune diseases, trauma, borderline personality disorder, and attachment disorders.

In Part III of the book I have discussed the Navajo model of medicine. I did so because I believe that it offers a paradigm for bridging the traditional psyche/soma split in western medicine *and* a model for bringing to bear and integrating transrational reality as a powerful tool in healing illnesses that otherwise appear to defy western treatment approaches. It seems to me that one obvious area of potential exploration in this regard is environmental illness complex (EIC). Another is the treatment of trauma.

As discussed in Chapters 12–15, Navajo cosmology and the resultant diagnostic system that derives from it holds that many illnesses[5] result from a wound/transgression to or from nature. And, as described in Chapter 17, nature herself is experienced as the source[6] of illness/trauma for those with EIC. *Here*, then, is a diagnostic framework that can hold those dimensions of environmental illness complex that the western medical model seems to be unable to hold. This is not to say that those with EIC should seek out Navajo practitioners. Even with a Borderland personality, these individuals function with a western ego, as all non-Natives do in this culture. Most people with EIC *do* need some of the benefits of treatment modalities offered by western medicine. However, I am suggesting that a team of western and Navajo practitioners can offer a single transcendent treatment model that at one in the same time embraces the (western) medical, psychological, and Borderland/ transrational dynamics of EIC without falling into many of the conundrums described in the previous chapter. The same model would be efficacious in the treatment of trauma wounds as well.

In my clinical experience with individuals who have suffered trauma, particularly in their primary years, nearly one-third of them have had animals associated with their experience of trauma, e.g. their favorite dog being tortured or killed by a family member. Some of these experiences have been described in previous chapters. For some, their trauma is never adequately addressed *until the trauma of their beloved animal is addressed and healed directly*. The western medical model and the various psychotherapeutic paradigms are wanting in this regard.[7] The Navajo model, as discussed in Chapter 13, addresses this level of wound *directly*.

Although I have not attempted such an integrated approach, i.e. western + Navajo practitioners working as a team with patients with EIC, I have consulted with Navajo medicine men regarding some of my patients with trauma wounds. I have held Navajo healing ceremonies in my office with select patients. Although it is too early to draw definitive conclusions from these efforts, so far the experience has been positive with visible results.

Ultimately, I imagine a team of environmental physicians, Navajo medicine men, analytical psychologists, and other practitioners exploring new and unified treatment approaches with EIC patients, each learning to apprehend and integrate the wisdom and science of the other's discipline. Hopefully funding institutions can be persuaded of the value of such research, since, like much of medical research, exploring these new treatment paradigms in a manner that will yield definitive data (statistical and non-statistical) will be expensive.

The notion of such interdisciplinary research involving Navajo medicine men and western-trained physicians is not as far beyond reach as it may seem. In 1998 the *Journal of the American Medical Association* (JAMA), one of the most prestigious and authoritative organs of allopathic medical research, published an article addressing the "Traditional Chinese medicine uses [of] moxibustion (["moxa"] burning herbs to stimulate acupuncture points . . . located beside the outer corner of the fifth toenail), to promote version of fetuses in breech presentation." This double-blind study yielded statistically significant data that demonstrated that this ancient Chinese practice to correct breech presentation stimulated the fetus to turn from the breech presentation to the safer cephalic (head) presentation during the 33rd week of normal gestation.[8] So, here it is: "Face-to-face," as it were, confluence of transrational reality[9] with the hard science of allopathic medicine. That the study was published in *JAMA* at all is remarkable. That, to my knowledge, there was no follow-up to the study, is not. But a seemingly impossible threshold has been crossed. And, thresholds crossed cannot be uncrossed. It remains for others to follow a path that has been opened.

If, as I have theorized, the western psyche is being reconnected with nature from which it has been split for the past three millennia, then with that reconnection comes a link to a transpersonal dimension that holds promise of mitigating the inflation of the western ego. On the one hand, the globalization movement as we know it today can be seen as a steamroller, symbolized by the multinational corporation, devoted to economic expediency as the greater good, threatening to crush everything in its path. On the other hand, an ego that is confronted by moral consciousness emanating from the Self,[10] holds potential for revolutionizing that thrust into a force for global transformation. Brian Swimme, a mathematician and cosmologist, and historian, Thomas Berry, address such possible transformation in their book, *The Universe Story*:

As industrial humans multiplied into the billions to become the most numerous of all of Earth's complex organisms, as they decisively inserted themselves into the ecosystemic communities throughout the planet, drastically reducing Earth's diversity and channeling the majority of the Gross Earth Product into human social systems, a momentous change in human consciousness was in process. Humans discovered that the universe as a whole is not simply a background, not simply an existing place; the universe itself is a developing community of beings. Humans discovered by empirical investigation that they were participants in this fifteen-billion-year sequence of transformations that had eventuated into the complex functioning Earth. A sustained and even violent assault by western intelligence upon the universe, through the work of Copernicus, Kepler, Galileo, Newton . . . Darwin . . . Curie, Hubble . . . Einstein, and the entire modern scientific enterprise, had brought forth a radically new understanding of the universe, not simply as a cosmos, but as a cosmogenesis, a developing community, one with an important role for the human in the midst of the process . . .

[The] future will be worked out in the tensions between those committed to the Technozoic, a future of increased exploitation of Earth as resource, all for the benefit of humans, and those committed to the Ecozoic, a new mode of human-Earth relations, one where the well-being of the entire Earth community is the primary concern.[11,12]

It is difficult at this juncture to imagine the form that such a transformation might take, since, by definition, the transcendent function produces a "third" which is different in nature from the two antagonistic dynamics. For example, a dynamic that holds antagonistic tension and gives balanced value to the well-being of lumbermen as well as to trees and the ecology, offers a prospect beyond what we have come to experience in the environmental movement. Through a mutual encounter with the "Great Grief" of the dilemma of the human condition, we are offered a possibility about which we can barely speculate. But if we can *imagine* sufficiently to articulate the dilemma and hold the grief, we should be open to embracing them. *Then* we are opened to noticing new thresholds of consciousness and possibility. That is the challenge as well as the potential promise of the Borderland.

Notes

1 Ryley, 1998, quoting Thomas Berry, historian and eco-theologian.
2 *Microsoft® Encarta® Encyclopedia 2000.* © 1993–1999 Microsoft Corporation.
3 For some, the New Age movement is their "spiritual bypass." These individuals do harm to the legitimate dimensions of that movement as well as to themselves personally.
4 See Chapter 14.
5 Bearing in mind, again, that there is no distinction between psyche and soma in the Navajo system.
6 But not necessarily the *cause* of EIC.
7 It is noted that mind/body treatment modalities such as EMDR, DNMS, and

SctD tend to address trauma at this level, i.e. injury to the beloved animal itself. However, they tend not to go beyond addressing the trauma to the patient *about* what happened to the animal and stop short of treating the trauma to the animal as well as to the patient. In Navajo way, a ceremony would be required to treat the animal as "patient" as well as well as the individual, so as to release the latter from his trauma. (For an explication of this point, see the discussion in Chapter 13 of the Navajo case presentation where the father of a child killed a dog while the child was in utero.)

8 Cardini, 1998; JAMA, 1998, 280(18):1580–4.

9 In this context, by "transrational reality" is meant that *what* took place as a result of burning moxa against the nail of the little toe of the mother – spontaneous turning of the fetus in utero from the breech to the cephalic position – did occur. *The nature of the dynamic* that brought about the results remains a mystery. In short, we know that the procedure works; we do not know *why* it works.

10 See Chapter 7.

11 Swimme, 1994: 14–15.

12 What is being alluded to by Swimme and Berry here is what I have addressed in terms of psychic evolution in Chapter 7.

Epilogue: The Borderland – the place-of-potential-meeting

Long, long ago, in a time before time and a time after time, in a time when time was circular, and East met West, before the separation of the worlds, and long, long after the separation of the worlds, then, in that time, this story begins.

In the East was the world of the White Brothers. (There were also White sisters in the World to the East, but no one spoke of them.) They were also known as the People of the Word. Words were very important to them and after a long time of only speaking words they learned to write words. Then there was no stopping them. They wrote words upon words, books upon books, laws upon laws. They had a word for everything. They knew a lot. And they wrote it all down. Nothing was left unwritten.

In the West were the Rainbow People, the Below and Above Earth People, the People of the Four Directions. And they had other names too, many of them – beautiful names. (Sometimes when one of them might feel sad, she might just sit and listen for the One-Who-Sang-Songs, for twice every day – at sunup and at sunset – she would sing the names of the Rainbow People. And then, the one who felt sad would feel better.)

The People of the Word and the Rainbow People did not know that the other existed. All were busy doing what they did. The Rainbow People tilled the earth and hunted and made ceremonies as the Holy People instructed them to do. They knew that their ceremonies were part of the Four Directions, that it would not rain or would flood without them, that they made people well when they were sick and that they were essential for Harmony and Beauty. This they did. And in winter when it was dark and the earth was quiet and cold, they huddled around fires in their houses and told stories of the way it was and the way it is and of the exploits of coyote and snake and Big Fly, of hawk, panther, and snail, and all the other creatures of the earth, the sky and the below worlds.

The People of the Word also tilled the land and hunted and did many of the same things that the Rainbow People did. But once they learned to write words, they became obsessed with learning. The more they learned the more they had to learn, for each answer led to the next question and there were more questions than anyone could possibly count. They studied everything and they learned everything and they wrote it all down and organized it so that everyone could understand. And after a while they developed something called "science." It was a wonderful thing and with it they devised all manner of machines and tools.

The People of the Word did not know that time was circular; they thought that all time moved in a straight line. Because they thought time only moved in a straight line and that one could never return to a place once passed, they became very clever about using time. But after a while, because they were so smart and learned so much and had to write everything down, they began to find that more and more time was taken up with more and more learning and the building of more and more machines and the building of something else they called "culture." There was less and less time for tilling the earth and hunting and the kinds of things that the People of the Rainbow did.

But the People of the Word were very smart and they invented machines that would do these things for them. The People of the Word thought that these machines would bring them more time and that they would not have to work so hard.

After a while, because their machines did so much for them, the People of the Word began to forget the rituals and ceremonies that they knew in the time of hunting and tilling. They began to forget the language of the creatures, the songs of the earth, the whisperings of the trees, and the reasons for all being creatures. But they didn't mourn this loss – they didn't even know they were losing something. They were very busy learning and writing things down and making machines.

Soon they learned to build cities – first small ones and then big ones and then cities bigger than all the villages of the People of the Rainbow combined. They were marvelous cities and each new one had something that the cities built before did not. Because their cities made it possible to put more things and people in one space, their numbers grew and grew. And soon their entire world was filled with cities and people.

As the People of the Word lost their rituals and ceremonies, these began to be replaced by things. At first the things they coveted were tools, and then later metals and stones which they called precious, and then very complicated machines. Unlike the Rainbow People, who found stones and metals to be precious because of what lived within them and their Beauty, the People of the Word valued these things because other people valued them. The more someone else valued something, the more someone else would want it and the more it would cost. And soon value was determined not by the Beauty within, but by greed. Some things became so valuable that they could no longer be seen. They were kept in a place called a "vault" and were brought out once or twice a year when someone else would ask to see the "thing-so-valuable-that-it-could-not-be-seen." These things-so-valuable-that-they-could-not-be-seen lived in darkness and became sad.

While all of these very important things were happening in the World to the East, nothing much changed in the World to the West. The Rainbow People tilled their land, hunted for their food, performed their rituals and ceremonies, told stories in the dark winter nights, and Walked in Beauty. It is true that they did not know how to read and to write things down or to make machines or build tall cities like the People of the East, but they seemed content.

When they learned to write down their words, their written words led the People of the Word towards a new kind of God. He was a God who created with his mind and his will. He would think things and then will them and then they would happen. The men He created in His image were like Him in this respect. They too became more and more fixed on their will and their use of power to create things, and before too long they believed (although many of them did not know this) that all things were created by their individual minds and their individual wills. And although they talked much of their Father God, they behaved as if they had as much power as He.

The Father God was very wise and made many laws for His people to govern their lives. He taught them the rules for living together, and above all else for worshipping Him. Sometimes His people would have great difficulty obeying His words and then He would become very angry. Even when they tried as hard as they could and did almost everything the way He wanted them to, somehow that would not be enough and He would become angry and destroy much of His creation and even the People He loved.

The People of the Word struggled and struggled to understand why the Father God was always so angry at them. They knew that they did bad things sometimes, but they didn't do them all of the time and deep down, secretly within, they did not believe that they were so bad. (They couldn't let the Father God know this thought because they knew it would make Him more angry than ever.) The Father God over and over said how special His people were to him and how He would treat them above all others. But eventually He would accuse them of breaking his rules and would rage at them anew. Sometimes they would even become angry, although they dared not let the Father God know they were angry.

Later the Father God gave the People of the East His Son to help them. His secret was that He needed a Son in the World to help Him with His temper, which He could not seem to get under control. And although His Son was much different from Himself and could love more than He could be angry, the people grew more hostile. Soon the followers of the Son decided that the Word of the Son was the Word to follow and that those who did not follow His Word were not true believers. In the World of the East it was not a good thing to not be a true believer. As a result there were many wars and many killings.

As the People of the Word struggled to understand their relationship with the Father God, they became more and more aware of themselves. The more they struggled to understand Him, the more they came to know about themselves. After a time a few of them became very thoughtful and began to stop doing, so that they could think about who they were. Some of them even spent time reflecting on what took place inside them. And over time, this capacity for self-reflecting developed into a new thing which they called "Ego."

This Ego was a wonderful thing and a terrible thing. It enabled the People of the Word to write even more books about more things, it enabled them to develop a healing system called "medicine," and after a while they learned to write down music as well as words. This was truly a wonderful thing, they thought, since no songs ever sung would be forgotten. But they had forgotten that music that came from a written page no longer carried the blessings of the plants and animals and of Wind who sang the first songs long ago.

Ego also enabled them to make the most terrible weapons of war and there were more wars and more and more people were killed. But most important to most of them, Ego made them feel that they were above all the animals and plants and all things of being. They knew that nothing was greater than they and that they could do anything they wished. This thought made them feel safe. It also made them arrogant.

All things would be subject to their will and they could even change the way the rivers ran and take down whole forests to build their cities and look for precious metals which would be worn or stored in vaults to be safe. They didn't want to hurt the feelings of the Father God by letting Him know that they were beginning to feel that they were more powerful than He, so they pretended that they still believed He was more powerful than they.

The world of the Rainbow People changed hardly at all. They were happy to do what they did, to plant and grow and hunt and carry out the rituals and ceremonies taught to them all by First Man. This they did year in and year out. Because they did not forget the rituals and ceremonies, they were not plagued with greed for things like the People of the Word. But sometimes they were infected by jealousy of each other, and because of this sometimes they felt witched by each other and bad things would happen.

Rainbow People had no Father God like the People of the Word. In fact, they had no gods at all. They knew that life emerged from below and was not created by anything or anyone. What was below had always been, and when it was time, the People emerged from below and took their place in the balance of all things. There were no superior beings. All things, including the Holy People, even Talking God himself, were what they were, and each did what it was right for them to do.

The Rainbow People knew the story of the Emergence because the Holy People told it to them, and they could see it in all the living things and things of being about them. There were special people known as Medicine People who not only knew the stories of the Emergence and what took place in each world, but knew the secrets for sending evil thoughts to the North, and which ceremony was necessary for each illness and how to re-establish harmony when someone did something wrong or had a bad dream or when lightning struck. Usually when someone was witched he would have to go to a Medicine Person to break the spell. Often the Medicine Person would protect him if the People would perform special rituals and think good thoughts.

Rainbow People fought with each other some of the time. But they did not have "Ego" and "science," and most important, they did not have "Horse" like The People of the Word. They fought with the same weapons they had always had. So their fights were short and far between and not many people were killed or hurt. In fact, before the Great Crossing, they seldom killed in their wars, and vanquished their enemy by making coup on each other as a matter of pride, and by taking prisoners. They even took and sold slaves. When they made war and killed, they also knew when to stop – when enough were killed.

After a long long time and when the People of the Word began to run out of space in the Land to the East, a great argument broke out as to whether the Earth was round or flat. This argument was part of the learning of the People of the Word, and much depended on the answer, for their greed had no other place to go. And as a result of this argument great ships were built because it had been decided that the only way to know the answer to this question was to sail to the end of the ocean.

And so it was undertaken. The Waters-Not-To-Be-Crossed were crossed and the Great Crossing was undertaken. And indeed an answer was found. The Earth was round. The People of the Word rejoiced, especially the Father King, because a new place was found for the search for the precious metal "gold" and a new home was found for their greed. This meant that fewer people would be killed in the Land to the East, and they were happy because of this belief. But they found there were different people on the other side of the round Earth.

To the people who inhabited the Land to the West, to the Rainbow People, the People of the Word became known by their color. This was a wise decision since the People of the Word did not trust anyone who was not the same color as they – even if they were named Rainbow People.

Because the People of the Word had lost their rituals and ceremonies so long ago and no longer could be made to feel safe by them, they were frightened at their encounter with the Rainbow People. These new people were a different color, a darker color than the People of the Word. Their ways were strange, they showed their bodies, and they showed little fear and welcomed the stranger Whites. They still understood the rituals and ceremonies long since forgotten by the People of the Word, who found them very strange and even frightening. They also did not understand greed. This last was the most unsettling fact of all about the Rainbow People. How could anyone trust people who did not understand greed?

The People of the Rainbow found the People of the Word just as strange. Although they were very impressed and attracted to their magical color, they could not understand why the People of the Word always had to fight for what was there to be shared. It seemed a very strange way to live. They wore very heavy clothes and metal and seemed ashamed of their bodies, and they knew no rituals at all except that of reading from their books. Some Rainbow People wondered if the People of the Word knew anything at all that was not written in a book.

There were special people who came with the People of the Word. At first the Rainbow People thought these were the Medicine People of the Whites, especially since they wore brightly colored robes in addition to their black uniforms. They seemed more sensible than the other Whites since they did not wear metal clothes in the heat of the sun. They also brought with them a special symbol, a cross made of metal, which they carried everywhere and it was the first and only thing about the Whites that meant something to the Rainbow People. "Ah," they thought, "these are their Medicine People, for they know the wonders of Messenger Dragonfly, and the place of Emergence." But finally, when they learned to talk with the Whites, they found that the cross had a different meaning for them, and that the Whites knew nothing of the Emergence and the Below Worlds.

When these strange Medicine People could converse with the People of the Rainbow, they asked them about their gods. Since the Rainbow People had no gods, they thought that the White Medicine People were asking about their rituals and ceremonies and the Holy People, and they answered, "Wil-a'-Che," meaning, "We do not speak of it." The White Medicine People misunderstood their meaning and took their response to mean, "We don't know," – that the Rainbow People had no god like theirs at all. In a strange way this seemed to please the White Medicine People, who then began to treat the Rainbow People as if they knew nothing at all.

It was a very bad answer to give the White Medicine People, even if it was true. (After all, how could one speak of one's rituals and ceremonies and of the Holy People to someone who knew nothing of the Emergence and the Below Worlds?) But it was a very bad answer nonetheless. For what followed was many years of torture and killing in the name of the loving god of the People of the Word. And although the People of the Rainbow were told over and over again that the Father God of the Whites and His Son loved them, and although they had to say that they understood this in order not to be killed, they never did understand how a God of Love would have it so. They did not understand how this god cared only about words and nothing about the plants and trees and animals and the things of being. But that was the way it was.

There followed many more years (even more than the Medicine People who remembered everything could remember) of punishment, especially for performing their rituals and ceremonies that the People of the Rainbow had to hide and perform in secret.

Then the Great Sickness descended. It was unlike anything that had ever happened to the Rainbow People before and caused terrible pain and death.

Whole villages died and even whole peoples who were the Keepers of the Sacred Language. Soon there was no one to remember the words of the Holy People and the Holy People themselves wept and grieved. It was the Time-of-Great-Sadness and everywhere there was death, grief, and mourning without relief.

Then, many years later, in the north part of the Land to the East, a different group of White people came. They spoke a different language from those to the South, and they did not seem so cruel. They were still People of the Word and did many of the same things as the Whites to the South.

At first these Whites lived in harmony with the People of the Rainbow and there was peace. But more and more came across the Waters-Not-To-Be-Crossed and soon there was no room for everyone. The Whites began to kill the People of the Rainbow and force them off the lands on which they had lived since the Emergence and then there was no longer Harmony and Peace.

They, too, asked the People of the Rainbow about their rituals and ceremonies. And again, the People of the Rainbow gave the same answer, "Wil-a'-Che," meaning, "We do not speak of it." The White Medicine People from the North misunderstood their meaning just like the White Medicine People to the South and took their response to mean, "We don't know" – that the Rainbow People didn't have any of what the White Medicine People called "religion." This time, although they did kill many Rainbow People, they also sent White Medicine People called Missionaries to "save" the Rainbow People, and they brought the religion of the Father God like the White people to the South. Many Rainbow People who lived in the North were permitted to live, but they too had to hide their rituals and ceremonies like the Rainbow People to the South. They were told too that they had to wear the same clothes as the Whites, that they could no longer speak their language, that their language was not good for them, and that their children had to be sent away to schools so that they could learn to read and write like the People of the Word. They also said that they knew better where it was best for Rainbow People to live and made them put "x"s on papers, which they said explained where and why. These they called "Treaties" and although the Rainbow People still could not understand them, they knew that they were important to the People of the Word and that someday they might be important to the Rainbow People as well.

There was much that was the same for the Rainbow People to the North as what happened to the Rainbow People to the South, but this time something different occurred as well. The White People of the North brought Horse and guns and firewater with them. And when they gave these to the Rainbow People, this time the Rainbow People could not laugh and shrug their shoulders at the strange ways of the Whites. It was as if these three things – especially firewater – were infected with the germ of greed, and for the first time the Rainbow People began to forget their rituals and ceremonies and the teachings of First Man and First Woman and the other Holy People, and some of them began to act like Whites. They even fought in the White Men's wars against other Rainbow People, not out of need or pride like in the past, but out of greed and even to steal possessions and land. And this time they did not just strike coup against their Rainbow brothers and take prisoners – this time they killed.

Never before had anyone seen Rainbow People behave this way, and those who kept the rituals and ceremonies and listened to the Holy People were truly confused. No one, not even the Medicine People, could stop this craziness.

And the Whites came and came from across the Waters-Not-To-Be-Crossed, like an unending herd of buffalo, trampling everything in their path. And soon they were building big cities in the Land to the West and the Rainbow People were pushed farther and farther away from the lands they had known. It was as if the ants and other insects from the First World had gone up the Great Reed, through all four of the Below Worlds, and were taking over all of the Fifth World. Surely Monster Slayer and his brother were needed again. But the Whites came in such numbers and with such ferocity that there was not time to perform the rituals and ceremonies to bring things into enough balance to call them forth. It was surely a dangerous and uncertain time for the Rainbow People.

Then something happened that gave the Rainbow People some new hope. The Whites themselves began to fight a terrible war with each other. The Rainbow People tried to stay out of the way and lie low while the Whites killed each other. But this only helped a little, and although the Whites killed each other with a ferocity that no one had ever seen before, that did not keep them from also killing Rainbow People whenever they encountered them. After a while the Medicine People and the Elders would just say, "Those White People, those People of the Word, are surely crazy, because all they want to do is to kill. They kill us and they kill each other and they are killing all of our buffalo as well. Soon there will be no food; not for us and not for them. They are surely crazy!" And the Medicine People and the Elders were right – except the Whites did have enough food for themselves.

Another problem for the Rainbow People was the sicknesses which the People of the Word gave them. They were new kinds of sicknesses and none of the Medicine People could help. Many many people died and some tribes lost nearly all of their members. When certain clans would die out, their songs and dances would die with them, and the people worried about how they would marry and make children with so few clans to marry with. The dying from the White Man's sickness went on for a long time and no Medicine People could help.

In spite of many new rituals and dances devised to ward off the evils brought by the White Brothers and many meetings with the Great White Father in a city near the Waters-Not-To-Be-Crossed, and many more treaties that were given Rainbow People, the new hope among the Rainbow People that came when the Whites began to fight their terrible war, did not last long.

No matter what they did or said, the Rainbow People were killed and their lands were taken. And after the big war between the Blue Whites and the Gray Whites, it got even worse. Before too long there were no more buffalo to hunt. It was the worst of times, and no one knew what would come to pass. Many Rainbow People thought that they would all die and then there would be no one to sing the songs, perform the rituals and ceremonies, and that Mother Earth, Herself, would surely become sick and die.

But a new time came which the Whites called the "20th century." And for reasons that no one understood, the Whites began to get quiet and did not hunt down the Rainbow People anymore. Finally, the killing stopped. There were no more buffalo to hunt. But the killing stopped. And the Rainbow People, who were now broken up into many small bands in many strange lands picked by the Whites, were allowed to live in peace. Some were even permitted to go home to the lands from which they were taken. They were poor and didn't have enough to eat and many had rags for clothes, but they were allowed to live in peace.

These were still terrible times for the Rainbow People – many bands were not allowed to perform the rituals and ceremonies, many were given strange new names in the White Man's language and were forced to speak the White's language and were not permitted to speak their own. Their children were taken away to schools in far off places that no one knew, and sometimes they were never seen again. But the killing had stopped.

The Medicine People and the Elders were right about the White Brothers – they were crazy. They had learned nothing from the killing in the age that just passed. The 20th century became the age of the Great Wars, and the Rainbow People fought with their White Brothers on the other side of the Waters-Not-To-Be-Crossed. These wars were even more terrible than the wars between the Blue and Gray Whites and the wars against the Rainbow People. And it seemed that all of their learning was fixed on making more powerful weapons for killing the most people possible, even for killing people who were not fighting in the war. No one among the Rainbow People understood them.

Then a very strange thing happened. Twenty-five or 30 years after they stopped killing Rainbow People, the White Brothers decided to make them citizens of their new country. No one among the Rainbow People was sure what that meant, but they were told that now the Rainbow People could do what the People of the Word could do. That seemed very strange and the Great White Father in the great city near the Waters-Not-To-Be-Crossed sent some people to work with the tribes of Rainbow People to show them how to use words and to write them down and to make laws and rules for themselves. These were strange ways that no one really understood. But by now, the old ways did not work well anymore and some had been lost and forgotten. The Rainbow People were in disarray. They could not go back to the old ways. There was no going back. They were alone in the Fifth World with the White

Brothers and if they were going to survive, they realized that they would have to learn these new ways. It was a sorrowful and painful time. It was a time of the Great Sadness and there was a quiet mourning everywhere. But there was nothing else they could do.

In the meantime, the White Brothers fought two Great Wars. Many Rainbow Warriors felt that now that they were citizens of the White Man's country that honor and loyalty required them to help their White Brothers fight the enemy in the Second Great War. And they did. Some became Code Talkers and great heroes in the war across the Waters-Not-To-Be-Crossed. The Whites were impressed with the prowess of the Rainbow Warriors and honored them in many ways.

Because the People of the Word had learned so much and written down everything they learned, their Science and its son, Technology, could make the most awesome weapons and perform the most awesome feats. By the end of the Second Great War, the People of the Word had made a terrible new weapon of war. Some said that it was more powerful than the power of the sun. Everyone was amazed – even the People of the Word themselves. Then, towards the end of this new age they called the 20th century, they stopped fighting Great Wars and all the Word People's energy and resources went into making these and even more powerful weapons of war that were so powerful that everyone was afraid to use them. So they entered a strange period where they only threatened to make war on each other over and over and over again. But they never did make a Great War on each other because they were afraid of their own weapons as well as those of their enemy. This was truly a new age.

Towards the end of this new age, the People of the Word began to speak of the Terrible Awareness. At first it was just a small band of White Brothers who did so, and the others made fun of them and got angry at them. But their words made sense to the Rainbow People who had learned by now to listen quietly. They knew not to enter the argument that was beginning between the People of the Word.

Again greed played a major role as always in the arguments between the different bands of the People of the Word. But those who spoke of Mother Earth, of the poisons that had been spilled on her skin, the rape of her womb, the cutting of her hair, the poisoning of the domain of Father Sky, spoke louder and with more passion than ever. There were many words spoken for a long long time and many arguments took place. And the Word People even began to speak of their own greed and how it was poisoning everything and how they would all die if it did not stop. After a time more and more People of the Word began to listen.

The People of the Word in the new country began to tell the People of the Word in the old country on the other side of the Waters-Not-To-Be-Crossed and even they began to listen too. And the Terrible Awareness began to grow on them and more and more they began to realize that the thing called Ego had become too arrogant and had created new monsters even more frightening than those killed by Monster Slayer and Child-Born-of-Water. These monsters could not be killed, they could only be understood and tamed. Most important of all, they began to become aware that Ego not only could not control these new monsters, but if they were not careful, Ego would be seduced into working for these new monsters. And the People of the Word became very afraid. And the Rainbow People became amazed when they saw this.

Even the power of the Medicine of the People of the Word began to be questioned by some. Some of the Medicine created by Ego and its son, Technology, not only began to stop healing, it began to become a problem itself. Somehow the Medicine resulted in even stronger diseases that could not be cured by any Medicine anyone knew. And some began to suggest that perhaps some of the plants and herbs of the People of the Rainbow were indeed powerful and could help. Some even became interested in the healing ceremonies of the Rainbow People. This was the most shocking thing of all because the White Brothers had always made fun of their healing ceremonies. And the Rainbow People listened and watched with amazement.

There stirred a murmur of excitement among the Rainbow People. They were happy that their Medicine People and the Elders had told them the truth, even during the darkest times. And they were proud to know that at last a few of the People of the Word were beginning to discover the wisdom of the Ways of the Rainbow People. But they were also sad since so many of their rituals and ceremonies and medicines, even their languages, had been forgotten, and so many of their Medicine People and Elders had died and taken with them many of the songs and stories which would never again be sung or told.

But the Rainbow People also were afraid, because now they were dependent on many of the ways of the People of the Word. They had already begun to realize that they needed more of this thing called Ego that was so important to the People of the Word and so confusing to the Rainbow People. Although they knew that it was sometimes destructive to the People of the Word, they also knew that they could no longer live and survive without getting more of it for themselves.

They were even dependent on some of the Medicine of the People of the Word, because many of their illnesses were illnesses given to them long ago by the Whites. So it was not enough, they knew, for their Rainbow Medicine to be recognized by the People of the Word. Soon some of them began to realize that it would be necessary for the Medicine People of both Peoples to meet and speak with one another. And as they pondered this, some of the Wise People and Elders of the People of the Word pondered the same thoughts.

So each sat and pondered and reflected. And every once in a while one or two of the Wise People of the People of the Word would look up and would see one or two of the Wise People of the Rainbow People look up and they would each look across the Borderland that separated the two Peoples and see one another, and their eyes would meet.

So this is how the new age called 20th century came to a close, with the Rainbow People and the People of the Word together at the Borderland, the Place-of-Potential-Meeting. Here, there was an ending. And here, perhaps, a new beginning. Here, at the Borderland, at the Place-of-Potential-Meeting is where that story may yet be told . . .

Appendix

July 9, 2001

Dear Responder to my "Borderland" Article in either *The Salt Journal* or *The IONS Review*:

As an update, the book is well along the way. I am hoping for a publication date sometime in 2002. The tentative title, for now, is *Listening in the Borderland: Discriminating the Pathological from the Sacred.*

You have responded to my article "On the Borderland." Some of you have been quite generous and trusting in sharing your personal experiences, for which I am most grateful. I am writing you now because I am at a place in my own writing on the "Borderland" experience where more direct input from you would be most helpful in exploring, challenging, and validating some of my own thinking about the "Borderland." For now, I have concluded that in terms of personal psychology there are three portals to the Borderland:

1 evolution
2 character or personality structure (i.e. the type of psyche we are born with)
3 trauma.

It is about the third, trauma, that I am writing you.

Most of you have acknowledged that you have had some form of early childhood trauma/abuse (psychological/emotional, physical non-sexual, or physical sexual) in your life experience. In one way or another, you have indicated that you consider that abuse/trauma as significant in opening up the Borderland in your life experience. I have formulated several questions to which your responses would be very helpful to me in better understanding your past *and present* relationship to the Borderland in the context of your trauma/abuse history. I would appreciate responses to all of these questions. I invite you to be both concrete (e.g. yes, no, age 8, etc.) and to elaborate your response with as much detail as you care to share.

I am aware that the questions that follow are both daunting and a lot to ask. Frankly, when I read them over myself, they began to feel like an exam! I have asked for a lot of narrative response because it is in that context that the depth of personal connection and understanding comes through – particularly in sharing your images and feelings about your Borderland experience. That is what has been most valuable to me.

Some of you may find that you don't wish to answer them all. If so, please answer those that speak to you. At this juncture in my work, it would be particularly helpful to me if you would answer questions 12, 16, 17, and 18. Also, I am aware that some of you have already provided me with some of the information sought in some of the questions. I still have your earlier communications, if you are willing, I would encourage you to respond to all of the questions fully, including those for which you have already partially provided information.

Since I am sending you this communication via email, the best format for me is if you would use the "Reply" button to respond to this Questionnaire and if you would respond to each question in the same paragraph as the question, e.g. hit the "Enter" key after the question and respond to the given question before going on to the next question. If this doesn't make sense, just respond in the manner that is most convenient for you indicating the number of the question you are responding to.

As in previous correspondence, your individual responses will be treated with respect and confidentiality. So, again, my thanks for your cooperation and support. It would be most helpful if I could have your response by July 23 if at all possible. If that is not possible, I would like your response whenever you can send it.

Questionnaire

1. Your age.
2. Marital status (including the number of marriages/partnerships if more than one).
3. Number of children: Age and sex
4. From your perspective today, how old were you when you had your first Borderland experience? How long have you been aware of the Borderland – even if at the time you did not have words to describe it – and when do you first recalling telling anyone about it?
5. How did you come to know of your Borderland connection? Did you keep that awareness a secret or did you share it? What types of people did you share it with and from what types of individual did you keep it a secret? What kind of reception did you receive from those with whom you shared your Borderland connection?
6. Would you say that you have led parallel lives: One, more or less, known to others; another, more connected to the Borderland which you did not make known to the majority of your intimates? Please give details.
7. How has your Borderland life experience impacted your relationships

with those most intimate to you: Spouse/partner, parents, children, intimate friends? Please indicate both positive and negative factors.

8. How has your Borderland life experience impacted your relationships with the culture at large, e.g. on the job, with less intimate acquaintances, in school, etc.? please indicate both positive and negative factors.

9. Looking back, with regard to questions #7 and #8, what would you have changed in terms of *your* actions?

10. Do you observe a religious/spiritual practice? What kind? Please describe.

11. Describe your relationship with your children and intimate family members, e.g. are they close, distant, good, bad, extraordinary: indicate problems, most positive aspects, etc.

12. Please describe in some detail the nature of the trauma(s) that you encountered *that you consider to be instrumental in opening up the Border-land* to you. At what age did the trauma(s) take place? What connection do you see between those events you have just described and the opening of the Borderland to you?

13. Have you been in therapy? At what age(s)? How many therapies? How long for each therapy (weeks, months, years)? What gender was your therapist(s)? What kind of therapy(ies) was it (e.g. cognitive, behavioral, supportive, hypnosis, psychoanalytic, etc.)? Did you choose to go into therapy or was that choice made for you? By whom? Was the therapy(ies) beneficial, not helpful, or a negative experience? Why?

14. What role did your therapy(ies) play in discovering your history of trauma? Was that helpful? Did you discover your Borderland connection while in therapy? *Did you discuss your Borderland experience with your therapist*?

15. How would you distinguish the difference between psychic experience(s) and Borderland experience(s)?

16. If you could have realized significantly better intimacy with others in the first half of your life, would you choose to do so if it meant sacrificing some of the Borderland connection/experience that you had? Would you choose to do so now if that choice were available to you?

17. What do you fear most in sharing the existence of your Borderland experience with others? (Some of you have informed me that you have taken such a risk since reading my article. What has been your experience since then and/or our last communication?)

18. Below is a quote from a book regarding trauma and its treatment by a noted authority in the field. Do you agree/disagree with the sentiment of this paragraph and in what ways?

When our ... patients get better, even as their outer lives become more animated with their true selves, they go through a mournful period of dreaded loss of their inner worlds – or so it feels to them – a kind of agonizing sacrifice of what feels like their "childhoods." They do not want to give up "God's world" for the hollow superficialities of life in "this world," with its banalities and falsehoods. Yet life in the outer world is beginning to be more real and authentic . . . they are challenged to give up their identification with the inflated world of bewitchment. This is what "happily ever after" means in . . . fairy tales – neither living in bliss, on the one hand, nor a hollow "reality" on the other, but living in a world where the wall between imagination and reality comes down and becomes a flexible boundary . . . it is living a life one can dream about and in which the struggle to realize that dream can be shared with others who are doing the same thing.

Thank you so much,
Jerome S. Bernstein

Bibliography

Abram, D. (1996). *The Spell of the Sensuous*. New York, Random House.

American Academy of Environmental Medicine (2003). *Optimal Health in a Healthy Environment*. www.aaem.com

American Medical Association (A. M. A.) (2003). *Physician ICD-9-CM2003: International Classification of Diseases*, Hyattsville, MD, NCHS.

Andersen, H. C. (1871, printed version first published; 1972, film). The Emperor's New Clothes.

Anson, S. (1997). "Post-traumatic Stress Disorder, Somatization, Trauma, and Multiple Losses". In *Mind-Body Problems: Psychotherapy with Psychosomatic Disorders*. J. S. Finell (Ed.). Northvale, NJ, Jason Aronson, pp. 95–119.

Avila, E. w. J. P. (1999). *Woman Who Glows in the Dark: A Curandera Reveals Traditional Aztec Secrets of Physical and Spiritual Health*. New York, Jeremy P. Tarcher/Putnam.

Balint, M. (1969). *Basic Fault: Therapeutic Aspects of Regression*. New York, Brunner/Mazel.

Bartha, L. et al. (1999). Multiple Chemical Sensitivity: a 1999 Consensus. *Archives of Environmental Health*, 54(3), 147–149.

Bell, I. R. (2003). The Complicated Patient: Multiple Chemical Sensitivities. *Psychiatric Times,* 20(1).

Bernstein, J. (1989). *Power and Politics: The Psychology of Soviet-American Partnership*. Boston, Shambhala.

Bernstein, J. S. (1993). "Beyond the Individual: Analytical Psychology Applied to Groups and Nations". In *Carl Gustave Jung: Critical Assessments*. R. Popadopoulos (Ed.). London, Routledge.

Bernstein, J. (2000). Listening in the Borderlands. *The Salt Journal* 2(2), 13–21.

Bernstein, J. (2000). On the Borderland. *IONS Noetic Sciences Review* 53, 8–13, 44–46.

The Bible (1987) Nashville, TN, Gideons International.

Blum, A. and Danson, M., et al. (1997). Problems of Sexual Expression in Adult Gay Men: A Psychoanalytic Reconsideration. *Psychoanalytic Psychology: A Journal of Theory, Practice, Research, and Criticism*, 14(1), 1–11.

Boas, F. (1938). *The Mind of Primitive Man*. Toronto, Free Press and Macmillian.

Bohm, D. (1980). *Wholeness and the Implicate Order*. London and New York, Routledge.

Bohm, D. (1985). *Unfolding Meaning*. London and New York, Routledge.

Bolen, J. S. (1987). Healing the Psyche, Healing the Earth. *Psychological Perpectives*, 18(1), 26–37.

Bruchac, J. (1993). *The Native American Sweat Lodge: History and Legends*. Freedom, CA, The Crossing Press.

Buirski, P. (Ed.) (1994). *Comparing Schools of Analytic Therapy*. NJ, Jason Aronson.

Callaway, S. M., G. Witherspoon et al. (1974). *Grandfather Stories of the Navajos*. Rough Rock, AZ, Navajo Curriculum Center.

Campbell, R. J. (1996). *Psychiatric Dictionary*. New York, Oxford University Press.

Cardini F. and Weixin, H. (1998). Moxibustion for Correction of Breech Presentation: A Randomized Controlled Trial. *Journal of the American Medical Association (JAMA)*, 280(18), 1580–4.

Carlson, V. and Witherspoon, G. (1974). *Black Mountain Boy: A Story of the Boyhood of John Honie*. Phoenix, AZ, Navajo Curriculum Center.

Cavendish, R. (1970) *Man, Myth & Magic: An Illustrated Encyclopedia of the Supernatural*. New York, Marshall Cavendish.

Chambers English Dictionary (1988). Edinburgh, W. & R. Chambers Ltd. and The Press Syndicate of the University of Cambridge.

Cirieux, M. D. (1980). *Watunna: An Orinoco Creation Cycle*. Berkeley, CA, North Point Press.

Compton's NewMedia (1993). Compton's NewMedia.

Conforti, M. (1996). On Archetypal Fields. *Review of Contemporary Contributions to Jungian Psychology*, 4(2), 1–4.

Cousins, N. (1987). Mind-Body Healing Comes of Age. *Psychological Perpectives*, 18(1), 98–104.

Cowan, L. (1996). Surfing in America. *Review of Contemporary Contributions to Jungian Psychology*, 3(4), 3.

Curran, D. K. (1996). *Tyranny of the Spirit: Domination and Submission in Adolescent Relationships*. Northvale, NJ, Jason Aronson.

Damasio, A. (1999). *The Feeling of What Happens: Body and Emotion in the Making of Consciousness*. New York, Harcourt.

Darwin, C. (1859). *The Origin of Species by Means of Natural Selection*. New York, Random House.

Darwin, C. (1871). *The Descent of Man*. New York, Random House.

David, J. (1991). *Interweaving Symbols of Individuation in African and European Fairy Tales*. Cape Town, Kaggen.

de Chardin, T. (1959). *The Phenomenon of Man*. New York, Harper & Row.

Deloria, P. J. (1998). *Playing Indian*. New Haven, Yale University Press.

Descartes, R. Philosophical Reflections.

Descartes, R. (1934). *A Discourse on Method*. New York, E.P. Dutton & Co.

Dockstader, F. J. (1987). *The Song of the Loom: New Traditions in Navajo Weaving*. New York, Hudson Hills.

Dossey, L. (1999). *Reinventing Medicine: Beyond Mind-Body to a New Era of Healing*. New York, HarperCollins.

Duff, A. (1990). *Once Were Warriors*. New York, Vintage Books.

Durant (1966). *Our Oriental Heritage*. New York, Simon and Schuster.

Durant, W. (1966). *The Life of Greece*. New York, Simon and Schuster.

Edinger, E. F. (1972). *Ego and Archetype: Individuation and the Religious Function of the Psyche*. New York, G. P. Putnam.

Edinger, E. F. (1983). The Transformation of God. *Quadrant: Journal of the C.G. Jung Foundation for Analytical Psychology*, 16(2), 23–37.

Edinger, E. F. (1999). *The Psyche in Antiquity: Early Greek Philosophy*. Toronto, Inner City Books.

Edinger, E. F. (1999). *The Psyche in Antiquity: Gnosticism and Early Christianity: From Paul of Tarsus to Augustine*. Toronto, Inner City Press.

Edinger, E. F. (1999). *Archetype of the Apocalypse: Divine Vengeance, Terrorism, and the End of the World*. Peru, IL, Open Court.

Eisenberg, D., Davis, R., Ettner, S., Appel, S., Wilkey, S., van Rompay, M., Kessler, R. (1998). Trends in Alternative Medicine Use in the United States, 1990–1997: Results of a Follow-up National Survey. *Journal of the American Medical Association* (JAMA), 280(18), 1569–75.

Eliade, M. (1958). *Rites and Symbols of Initiation: The Mysteries of Birth and Rebirth*. New York, Harper & Row.

Eliade, M. (1963). *Myth and Reality*. New York, Harper Colophon.

Ellenberger, H. F. (1970). *The Discovery of the Unconscious: The History and Evolution of Dynamic Psychiatry*. New York, Basic Books.

Elliott, E. M. (2001). *On Depression*. Paper, Santa Fe, NM.

Elliott, W. (1995). *Tying Rocks to Clouds: Meetings and Conversations with Wise and Spiritual People*. New York, Doubleday.

Encyclopedia Britannica (1922). "General Background to Human Evolution" (G. E. Robert McHenry.) Chicago, Encyclopedia Britannica.

Encyclopedia Britannica Book of the Year (2001). Chicago, Encyclopedia Britannica.

Epstein, B. S. (1997). "A Case of Severe Anxiety and Panic Manifested as Psychosomatic Illness". In *Mind-Body Problems: Psychotherapy with Psychosomatic Disorders*. J. S. Finell (Ed.). Northvale, NJ, Jason Aronson, pp. 185–210.

Erskine, A. and Dorothy, J. (Ed.) (1994). *The Imaginative Body: Psychodynamic Therapy in Health Care*. Northvale, NJ, Jason Aronson.

Farella, J. R. (1984). *The Main Stalk: A Synthesis of Navajo Philosophy*. Tucson, AZ, University of Arizona Press.

Fathers, F. (1968). *An Ethnologic Dictionary of the Navajo Language*. Saint Michaels, AZ, St. Michaels Press.

Feldman, B. (1995). "Bulimia in Adolescent Women: An exploration of Personal and Archetypal Dynamics in Analysis". In *Incest Fantasies & Self Destructive Acts: Jungian and Post-Jungian Psychotherapy in Adolescence*. M. Sidoli and B. Gustav (Eds.). New Brunswick, NJ, Transaction, pp. 173–186.

Finell, J. S. (1997). "Alexithymia and Mind-Body Problems". In *Mind-Body Problems: Psychotherapy with Psychosomatic Disorders*. J. S. Finell (Ed.). Northvale, NJ, Jason Aronson, pp. 3–18.

Foehrenbach, L., Celentano, C., Kirby, J., and Lane, R. C. (1997). "Developmental Determinants of Psychosomatic Symptoms". In *Mind-Body Problems: Psychotherapy with Psychosomatic Disorders*. J. S. Finell (Ed.). Northvale, NJ, Jason Aronson, pp. 19–38.

Fordham, M. (1957). *New Developments in Analytic Psychology*. London, Routledge & Kegan Paul.

Franz, M.-L. v. (1972). *Creation Myths*. Zurich, Spring.

Friedman, R. M. D. (2002). Like Drugs, Talk Therapy Can Change Brain Chemistry. *New York Times*.

Frisbie, C. J. (1987). *Navajo Madicine Bundles or Jish: Acquisition, Transmission, and*

Disposition in the Past and Present. Albuquerque, NM, University of New Mexico Press.

Gaddis, J. L. (1992/93). International Relations Theory and the End of the Cold War, *Journal of International Security*, 17(3), 5–58.

Gafni, M. (2003). The Erotic and the Ethical. *Tikkun*, 18(2), 33–54.

Gartner, R. B. (1997). Considerations in the Psychoanalytic Treatment of Men Who Were Sexually Abused as Children. *Psychoanalytic Psychology: A Journal of Theory, Practice, Research, and Criticism*, 14(1), 13–41.

Gebser, J. (1949, 1953). *The Ever-Present Origin*. Athens, OH, Ohio University Press.

Geer, G. (1988). Through the Prism of Ameri. *Quadrant: Journal of the C.G. Jung Foundation for Analytical Psychology*, 21(2), 21–29.

George A., Cowan, D.P., Meltzer, D. (Eds.) (1994). *Complexity: Metaphors, Models, and Reality*, Santa Fe Institute Studies in the Sciences of Complexity. Reading, Addison-Wesley.

Giessler, B. K. M. (1995,1996,1997,1998). *Non-Native American Indian: A Smoki Deal*. Arizona Republic/Phoenix Gazette.

Goode, E. (2000). How Culture Molds Habits of Thought. *The New York Times*, D1, D4.

Goodwin, F., Lineham, M. and Porr, V. (1999). *Borderline Personality Disorder: The Infinite Mind*. New York, TARA Association for Personality Disorder.

Gordon, R. (1979). Reflections on Curing and Healing. *The Journal of Analytic Psychology* 24(3), 207–217.

Gore, A. (2000). *Earth in the Balance: Ecology and the Human Spirit*. New York, Houghton-Mifflin.

Gorman, C. N. (1971). *Carl Gorman's Description of Navajo Religion*. Fort Defiance, Arizona.

Gray, J. P. D. (1992). *Men are from Mars, Women are from Venus: A Practical Guide for Improving Communication and Getting What You Want in Your Relationships*. New York, HarperCollins.

Greene, M. (1995). *The Birth of Changing Woman*. www.cgjungpage.org.

Greene, M. (1995). *The Emergence of Land and the Importance of the Word in the Popul Vuh and Several Origin Myths of the Southwest Indians*. www.cgjungpage.org

Griffin, S. (1999). *What Her Body Thought: A Journey into the Shadows*. New York, HarperCollins.

Griffin-Pierce, T. (1992). *Earth is My Mother, Sky is My Father: Space, Time, and Astronomy in Navajo Sandpainting*. Albuquerque, NM, University of New Mexico Press.

Grinker, R. S. S. and Werble, B. (1977). *The Borderline Patient*. New York, Jason Aronson.

Guggenbuhl-Craig, A. (1971). *Power in the Helping Professions*. New York, Spring.

Guy-Gillet, G. (1990). The Dynamics of the Transference in Narcissistic Restorations, *The Journal of Analytic Psychology*, 35(2), 99–110.

Haile, B. (1947). *Head and Face Masks in Navaho Ceremonialism*. Saint Michaels, AZ, St. Michaels Press.

Haile, B. (1950). *Legend of the Ghostway Ritual in the Male Branch of Shootingway*. Saint Michaels, AZ, St. Michaels Press.

Haile, B. (1950). *Suckingway: Its Legend and Practice*. Saint Michaels, AZ, St. Michaels Press.

Haile, B. (1981). *Upward Moving and Emergence Way*. Lincoln, NE, University of Nebraska Press.

Haile, B. and Oakes, M. (1957). *Beautyway: A Navaho Ceremonial*. New York, Pantheon.

Harding, M. E. (1947). *Psychic Energy: Its Source and Goal*. New York, Pantheon Books.

Harman, W. (1998). *Global Mind Changing*. San Francisco, Berrett-Knechler.

Harner, M. (1998). "What is a Shaman?" In *Shaman's Path: Healing Personal Growth and Empowerment*. G. Doore (Ed.). Boston, Shambhala, pp. 7–15.

Haule, J. R. (1988). Response to America as "The New World". *Quadrant: Journal of the C. G. Jung Foundation for Analytical Psychology*, 21(2), 71–81.

Hausman, G. (1993). *The Gift of the Gila Monster: Navajo Ceremonial Tales*. New York, Simon & Schuster.

Henderson, J. L. (1988). The Cultural Unconscious. *Quadrant: Journal of the C. G. Jung Foundation for Analytical Psychology*, 21(2), 7–16.

Herman, J. L. (1992). *Trauma and Recovery: The Aftermath of Violence: from Domestic Abuse to Political Terror*. New York, Basic.

Hermann, M. (1973). *Herbs and Medicinal Flowers*. New York, Galahad Books.

Hollis, J. (1997). The Image Behind the Emotion: Practicing Active Imagination. *Review of Contemporary Contributions to Jungian Psychology*, 4(3), 4–10.

Hopcke, R. H. (1988). Synchronicity in Analysis: Various Types and Their Various Roles for Patient and Analyst. *Quadrant: Journal of the C. G. Jung Foundation for Analytical Psychology*, 21(1), 55–64.

Hubback, J. (1990). The Changing Person and the Unchanging Archetype. *The Journal of Analytic Psychology*, 35(2), 111–123.

Hultkranz, A. (1997). *Soul and Native Americans*. Woodstock, CT, Spring.

Hutchens, A. R. (1973). *Indian Herbology of North America*. Ontario, Merco.

IAAP Newsletter (1996). (16).

Jahoda, G. (1975). *The Trail of Tears: The Story of the American Indian Removals, 1813–1855*. New York, Wings.

Jarrett, J. L. (Ed.) (1988). *Nietzsche's Zarathustra*. Princeton, NJ, Princeton University Press.

Jenks, K. (1986). "Changing Woman": The Navajo Therapist Goddess. *Psychological Perpectives: Contemplative Life*, 17(2), 202–221.

Jensen, D. (2000). Where the Buffalo Go: How Science Ignores the Living World – An Interview with Vine Deloria. *The Sun Magazine*, 4–13.

Jerusalem Bible (1966). Doubleday.

Johnson, S. M. (1985). *Characterological Transformation: The Hard Work Miracle*. New York, W.W. Norton.

Josey, A. (1996). A New Ethic for Our Time: Reflections on Erich Neumann's "Depth Psychology and a New Ethic". *Review of Contemporary Contributions to Jungian Psychology*, 3(5), 4–9.

Jung, C. G. Most quotations in the text are taken from *The Collected Works of C. G. Jung*, edited by H. Read, M. Fordham and G. Adler, translated from the German by R. F. C. Hull, and published in London by Routledge & Kegan Paul, 1953–78, in New York by Pantheon Books, 1953–60, and the Bollingen Foundation, 1961–7, and in Princeton, New Jersey, 1967–78. Quotation sources are indicated by the year, the title of the essay, and the volume number followed by the page numbers. Sources other than the *Collected Works* are listed chronologically.

—1911–1912: "Two Kinds of Thinking". *CW* 5: 7–33.

—1921: "Psychological Types". *CW* 6: entire volume.

—1921: "The Type Problem in Classical and Medieval Thought". *CW* 6: pp. 3–66.

—1931: "Archaic Man". *CW* 10: 50–73

—1933: "The Meaning of Psychology for Modern Man". *CW* 10: 134–156.

—1935: "Psychotherapy and a Philosophy of Life". *CW* 16: 384.

—1938: "The Relations Between the Ego and the Unconscious": *CW* 6:123–241.

—1945: "Medicine and Psychotherpay". *CW* 16: pp. 84–93.

—1948: "On Psychic Energy". *CW* 8: 3–66.

—1951: "The Psychology of the Child Archetype". *CW* 9I: 151–181.

—1952: "Answer to Job". *CW* 11: pp. 355–470.

—1954: "The Psychology of the Transference". *CW* 16: pp. 163–323.

—1954: "The Vision of Zosimos". *CW* 13: pp. 57–108.

—1955 and 1956: "Mysterium Conjunctionis

—1959: "The Transcendent Function". *CW* 8: 67–91.

—1961: "Healing the Split". *CW* 18: 253–264.

—1961: "Symbols and the Interpretation of Dreams 1". *CW* 18: 185–195.

—1961: "Symbols and the Interpretation of Dreams 2". *CW* 18: 196–202.

—1961: "Symbols and the Interpretation of Dreams 3". *CW* 18: 203–215.

Jung, C. G. (1955 and 1956). *Mysterium Conjunctionis: An Inquiry into the Separation and Synthesis of Psychic Opposites in Alchemy. Collected Works*, Vol 14.

Jung, C. G. (and after his death von Franz, M-L., Hendwerson, J., Jacobi, J., and Jaffe, A.) (1964). *Man and His Symbols*. Garden City, NY, Doubleday.

Jung, C. G. (1960) "Letter to the Earl of Sandwich". In *C.G. Jung Letters, Vol 2, 1951–61*, G. Adler (Ed.), Routledge, London, pp. 579–580.

Jung, C. G. (1960) "Letter to A.D. Cornell". In *C.G. Jung Letters, Vol 2, 1951–61*, G. Adler (Ed.), Routledge, London pp. 537–543.

Jung, C. G. (1963). *Memories, Dreams, Reflections*. New York, Vintage Books.

Jung, C. G. (1968) Analytical Psychology: Its Theory and Practice (Tavistock Lectures). Routledge, London.

Jung, C. G. (1972). *The Structure and Dynamics of the Psyche. Collected Works*, Vol 8.

Kalsched, D. (1996). *The Inner World of Trauma*. New York, Routledge.

Kauffman, S. (1993). *The Origins of Order: Self-Organization and Selection in Evolution*. New York, Oxford University Press.

Kauffman, S. (1995). *At Home in the Universe: The Search for the Laws of Self-Organization and Complexity*. New York, Oxford University Press.

Kauffman, Y. (1996). The Dreams of Gilgamesh: As a Mythic Layer of the Psyche. *Review of Contemporary Contributions to Jungian Psychology* 3(4), 1, 4–9.

Kavanaugh, J. (1991). *There Are Men Too Gentle to Live Among Wolves*. Kalamazoo, MI, Steven J. Nash.

Keller, S. (1999). *The Immune System: A Seminar for Health Professionals*. Albuquerque, NM, Institute for CorTexT Research and Development.

Kelman, H. C. (1997). Group Processes in the Resolution of International Conflicts: Experiences from the Israeli-Palestinian Case. *American Psychologist*, 52(3), 212–220.

Kernberg, O. F. (1975). *Borderline Conditions and Pathological Narcissism*. New York, Jason Aronson.

Keutzer, C. S. (1984). Synchronicity in Psychotherapy. *The Journal of Analytic Psychology*, 29(4), 373–381.

King, J. (1943). "Where the Two Came to Their Father: A Navaho War Ceremonial". In *Bollingen Series I*. Princeton, Princeton University Press.

Kingsolver, B. (2000). *Prodigal Summer*. New York, HarperCollins.

Klah, H. (1942). *Navajo Creation Myth: The Story of Emergence*. New York, AMS.

Kohut, H. (1971). *The Analysis of the Self*. New York, International Universities Press.

Lakoff, G. (2003). *Where Mathematics Comes From*. Santa Fe Institute Public Lecture, Santa Fe, NM.

Lakoff, G. and Nunez, R. E. (2000). *Where Mathematics Comes From: How the Embodied Mind Brings Mathematics into Being*. New York, Basic.

Langley, G. (1996). A Fistful of Dreams: Taming the Wild West in the Old World. *Munich Found: Bavaria's City Magazine in English*, VIII(8), 33–35.

Lessing, D. (1987). *Prisons We Choose to Live Inside*. New York, Harper & Row.

Levine, P. A. and Frederick, A. (1997). Waking the Tiger: Healing Trauma. Berkeley, CA.

Levy-Bruhl, L. (1910, English translation, 1926). *Les Fonctions Mentales Dans les Societes Inferieures: How Natives Think*. New York, Washington Square Press.

Levy-Bruhl, L. (1966). *How Natives Think*. New York, Washington Square Press.

Lewontin, R. C. (2003). *The Coevolution of Organism and Environment*. Tenth Annual Stanislaw Ulam Memorial Lecture Series, 13 November 2003, Santa Fe, NM, The Santa Fe Institute.

Lietaer, B. A. (1994). Community Currencies: A New Tool for the 21st Century. *World Business Academy Perspective*, 8(2), 80–98.

Lightman, A. (1999). A Cataclysm of Thought. *The Atlantic Monthly*, (283) 88–96.

Link, M. S. (1956). *The Pollen Path: A Collection of Navajo Myths*. Stanford, CA, Stanford University Press.

Locke, R. F. (1992). *The Book of the Navajo*. Los Angeles, Mankind.

Lomatewama, R. (1993). *Drifting Through Ancestor Dreams*. Flagstaff, AZ, Entrada.

Loomis, M. (1988). *Balancing the Shields: Native American Teachings and the Individuation Process*. Audiotape, www.jungatlanta.com

Luckert, K. W. (1979). *Coyoteway: A Navajo Holyway Healing Ceremonial*. Tucson and Flagstaf, AZ, University of Arizona Press and Museum of Northern Arizona Press.

Maier, S. F., Watkins, L. R., and Fleshner, M. (1994). Psychoneuroimmunology: The Interface Between Behavior, Brain, and Immunity. *American Psychologist*, 49(12), 1004–1017.

Mandela, N. (1994). *Long Walk to Freedom: The Autobiography of Nelson Mandela*. New York, Little, Brown & Company.

Mander, J. (1991). *In the Absence of the Sacred: The Failure of Technology and the Survival of the Indian Nations*. San Francisco, Sierra Club Books.

Mander, J. and Goldsmith, E. (Eds.) (1996). *The Case Against the Global Economy and For a Turn Toward the Local*. San Francisco, Sierra Club Books.

Martin, L. (2003). Who Causes this Sickness? The Sun : 28–33.

Masterson, J. F., M.D. (1976). *Psychotherapy of the Borderline Adult: A Developmental Approach*. New York, Brunner/Mazel.

Masterson, J. F. (1981). *Narcissistic and Borderline Disorders: An Integrated Developmental Approach*. New York, Brunner/Mazel.

Matthews, W. (1902). *The Night Chant, A Navaho Ceremony*. New York, AMS.

Matthews, W. (1994). *Navaho Legends*. Salt Lake City, UT, University of Utah Press.

McCampbell, A. (1998). *Multiple Chemical Sensitivity*. Belmont, VA, Environmental Health Connection.

McCarthy, J. B. (1997). Narcissistic Adolescents' Object Relations. *Psychoanalytic Psychology: A Journal of Theory, Practice, Research, and Criticism*, 14(1), 97–112.

McCormack, C. (1990). *Projective-Identification in the Borderline-Schizoid Relationship*, Washington, DC, Washington School of Psychiatry.

McDougall, J. (1989). *Theaters of the Body: A Psychoanalytic Approach to Psychosomatic Illness*. Oral presentation. New York, W. W. Norton.

McNeley, J. K. (1981). *Holy Wind in Navajo Philosophy*. Tucson, AZ, University of Arizona Press.

Mehl-Madrona, L. (1997). *Coyote Medicine*. New York, Scribner.

Miller, A. (1984). *Thou Shalt Not Be Aware: Society's Betrayal of the Child*. New York, Farrar Strauss Giroux.

Mindell, A. (2000). *Quantum Mind: The Edge between Physics and Psychology*. Portland, OR, Lao Tse Press.

Momaday, N. S. (1968). *A House Made of Dawn*. New York, Harper & Row.

Moon, S. (1970). *A Magic Dwells: A Poetic and Psychological Study of the Navaho Emergence Myth*. San Francisco, Guild for Psychological Studies.

Moon, S. (1984). *Changing Woman and Her Sisters*. San Francisco, Guild for Psychological Studies.

Morrison, A. P. (1989). *Shame: The Underside of Narcissism*. Hillsdale, NJ, The Analytic Press.

Nebert, D. (2003). Multiple Chemical Sensitivities Syndrome (MCSS): What is it and What is Known About it? *Interface: Genes and the Environment*, University of Cincinnati Center for Environmental Genetics newsletter.

Nelson, J. E. (1994). *Healing the Split: Integrating Spirit into Our Understanding of the Mentally Ill*. New York, State University of New York Press.

Neumann, E. (1976). On the Psychological Meaning of Ritual. *Quadrant: Journal of the C.G. Jung Foundation for Analytical Psychology*, 9(2), 5–34.

New Dimensions: The Journal of New Dimensions Radio (1996).

New Shorter Oxford English Dictionary (1996). Oxford, Oxford University Press.

Noll, R. (1990). Comment on 'Individualism and Shamanism. *The Journal of Analytic Psychology*, 35(2), 213–217.

Novick, J. and Novick, K. K. (1996). *Fearful Symmetry: The Development and Treatment of Sadomasochism*. Northvale, NJ, Jason Aronson.

Nucleus: The Magazine of the Union of Concerned Scientists (1996).

O'Bryan, A. (1993). *Navaho Indian Myths*. New York, Warner.

Onions, C.T. (Ed.) (1966). *Oxford Dictionary of English Etymology*. Oxford University Press, Oxford.

O'Regan, B. and Hirshberg, C. (1993). *Spontaneous Remission: An Annotated Bibliography*. Sausalito, CA, Institute of Noetic Sciences.

Otto, R. (1923). *The Idea of the Holy: An Inquiry into the Non-Rational Factor in the Idea of the Divine and Its Relation to the Rational*. New York, Oxford University Press.

Parabola: The Magazine of Myth and Tradition (1995). 20(4).

Peat, D. F. (1990). Unfolding the Subtle: Matter and Consciousness. Lecture presented at Temple University, Philadelphia, 27 February 1990. www.fdavidpeat.com/bibliography/essays/temple2.htm.

Perlman, M. (1995). *Hiroshima Forever: The Ecology of Mourning*. Barrytown, NY, Station Hill Arts;

Piontelli, A. (1987). Infant Observation From Before Birth. *International Journal of Psychoanalysis*, 68, 453–463.

Piontelli, A. (1992). *From Fetus to Child: An Observational and Psychoanalytic Study*. New York, Routledge.

Plato (2003). *Phaedrus*. Newbury, MA, Focus.

Podhoretz, H. (1997). "Psychoanalytic Psychotherapy of Borderline Patients with Anorexia". In *Mind-Body Problems: Psychotherapy with Psychosomatic Disorders*. J. S. Finell (Ed.). Northvale, NJ, Jason Aronson, pp. 263–280.

Psychoanalytic Dialogues: A Journal of Relational Perspectives (1995). 5(4).

Psychoanalytic Dialogues: A Journal of Relational Perspectives (1996). 6(1)

Psychoanalytic Psychology: A Journal of Theory, Practice, Research, and Criticism (1996). 13(1).

Psychoanalytic Psychology: A Journal of Theory, Practice, Research, and Criticism (1996). 13(2).

Psychological Perpectives: Dreaming (1996). (33).

Quadrant: The Journal of Contemporary Jungian Thought (1995). 26(1 & 2).

Quincey, D. (2002). *Radical Nature: Rediscovering the Soul of Matter*. Montpelier, VT, Invisible Cities.

Quincey, D. (2002). Stories Matter, Matter Stories. *IONS Noetic Sciences Review* (June-August), 8–13; 44–45.

Random House Dictionary of the English Language (1971). New York, Random House.

Raphael-Leff, J. (1994). "Imaginative Bodies of Childbearing: Visions and Revisions". In *The Imaginative Body: Psychodynamic Therapy in Health Care*. A. Erskin and D. Judd. Northvale, NJ, Jason Aronson, pp. 13–39.

Ray, P. H. and Anderson, S. (2000). *The Cultural Creatives: How 50 Million People Are Changing the World*. New York, Harmony.

Redfield, J. (1993). *The Celestine Prophecy*. New York, Warner Books.

Reichard, G. A. (1950). *Navaho Religion: A Study of Symbolism*. Princeton, Princeton University Press.

Review of Contemporary Contributions to Jungian Psychology (1996). 4(1).

Robertson, R. (2002). Synchronicity in a New Light. *Psychological Perpectives: Before the Phoenix*, 43, 92–109.

Roessel, R. A. and Patero, D. (Eds.) (1974). Coyote Stories of the Navajo People. Phoenix, AZ, Navajo Curriculum Center Press.

Rossi, E. L. (1986). Conversations with Marie-Louise von Franz at 70. *Psychological Perpectives: Contemplative Life*, 17(2), 151–160.

Rossi, E. L. (2000). The Numinosum and the Brain: The Weaving Thread of Consciousness. *Psychological Perpectives* 40, 94–103.

Rossi, E. L. (2001). Psyche, Soma, and Gene Expression. *Pscyhological Perspectives* 42, 81–88.

Russell, E. H. (1985). Psychological Modes: Elaboration of a Geometric Mandala. *Quadrant: Journal of the C.G. Jung Foundation for Analytical Psychology*, 16(2), 39–55.

Ryley, N. (1998). *The Forsaken Garden: Four Conversations on the Deep Meaning of Environmental Illness*. Wheaton, IL, Quest Books.

Sabini, M. (1987). On Hearing Inner Voices. *Psychological Perpectives*, 18(1), 70–81.

Sabini, M. (2000). Culture Dreams. *The Salt Journal*, 2(3), 42–46.

Sabini, M., (Ed.) (2002). *The Earth Has a Soul: The Nature Writings of C.G. Jung*. Berkeley, CA, North Atlantic Books.

Samuels, A. (1985). *Jung and the Post-Jungians*. Boston, Routledge & Kegan Paul.

San Francisco Jung Institute Library Journal (1995). 14(3).

San Francisco Jung Institute Library Journal (1996). 15(2).

Sandner, D. (1979). *Navaho Symbols of Healing*. New York, Harcourt Brace Jonanovich.

Sandner, D. (1988). Response to "Balancing the Shield". *Quadrant: The Journal of Contemporary Jungian Thought*, 21(2), 51–56.

Sandner, D. and Wong, S. (Eds.) (1997). *The Sacred Heritage: The Influence of Shamanism on Analytical Psychology*. New York, Routledge.

Schmall, S. (1997). Personal communication. Santa Fe, NM.

Schore, A. N. (1994). *Affect Regulation and the Origin of the Self: The Neurobiology of Emotional Development*. Hillsdale, NJ, Larence Erlbaum Associates.

Schore, A. N. (2003) *Affect Regulation and the Repair of the Self*. New York, W. W. Norton.

Schwartz-Salant, N. (1982). *Narcissism and Character Transformation: The Psychology of Narcissistic Character Disorders*. Toronto, Inner City Books.

Schwartz-Salant, N. (1989). *The Borderline Personality: Vision and Healing*. Wilmette, IL, Chrion.

Scott, A., Egin, D. et al. (1996). Consciousness in Dialogue: Responses to Ken Wilber. *Noetic Sciences Review*, 40, 17–21.

Scott, S. S. (2000). Like Trees Walking: Stories of Healing with Nature. *Quadrant: Journal of the C.G. Jung Foundation for Analytical Psychology* XXXII (2), 42–59.

Searles, H. F. (1986). *My Work with Borderline Patients*. Northvale, NJ, Jason Aronson.

Sedgwick, D. (1993). *Jung and Searles: A Comparative Study*. New York, Routledge.

Sheldrake, R. (1987). Society, Spirit, and Ritual. *Psychological Perpectives*. 18(2), 320–331.

Sheldrake, R. (1987). Mind, Memory, and Archetype. *Psychological Perpectives*. 18(1), 9–25.

Shlain, L. (1991). *Art & Physics: Parallel Visions in Space, Time & Light*. New York, William Morrow.

Shlain, L. (1998). *The Alphabet Versus the Goddess*. New York, Penguin.

Shorter, E. (1993). *From Paralysis to Fatigue: A History of Psychosomatic Illness in the Modern Era*. New York, Free Press.

Shulman, H. (1997). *Living at the Edge of Chaos: Complex Systems in Culture and Psyche*. Einsiedeln, Switzerland, Daimon.

Siegel, D. (1999). *The Developing Mind: Toward a Neurobiology of Interpersonal Experience*. New York, Guilford Press.

Simo, J. (1997). "Psychosomatic Telemachus: The Body as Oracle, Armor, and Battlefield". In *Mind-Body Problems: Psychotherapy with Psychosomatic Disorders*, J. S. Finell (Ed.), Northvale, NJ, Jason Aronson, pp. 237–262.

Smith, H. (2001). *Why Religion Matters: The Fate of the Human Spirit in an Age of Disbelief*. New York, HarperCollins Publishers.

Some, M. P. (1993). *Ritual: Power, Healing, and Community*. Portland, OR, Swan/ Raven & Company.

Spiegelman, J. M. (2002). Developments in the Concept of Synchronicity in the Analytic Relationship and in Theory. *Quadrant: Journal of the C.G. Jung Foundation for Analytical Psychology*, XXXII(1), 57–73.

Stamper, M. (1996). Understanding "Fields" Magnetic & Archetypal. *Review of Contemporary Contributions to Jungian Psychology*, 4(2), 4;6.

Stern, C. (Ed.) (1978) *Gates of Repentance: The New Union Prayerbook for the Days of Awe*. New York, Central Conference of American Rabbis and Union of Liberal and Progressive Synagogues.

Stern, D. (1985). *The Interpersonal World of the Infant*. New York, Basic.

Stevens, A. (1993). *The Two Million-Year-Old Self*. College Station, TX, Texas A&M University Press.

Stevens, A. (1999). *Ariadne's Clue: A Guide to the Symbols of Humankind*. Princeton, Princeton University Press.

Stevens, A. (2001). *Debate: Psychology and Biology*. Cambridge 2001: Proceedings of The Fifteenth International Congress for Analytical Psychology. R. Hinshaw (Ed.). Einsiedeln, Switzerland, Verlag, pp. 367–377.

Stevens, A., and Price, J. (1996). *Evolutionary Psychiatry: A New Beginning*. New York, Routledge.

Stieber, T. (2000). George Cowan: Changing the World in Measurable Ways. *SFI: Bulletin of the Santa Fe Institute*, 15, 2–5.

Stirling, M. W. (1940). Indian Tribes of Pueblo Land. *National Geographic*, 78, 549–588.

Stolorow, R. D., Atwood, G. E., and Brandschaft, B. (Eds.) (1994). *The Intersubjective Perspective*. Northvale, NJ, Jason Aronson.

Strickholm, S. (1983). Synchronicity and Chaos: Vision and Outer Reality in Black Elk Speaks. *Pscyhological Perspectives*, (14)1, 30–51.

Strong, L. (1995). I Have Become a Problem to Myself: Augustine's Theory of Will and the Notion of Human Inwardness. *The St. John's Review*, 43(1), 59–70.

Swedo, S. a. Leonard, H. (1996). *It's Not All in Your Head*. New York, HarperCollins.

Swimme, B. and Berry, T. (1994). *The Universe Story: From the Primordial Flaring Forth to the Ecozoic Era – A Celebration of the Unfolding of the Cosmos*. New York, HarperCollins.

Tacey, D. J. (1995). *Edge of the Sacred: Transformation in Australia*. Victoria, Australia, HarperCollins.

Tanach (1996). Brooklyn, Mesorah Publications.

Tanakh: The Holy Scriptures (1985). Philadelphia and Jerusalem, Jewish Publication Society.

Targ, R. and Hastings, A. (1987). Psychological Impact of Psychic Abilities. *Psychological Perpectives*, 18(1), 38–51.

Tarnas, R. (1991). *The Passion of the Western Mind: Understanding the Ideas that Have Shaped Our World View*. New York, Ballantine.

The Network: Ideas of God (1996). 13(3).

Turner, F. (1983). *Beyond Geography: The Western Spirit Against the Wilderness*. New Brunswick, NJ, Rutgers University Press.

Turner, V. W. (1969). *The Ritual Process: Sturcture and Anti-Structure*. Chicago, Aldine Press.

Tustin, F. (1992). *Autistic States in Children*. New York, Routledge.

TV-Turnoff Network (2002). *Facts and Figures about our TV Habit* Washington, D.C., TV-Turnoff Network. www. tvturnoff.org.

Tyler, H. A. (1964). *Pueblo Gods and Myths*. Norman, Oklahoma, University of Oklahoma Press.

Tyminski, R. (1999). When the Therapist Must Symbolize Because the Patient Cannot: Therapeutic Trial by Fire. *Journal of Jungian Theory and Practice*, 1, 27–49.

Tyminski, R. (2003). The Symbol and The Neuron: Two Developmental Paths, Two Theories, and Two Puzzles. *The San Francisco Jung Institute Library Journal*, 22(1), 29–48.

Ulanov, A. (1999). Countertransference and the Self. *Journal of Jungian Theory and Practice*, 1, 5–26.

Ulanov, A. (2001). *Attacked by Poison Ivy: A Psychological Understanding*. York Beach, ME, Nicholas Hays.

Vennum, T. J. (1994). *American Indian Lacrosse: Little Brother of War*. Washington, D.C., Smithsonian Institution Press.

Volkan, V. D. (1981*)*. *Linking Objects and Linking Phenomena: A Study of the Forms, Symptoms, Metapsychology, and Therapy of Complicated Mourning*. New York, International Universities Press.

Waldrop, M. M. (1992). *Complexity*. New York, Simon and Schuster.

Waters, F. (1963). *Book of the Hopi: The First Revelation of the Hopi's Historical and Religious World-View of Life*. New York, Ballantine.

Waters, F. (1987). *The Woman at Otowi Crossing*. Athens, OH, Swallow Press and Ohio University Press.

Welwood, J. (2002). *Toward a Psychology of Awakening: Buddhism, Psychotherapy, and the Path of Personal and Spiritual Transformation*. Boston, Shambhala.

Wheelwright, M. and Haile, B. (1949). *Emergence Myth According to the Hanelthnayhe or Upward-Reaching Rite*. Santa Fe, NM, Museum of Navajo Ceremonial Art.

Wheelwright, M. C. (1988). *The Myths and Prayers of the Great Star Chant and the Myth of the Coyote Chant*. Tsaile, AZ, Navajo Community College Press.

Whitmont, E. C. (1969). *The Symbolic Quest*. Princeton, Princeton University Press.

Whitmont, E. C. (1980*)*. *Psyche and Substance: Essays on Homeopathy in the Light of Jungian Psychology*. Richmond, CA, North Atlantic.

Whitmont, E. C. (1982). *Return of the Goddess*. New York, Crossroad Publishing.

Whitmont, E. C., and Perera, S. B. (1989). *Dreams: A Portal to the Source: A Clinical Guide for Therapists*. London and New York, Routledge.

Whitmont, E. C. (1993). *The Alchemy of Healing: Psyche and Soma*. Berkeley, CA, North Atlantic Books.

Wiesel, E. (1999). *And the Sea is Never Full: Memoirs, 1969–*. New York, Alfred A. Knopf.

Wiggins, J. S., Renner, K.E. et al. (1971). The Psychology of Personality. Reading, MA, Addison-Wesley.

Wilford, J. N. (1999). Egypt Carvings Set Earlier Date for Alphabet. *New York Times*, 1, 10.

Willeford, W. (1984). Magic and Participating Consciousness. *The Journal of Analytic Psychology*, 29(4), 337–353.

Williams, R. (2000). Ecology as Religion. *The Salt Journal*, 2(3), 7.

Wilson, C. (1995). Dynamical Chaos: Some Implications of a Recent Discovery. *The St. John's Review*, 43(1), 1–20.

Winnicott, D. W. (1960). *Ego Distortion in Terms of True and False Self. The Maturational Processes and the Facilitating Environment*. London, Hogarth Press.

Winnicott, D. W. (1975). *Through Paediatrics to Psycho-Analysis*. New York, Basic.

Wishard, W. V. D. (2003). Understanding Our Moment in History. *Journal of Futures Studies*, February 2003.

Wolf, F. A. (1994). *The Dreaming Universe*. New York, Simon & Schuster.

Woolfson, T. (2002). Singing the Whole Garden. *The San Francisco Jung Institute Library Journal*, 21(3), 35–44.

Wyman, L. C. (1957). *Navaho Beautyway: Its Uses, Mythology, Songs and Geographical Setting*. New York, Pantheon.

Wyman, L. C. and Bailey, F. L. (1964). *Navaho Indian Ethnoentomology*. Albuquerque, NM, University of New Mexico Press.

Wyman, L. C. (1970). *Blessing Way*. Tucson, AZ, University of Arizona Press.

Yandell, J. (1987). Wasting Time: The Something of Nothing. *Psychological Perpectives*, 18(1), 82–97.

Zabriskie, B. (2002). Destructive Devotion: With Friends Like Us, Does Jung Need Enemies? *Journal of Jungian Theory and Practice*, 4(1), 5–17.

Zabriskie, P. T. (1988). America as 'The New World': Psychological Consequences of an Historical Image. *Quadrant: Journal of the C.G. Jung Foundation for Analytical Psychology*, 21(2), 57–70.

Zinkin, L. (1979). The Collective and the Personal. *The Journal of Analytic Psychology*, 24(3), 227–250.

Zolbrod, P. G. (1984). *Dine Bahane: The Navajo Creation Story*. Albuquerque, NM, University of New Mexico Press.

Zwillinger, R. (1999). *The Dispossessed: Living with Multiple Chemical Sensitivities*. Paulden, AZ, The Dispossessed Outreach Project.

Index